BROKEN

Broken

Illness and Disability in Antônio Francisco Lisboa, Camilo Castelo Branco, Clarice Lispector, Victor Willing, Paula Rego and Ana Palma

Maria Manuel Lisboa

https://www.openbookpublishers.com

©2025 Maria Manuel Lisboa

This work is licensed under the Creative Commons Attribution-NonCommercial 4.0 International (CC BY-NC 4.0). This license allows you to share, copy, distribute and transmit the text; to adapt the text for non-commercial purposes of the text providing attribution is made to the authors (but not in any way that suggests that they endorse you or your use of the work). Attribution should include the following information:

Maria Manuel Lisboa, *Broken: Illness and Disability in Antônio Francisco Lisboa, Camilo Castelo Branco, Clarice Lispector, Victor Willing, Paula Rego and Ana Palma*. Cambridge, UK: Open Book Publishers, 2025, https://doi.org/10.11647/OBP.0500

Further details about CC BY-NC licenses are available at
https://creativecommons.org/licenses/by-nc/4.0/

Copyright and permissions for the reuse of many of the images included in this publication differ from the above. This information is provided in the captions and in the list of illustrations. Unless otherwise stated, figures are reproduced under the fair dealing principle. Every effort has been made to identify and contact copyright holders and any omission or error will be corrected if notification is made to the publisher.

All external links were active at the time of publication unless otherwise stated and have been archived via the Internet Archive Wayback Machine at https://archive.org/web

Digital material and resources associated with this volume are available at
https://doi.org/10.11647/OBP.0500#resources
Information about any revised edition of this work will be provided at https://doi.org/10.11647/OBP.0500

ISBN Paperback: 978-1-80511-748-3

ISBN Hardback: 978-1-80511-749-0

ISBN Digital (PDF): 978-1-80511-750-6

ISBN HTML: 978-1-80511-752-0

ISBN Digital ebook (epub): 978-1-80511-751-3

DOI: 10.11647/OBP.0500

Cover images: Ana Palma (2012), CC BY-NC-SA 4.0; Paula Rego (1997), ©John Haynes. All Rights Reserved 2025/Bridgeman Images; Victor Willing in his London studio (1979), ©Victor Willing. All Rights Reserved 2025/Bridgeman Images; Clarice Lispector (Photo: Maureen Bisilliat), CC BY-SA 4.0, https://commons.wikimedia.org/wiki/File:Clarice_Lispector_por_Maureen_Bisilliat_em_agosto_de_1969._Acervo_IMS.jpg; Camilo Castelo Branco (Photo: Bohemia do Espirito), public domain, https://commons.wikimedia.org/wiki/File:Camilo_Castelo_Branco_Bohemia_do_Espirito.png; Antônio Francisco Lisboa (Photo: Inauguração do Museu de Congonhas), CC BY 2.0, https://commons.wikimedia.org/wiki/File:Inaugura%C3%A7%C3%A3o_do_Museu_de_Congonhas_(23425316429).jpg
Cover design: Jeevanjot Kaur Nagpal

For Bernard McGuirk
Bernard, after exactly forty years, this one is
for you, with love. Thanks for the memories.

Let's be perfectly clear boys and girls,
Cunts are still running the world.
Jarvis Cocker, 'Running the World'

Table of Contents

Acknowledgements	ix
Author's Biography	xi
List of Illustrations	xiii
A Note on Texts, Translations and Images	xxiii
Introduction: Faulty Merchandise	1
1. Little Cripples: Antônio Francisco Lisboa ('O Aleijadinho')	7
2. Camilo Castelo Branco's *A brasileira de Prazins*: 'When in Danger or in Doubt, Run in Circles, Scream and Shout'	31
3. 'I Know Where You Were Last Night': Clarice Lispector or When Stars Become Supernovas	57
4. Victor Willing: Being There	85
5. Paula Rego: A Brick through a Window Never Comes with a Love Note	119
6. Menstrous/Monstrous: Bleeding, Amenorrhea and Feminine Hygiene in the Art of Ana Palma and Paula Rego	147
INTERVIEWS AND RECOLLECTIONS	181
Interview with Lila Nunes	183
Interview with Ana Palma	187
In memoriam: Paula Rego and the Stories Left Untold Helder Macedo (*Translated by Maria Manuel Lisboa*)	195
Index	199

Acknowledgements

> Sister,
> you've been on my mind
> Sister, we're two of a kind
> So sister,
> I'm keepin' my eyes on you.
>
> (Táta Vega) Quincy Jones, 'Miss Celie's Blues'[1]

There are many reasons why I lament the death of Paula Rego. I would not be right to call her a friend. We weren't close. But I don't quite know how else to feel about someone who once offered to come and look after me when I was ill (bearing in mind the treatment of sick dogs in her works I said thanks very much, but no thanks); someone who offered do my portrait (I was afraid she'd make my legs look unfairly fat, so I didn't pursue the matter); but, more to the point, someone who allowed me to reproduce her images free of charge in two monographs and numerous articles, ensured they were made available to me without any problem and, over the years, even gave me a few hand-dedicated prints as a thank you for my writings on her. She changed my life and provided the visual narrative to many of my concerns. What she depicted, I often feel. Maybe we both belong in jail. The women in her images now smirk at me from my walls, somewhat menacing but also my kin. They know what's on my mind. Sometimes I feel the way they seem to. I'm not ashamed. And I'm not afraid of you, Paula! Sometimes we laughed, but who or what was she laughing at? Me? I was never sure. Wherever she may be right now, she is definitely not here, and the solution to the current cost and bureaucratic difficulties of reproducing images by her and by her late husband, Victor Willing, have been circumvented by

---

1 See https://www.youtube.com/watch?v=YQq7RqYVb38

giving internet links to them in this volume. Many of her images have also been reproduced in my other book, *Essays on Paula Rego: Smile When You Think about Hell*, which can be read for free on-line at https://www.openbookpublishers.com/books/10.11647/obp.0178

This is not ideal, but it is the best I can do. *Numquam desistas*. Or as the great Diane Keaton (aka Annie Hall) would say: 'la-di-da'.

Ana Palma has kindly allowed me to reproduce her art work and discussed it with me in an interview in a way that helped me tremendously.

I thank the following for helping me track down material used in this volume: Francisco Bethencourt, Helena Buescu, Helder Macedo, Viktor Mendes and Máire Ní Mhaonaigh.

A research grant from St. John's College, Cambridge covered the costs of image reproduction rights and editing this volume.

Last but absolutely not least, I thank the band of brothers and sisters I always mention in every book I have ever written, for making my life sweet, easy and fun. You know who you are. I am very lucky to have you.

Author's Biography

Maria Manuel Lisboa holds a Personal Chair in Portuguese Literature and Culture at the University of Cambridge and is a Fellow of St. John's College, Cambridge. She lectures and supervises on Portuguese, Brazilian and Mozambican Literatures, Film and Art. This is her eighth monograph. The others cover Literature, Film and Art from Portugal and Brazil as well as a comparative one on the theme of Apocalypse. She is also the author of approximately seventy articles and book chapters on all these areas.

See https://cambridge.academia.edu/MariaManuelLisboa

List of Illustrations

I.1	Kevin Carter, *The Vulture and the Little Girl* (1993), Wikipedia, https://en.wikipedia.org/wiki/File:Kevin-Carter-Child-Vulture-Sudan.jpg	p. 3
1.1	Antônio Francisco Lisboa, *Church of Saint Francis of Assisi* (1749–1809) São João del Rei, Congonhas, Brazil. Photo by Marinelson Almeida (2014), Wikimedia Commons, CC BY 2.0, https://commons.wikimedia.org/wiki/File:Igreja_de_S%C3%A3o_Francisco_de_Assis._A_joia_rara_de_S%C3%A3o_Jo%C3%A3o_Del_Rei_-_MG_(15277299478).jpg	p. 9
1.2	*Supposed Portrait of Aleijadinho*. Artist unknown (early nineteenth century), oil on parchment. Image size approx. 39.6 × 41.7 cm. Museu de Congonhas. Photo by Janine Moraes/Ministério da Cultura (2015), Wikimedia Commons, CC BY 2.0, https://commons.wikimedia.org/wiki/File:Inaugura%C3%A7%C3%A3o_do_Museu_de_Congonhas_(23425316429).jpg	p. 12
1.3	Antônio Francisco Lisboa, *Museum Casa dos Contos* (1782–84), Ouro Preto, Brazil. Photo by Cecioka (2019), Wikimedia Commons, CC BY-SA 4.0, https://commons.wikimedia.org/wiki/File:Museu_Casa_dos_Contos_2019_26.jpg	p. 13
1.4	Antônio Francisco Lisboa, *Church of Our Lady of Carmel* (1767–80), Ouro Preto, Brazil. Photo by Joedison Rocha (2019), Wikimedia Commons, CC BY-SA 4.0, https://commons.wikimedia.org/wiki/File:Igreja_de_Nossa_Senhora_do_Carmo,_Ouro_Preto-MG.jpg	p. 14

1.5	Antônio Francisco Lisboa, *The Ascent to Calgary* (1796–99), polychromed wood, life size sculptures. Sanctuary of Congonhas da Campo, Brazil. Photo by Rosino (2011), Wikimedia Commons, public domain, https://commons.wikimedia.org/wiki/File:Aleijadinho_01.jpg	p. 24
1.6	Antônio Francisco Lisboa, *Jesus' Crucifixion* (1796–99), polychromed wood, life size sculptures. Photo by Ricardo André Frantz (2015), Wikimedia Commons, CC BY 3.0, https://commons.wikimedia.org/wiki/File:A_crucifica%C3%A7%C3%A3o_de_Jesus_-_Aleijadinho_-_Congonhas.jpg	p. 25
1.7	Antônio Francisco Lisboa, *Church of the Good Lord of Matosinhos and the Twelve Prophets* (1800–05), life-size soapstone statues. Photo by Silvia Schumacher (2014), Wikimedia Commons, CC BY-SA 4.0, https://commons.wikimedia.org/wiki/File:Conjunto_da_Bas%C3%ADlica_do_Senhor_Bom_Jesus_de_Matosinhos3.JPG	p. 26
1.8	Tarsila do Amaral, *Workers* (1933). © Artistic-Cultural Collection of the Governmental Palaces of the State of São Paulo. Wikipedia, https://pt.wikipedia.org/wiki/Ficheiro:Operarios.jpg#/media/Ficheiro:Operarios.jpg	p. 27
4.1	Photograph of *Fernando Pessoa* (1914). Wikimedia Commons, public domain, https://commons.wikimedia.org/wiki/File:Pessoa_chapeu.jpg	p. 88
4.2	Victor Willing, *Rien* (1980, oil on canvas, 200 × 183 cm. ©The Estate of Victor Willing, https://www.tate.org.uk/art/artworks/willing-rien-t03187	p. 88
4.3	Victor Willing, *Self-Portrait at 70* (1987), oil on canvas, 56 × 56 cm. Pallant House Gallery, Chichester. ©The Estate of Victor Willing. Photo by Mark Bridge (2006), https://www.flickr.com/photos/markbridge/179893540	p. 91
4.4	Victor Willing, *Judge* (1982), oil on canvas, 250 × 200 cm. ©The Estate of Victor Willing, https://artuk.org/discover/artworks/judge-70485	p. 92

List of Illustrations xv

4.5	Victor Willing, *Standing Nude* (1952–53), oil paint on hardboard. Support: 1538 × 1234 mm; frame: 1583 × 1286 × 75 mm. ©The Estate of Victor Willing, https://www.tate.org.uk/art/artworks/willing-standing-nude-t07126	p. 93
4.6	Damien Hirst, *The Physical Impossibility of Death in the Mind of Someone Living* or *Death Denied* (2008), glass, steel, shark, acrylic and formaldehyde solution. Photo by Agent001 (2009), Wikimedia Commons, CC BY-SA 3.0, https://commons.wikimedia.org/wiki/File:Shark83.JPG	p. 97
4.7	Tribute, Mark Rothko Art Centre, Daugavpils (Latvia), October 2017. Photo by Traqueurdelumieres (2017), Wikimedia Commons, CC BY-SA 4.0, https://commons.wikimedia.org/wiki/File:Tribute,_Mark_Rothko_Art_Centre,_Daugavpils_(Latvia),_October_2017.jpg#/media/File:Tribute,_Mark_Rothko_Art_Centre,_Daugavpils_(Latvia),_October_2017.jpg	p. 100
4.8	Victor Willing, *Self-Portrait* (1957), oil on canvas, 56 × 56 cm. ©The Estate of Victor Willing, https://www.creativeboom.com/inspiration/visions-a-major-retrospective-of-the-mid-century-british-painter-victor-willing/	p. 102
4.9	Victor Willing, *Place of Exile* (1976), charcoal and pastel on paper, 31.4 × 50 cm. ©The Estate of Victor Willing, courtesy Marlborough Fine Art, https://artscouncilcollection.org.uk/artwork/place-exile	p. 104
4.10	Victor Willing, *Place Triptych* (1976–78), oil on canvas, 66 × 116 cm (left panel, 190 × 216 cm (centre panel), 166 × 116 cm (right panel). ©The Derek Williams Trust, https://derekwilliamstrust.org/news/victor-willing-takes-his-place-in-the-collection/#	p. 104
4.11	Paula Rego, *The Family* (1988), acrylic on paper on canvas, 213.4 × 213.4. ©Victoria Miro, https://www.victoria-miro.com/artworks/29907/	p. 105
4.12	Victor Willing, *Mud* (1979–80), oil on canvas, 183.2 × 426.1 cm. ©The Estate of Victor Willing. Arts Council Collection, Southbank Centre, London, https://artuk.org/discover/artworks/mud-64323	p. 106

4.13	Victor Willing, *Stepladder* (1976), oil on canvas, 183 × 152 cm. ©The Estate of Victor Willing. Pallant House Gallery, Chichester, https://artuk.org/discover/artworks/painting-with-stepladder-70480	p. 107
4.14	Victor Willing, *Swing* (1978), oil on canvas, 152 × 83 cm. ©The Estate of Victor Willing, https://artuk.org/discover/artworks/swing-70536	p. 107
4.15	Victor Willing, *Place with a Red Thing* (1980), oil on canvas, 200 × 250.2 cm. ©The Estate of Victor Willing, https://www.tate.org.uk/art/artworks/willing-place-with-a-red-thing-t03186	p. 108
4.16	Victor Willing, *Breathe* (1982), pastel and charcoal on paper, 42.2 × 30 cm. ©The Estate of Victor Willing, https://www.artsy.net/artwork/victor-willing-untitled-breathe	p. 109
4.17	Victor Willing, *Cart* (1978), oil on canvas, 188 × 208 cm. ©The Estate of Victor Willing. Bridgeman Images, https://www.bridgemanimages.com/en/willing/the-cart-1978-oil-on-canvas/oil-on-canvas/asset/1079709	p. 110
4.18	Victor Willing, *Effigy* (1978), crayon and pastel on paper, 25 × 32.5 cm. ©The Estate of Victor Willing. Timothy Taylor, https://www.timothytaylor.com/artworks/16711-victor-willing-effigy-1978/	p. 110
5.1	Paula Rego, *Crivelli's Garden* (1990–91), acrylic on canvas, 189.9 × 945.3 cm. ©National Gallery, London, https://artlyst.com/whats-on-archive/paula-rego-crivellis-garden/	p. 122
5.2	Artemisia Gentileschi, *Judith Beheading Holofernes* (1614–20), oil on canvas, 199 cm × 162.5 cm, Uffizi Gallery, Florence. Wikimedia Commons, public domain, https://commons.wikimedia.org/wiki/File:Judit_decapitando_a_Holofernes,_por_Artemisia_Gentileschi.jpg	p. 123
5.3	Jan Massys, *The Ill-matched Pair* (1566), oil on panel, 97 × 134 cm, National Museum, Sweden. Wikimedia Commons, public domain, https://commons.wikimedia.org/wiki/File:The_Ill-matched_Pair_(Jan_Massys)_-_Nationalmuseum_-_17511.tif	p. 123

5.4	Artemisia Gentileschi, *Samson and Delilah* (1930–38), oil on canvas, 90.5 cm × 109.5 cm, Palazzo Zevallos Stigliano, Naples. Wikimedia Commons, public domain, https://commons.wikimedia.org/wiki/File:Samson_und_delilah.jpg	p. 125
5.5	Paula Rego, *Red Monkey Beats His Wife* (1981), acrylic on paper. 65 × 105 cm. ©The Estate of Paula Rego. Victoria Miro, https://www.victoria-miro.com/artworks/29917/	p. 127
5.6	Paula Rego, *Dog Woman* (1952), pencil on paper, 15.5 × 21.5 cm. ©The Estate of Paula Rego, https://shop.tate.org.uk/paula-rego-dog-woman/paureg2122.html	p. 128
5.7	Paula Rego, *Dog Woman* (1994), pastel on canvas, 120 × 160 cm. ©The Estate of Paula Rego. Victoria Miro, https://www.victoria-miro.com/artworks/29910/	p. 128
5.8	Paula Rego, *Girl Lifting Up Her Skirt to a Dog* (1986), acrylic on paper mounted on canvas, 76 × 55.5 cm. ©The Estate Paula Rego. Bridgeman Images, https://www.bridgemanimages.com/en/rego/girl-lifting-up-her-skirt-to-a-dog-1986-acrylic-paint-on-paper-mounted-on-canvas/acrylic-paint-on-paper-mounted-on-canvas/asset/8369496?offline=1	p. 128
5.9	Antoine Watteau, *The Toilette* (first half of the eighteenth century), oil on canvas, 45.2 × 37.8 cm, the Wallace Collection, London. Wikimedia Commons, public domain, https://commons.wikimedia.org/wiki/File:Antoine_Watteau_-_The_Toilette_-_WGA25473.jpg	p. 129
5.10	Jean-Honoré Fragonard, *Two Girls on a Bed Playing with their Dogs* (date unknown), oil on canvas, 74.3 × 59.3 cm, Resnick Art Collection, Los Angeles. Photo by Sotheby's (2022), Wikimedia Commons, public domain, https://commons.wikimedia.org/wiki/File:Jean-Honor%C3%A9_Fragonard_-_Two_girls_on_a_bed_playing_with_their_dogs_-_collection_Resnick.jpg	p. 129

5.11   Jean-Honoré Fragonard, *Young Girl and her Dog* (1770–   p. 130
        75), oil on canvas, 89 × 70 cm, Alte Pinakothek, Munich.
        Photo by Jebulon (2014), Wikimedia Commons, public
        domain, https://commons.wikimedia.org/wiki/
        File:Jeune_fille_et_son_chien,_Jean-Honor%C3%A9_
        Fragonard,_HUW_35,_Alte_Pinakothek_Munich.jpg

5.12   Paula Rego, *The Betrothal: Lessons: The Shipwreck, after*   p. 131
        'Marriage à la Mode' by Hogarth (1999), pastel on paper
        mounted on aluminium, 165 × 500 cm, Tate, London.
        ©Paula Rego. Tate, https://www.tate.org.uk/art/
        artworks/rego-the-betrothal-lessons-the-shipwreck-
        after-marriage-a-la-mode-by-hogarth-t07919

5.13   William Hogarth, *Marriage A-la-Mode: The Tête à Tête*   p. 131
        (c. 1743), oil on canvas, 69.9 × 90.8 cm, the National
        Gallery, London. Wikimedia Commons, public
        domain, https://commons.wikimedia.org/wiki/
        File:William_Hogarth_-_Marriage_A-la-Mode_2_
        The_T%C3%AAte_%C3%A0_T%C3%AAte.jpg

5.14   William Hogarth, *A Harlot's Progress*, Plate 1 (1732),   p. 132
        etching and engraving on paper, 31.6 × 38.8 cm,
        British Museum. Wikimedia Commons, public
        domain, https://commons.wikimedia.org/
        wiki/File:A_Harlot%27s_Progress,_Plate_1_
        (BM_1858,0417.544).jpg

5.15   William Hogarth, *Hudibras and the Skimmington* (1725–   p. 132
        26), engraving (second plate of three), 26.9 × 50.8 cm,
        New York Metropolitan Museum of Art. Wikimedia
        Commons, CC0, https://commons.wikimedia.
        org/wiki/File:Hudibras_and_the_Skimmington_
        (Twelve_Large_Illustrations_for_Samuel_Butler%27s_
        Hudibras,_Plate_7)_MET_DP826937.jpg

5.16   Paula Rego, *Wife Cuts off Red Monkey's Tail* (1981),   p. 132
        acrylic on paper, 68 × 101 cm. ©The Estate of
        Paula Rego. Marlborough Fine Art, https://www.
        researchgate.net/figure/Paula-Rego-Wife-Cuts-off-
        Red-Monkeys-Tail-1981-Acrylic-on-paper-68-x-101-
        cm_fig3_335537543

List of Illustrations *xix*

5.17 Paula Rego, *Girl and Dog* (1986), acrylic on paper, 112 × 76 cm. ©The Estate of Paula Rego. Marlborough Fine Art, https://www.researchgate.net/figure/Paula-Rego-Girl-and-Dog-Untitled-b-1986-Acrylic-on-paper-112-x-76-cm-Photograph_fig11_335537284   p. 133

5.18 Paula Rego, *Snare* (1987), acrylic on paper on canvas, 150 × 150 cm. ©The Estate of Paula Rego / Bridgeman Images. British Council Collection, https://artuk.org/discover/artworks/snare-176993   p. 133

5.19 Paula Rego, *Two Girls and a Dog* (1987), acrylic paint on paper on canvas, 150 × 150 cm, Calouste Gulbenkian Foundation, Lisbon. ©The Estate of Paula Rego, https://gulbenkian.pt/cam/en/publications/paula-rego-4/   p. 134

5.20 Paula Rego, *Descent from the Cross* (2002), pastel on paper on aluminium, 75 × 72 cm. ©The Estate of Paula Rego. Bosc d'Anjou (2021), https://www.flickr.com/photos/boscdanjou/52136949210   p. 134

5.21 Paula Rego, *Lamentation* (2002), watercolour and ink on paper, 21 × 29 cm, property of the Portuguese State (Portuguese State Contemporary Art Collection). ©The Estate of Paula Rego. Victoria Miro, https://www.artsy.net/artwork/paula-rego-lamentation-at-the-foot-of-the-cross   p. 134

5.22 Paula Rego, *Deposition* (1998), pastel and graphite on paper mounted on aluminium, 160 × 120 cm, private collection, https://www.christies.com/en/lot/lot-5335320   p. 134

5.23 Paula Rego, *The Little Mermaid* (2003), pastel on paper mounted on aluminium, 140 × 110 cm, Kunsthal Charlottenborg, Copenhagen, https://www.christies.com/en/lot/lot-5608702   p. 136

5.24 Paula Rego, *Mermaid Drowning Wendy* (1992), coloured etching and aquatint, 27.7 × 20 cm, Cristea Roberts Gallery, London, https://cristearoberts.com/artists/206-paula-rego/works/90242/   p. 136

5.25	Winslow Homer, *The Blue Beard Tableau: Fatima Enters the Forbidden Closet* (1868), wood engraving, 11.4 × 11.7 cm, Boston Public Library, Print Department. Wikimedia Commons, public domain, https://commons.wikimedia.org/wiki/File:Blue_beard_tableau_(Boston_Public_Library).jpg	p. 138
5.26	Paula Rego, *Dressing Him Up as Bluebeard* (2002), lithograph, 73 × 54 cm, part of a limited set, Museum of Modern Art, Tate, The Metropolitan Museum of Art, Art Institute of Chicago, https://www.artsy.net/artwork/paula-rego-dressing-him-up-as-bluebeard-from-the-jane-eyre-series	p. 139
5.27	Paula Rego, *Mother Takes Revenge* (2003), pastel on paper, 104 × 79 cm. © The State of Paula Rego. Bridgeman Images, https://www.bridgemanimages.com/en/rego/mother-takes-revenge-red-riding-hood-series-2003-pastel-on-paper/pastel-on-paper/asset/8835840?offline=1	p. 140
5.28	Paula Rego, *Mother Wears Wolf's Pelt* (2003), pastel on paper, 84 × 67 cm. © The Estate of Paula Rego. Bridgeman Images, https://www.bridgemanimages.com/en/rego/mother-wears-the-wolf-s-pelt-red-riding-hood-series-2003-pastel-on-paper/pastel-on-paper/asset/8835842?offline=1	p. 141
5.29	Paula Rego, *Night Bride* (2009), etching and aquatint, 36.5 × 50 cm, Royal Academy Collection, https://www.royalacademy.org.uk/art-artists/work-of-art/night-bride	p. 141
5.30	Paula Rego, *Escape* (2009), etching and aquatint, 49 × 36.5 cm. ©Ostrich Arts Ltd/Amgueddfa Cymru - Museum Wales, https://museum.wales/collections/online/object/2e7a7812-96c6-357f-98d1-681ff3ae4012/Escape/?field0=string&value0=roman&field1=with_images&value1=1&page=196	p. 144
6.1	Paula Rego, *Nativity* (2002), property of the Portuguese State (Portuguese State Contemporary Art Collection), https://www.researchgate.net/figure/Paula-Rego-Nativity-2002-Pastel-on-paper-mounted-on-aluminium-54-x-52-cm-Belem_fig1_335537454	p. 151

List of Illustrations xxi

6.2	'We Won't Go Back', coat hanger sign from demonstration in front of SCOTUS, 3 May 2022. Photo by Janni Rye (2022), Wikimedia Commons, CC0, https://commons.wikimedia.org/wiki/File:We_wont_go_back_-_coat_hanger_-_sign_-_Demonstration_in_front_of_SCOTUS_May_3_2022_754.jpg	p. 159
6.3	Paula Rego, *Untitled Triptych; Abortion* (left-hand panel) (1998–99). Pastel on paper mounted on aluminium, 110 xx 100 cm. ©The Estate of Paula Rego and Victoria Miro, https://womensartblog.wordpress.com/2018/05/21/the-abortion-pastels-paula-rego/	p. 159
6.4	Paula Rego, *Untitled* (Abortion) (1988), pastel on paper mounted on aluminium, 110 × 100 cm. ©The Estate of Paula Rego and Victoria Miro, https://www.nationalgalleries.org/sites/default/files/features/EFENJJWW4AADxdy_1.jpg	p. 159
6.5	Paula Rego, *Agony in the Garden* (2002), pastel on paper on aluminium, 79.5 × 76.5 × 4.5 cm, Virgin Mary Series. ©Paula Rego. All rights reserved 2025/Bridgeman Images, https://www.bridgemanimages.com/en/rego/agony-in-the-garden-2002-pastel-on-paper-on-aluminium/pastel-on-paper-on-aluminium/asset/8617906	p. 162
6.6	Ana Palma, *Entrails II* (2021), acrylic and watercolour pencil on paper, 35 × 50 cm, CC BY-NC-SA 4.0.	p. 163
6.7	Ana Palma, *The Cycle* (2016–19), graphite pencil and acrylic on paper, 59.4 × 84.1 cm, CC BY-NC-SA 4.0.	p. 164
6.8	Ana Palma, *You Died on Me* (2013), graphite and watercolour on paper, 47 × 42.5 cm, CC BY-NC-SA 4.0.	p. 165
6.9	Ana Palma, *Orange* (2017), watercolour on paper, 29.7 × 42 cm, CC BY-NC-SA 4.0.	p. 166
6.10	Ana Palma *Rebirth* (2017), coloured pencil and acrylic on paper, 42 × 59.4 cm, CC BY-NC-SA 4.0.	p. 167
6.11	Ana Palma, *Truth* (2019), graphite pencil and acrylic on paper, 29.7 × 42 cm, CC BY-NC-SA 4.0.	p. 169
6.12	Ana Palma, *Found It!* (2017), watercolour pencils on paper, 70 × 50 cm, CC BY-NC-SA 4.0.	p. 169

6.13	Ana Palma, *Inner Spring* (2019), graphite, watercolour pencils and acrylic on paper, 29.2 × 42 cm, CC BY-NC-SA 4.0.	p. 170
6.14	Ana Palma, *Demeter* (2021), graphite and watercolour on paper, 29.7 × 42 cm, CC BY-NC-SA 4.0.	p. 172
6.15	Ana Palma, *Persephone* (2021), graphite and watercolour on paper, 29.7 × 42 cm, CC BY-NC-SA 4.0.	p. 173
6.16	Siena, *Sibilla Cumea*, Sienna Cathedral, mosaic floor detail. Photo by Sailko (2011), Wikimedia Commons, CC BY-SA 3.0, https://commons.wikimedia.org/wiki/File:Siena,_sibilla_cumea_01.JPG	p. 176

A Note on Texts, Translations and Images

All translations from Portuguese are by Maria Manuel Lisboa. Although not all academics would opt to use on-line texts rather than established editions, this author follows a different logic: where a text is available on-line in an accurate rendition, it is more democratic to refer to that than favouring one specific print edition over another in the case of texts widely available under different presses in different countries, as is the case of works by Eça de Queirós, Camilo Castelo Branco, Fernando Pessoa, Clarice Lispector and others. This book contains two types of illustrations: images reproduced directly in the text, and external images accessible via stable URLs and QR codes, each accompanied by a thumbnail. Certain images are provided through links rather than full reproduction in print because of resolution, permissions or cost constraints.

Today, the 'polymath' [...] is distrusted. He has few colleagues. He will commit errors and oversights, perhaps trivial or readily corrected, but of a kind which exasperates the specialist, which casts doubt on the work as a whole. I have, on occasion, been careless over detail, over technical discriminations. Impatience, [...] the pressure of deadlines and public platforms [...] have marred texts which could have been, formally at least, unblemished. An unripe restlessness, [...] has made me drop subjects, problems, disciplines once I thought, erroneously perhaps, that I had seized their gist, that I knew where the matter led. My belief that cows have fields but that passions in motion are the privilege of the human mind has long been held against me.

George Steiner, *Errata*

Introduction: Faulty Merchandise

> The world breaks everyone, and afterward, some are strong at the broken places.
>
> Ernest Hemingway, *A Farewell to Arms*

Let us talk about disability. Are you physically impaired, incapacitated, crippled, debilitated, limited, restricted, maimed, paralyzed, disabled, paralytic, differently-abled? Or are you mentally ill, neurodiverse, mad, batty, barmy, insane, crazy, a lunatic, a psycho?

Or are you both? If you are extremely unlucky (in the words of the deeply politically-incorrect Ian Dury), are you spasticus/autisticus?[1] Are you either? Are you neither? Will it kill you? As is the case with most things, the answer to these questions depends partly on race, sex, age, class, occupation, tenacity, wear and tear, fatigue, despair.

One man's shell shock is another woman's hysteria (Showalter, 1987). If you are a young, promising university student, tough though life may be, the world of disability resources is your oyster. If you are an overweight, chain-smoking, unemployed, council-house mother-of-six, you are seen as a benefits scrounger. If you are somewhere in the middle, 'outcomes' may depend on whether or not you are someone who is able to 'self-advocate' (aka, a sufficiently-grumpy cripple).

In the enlightened world of academia, for example, where pigs definitely fly, one finds a whole industry of Disability Studies: Disability in Literature; Disability in Art; Disability in Film; Disability in Science Fiction ('there are no ramps in space'); Disability in History; Disability in Society; Cultural Studies and Disability; Queer Disabilities; Transnational Disabilities; Disability and Race;

---

[1] See further, https://dangerousminds.net/comments/spasticus_autisticus_the_day_the_bbc_banned_ian_dury/

Transgender Disability; Post-human Disability; etc. Just put the word 'disability' on Amazon or in your library's search engine and you will find that you will never walk alone (if you can walk at all). Praxis is a beautiful word, of course, but look out for Theory overburden. Bandwagons can be adapted for the disabled: blue-badges-for-all. Just don't annoy your line manager, lest (to use another over-used/abused/abusive term) you queer the patch for another cripple down the line.

In the past fifteen years or so, Disability Studies have mushroomed in universities, from books to dedicated journals, to forums, to workshops.[2] But why only now? Back whenever it was, Oedipus became blind through self-harming, the latter problem in its turn having been triggered by a dysfunctional family and polis. Cripples, like the poor, have always been with us.

Paraphrasing Tolstoy, all healthy people are alike; each unhealthy person is unhealthy in their own way. The modalities of being broken, be it in body or in mind, are as numerous as there are living organisms on the planet. One of the most obvious but thought-provoking comments anyone ever made to me was that in the wild all animals die a nasty death. The same, of course applies to many human beings, either in the wild or in one's own neighbourhood. And the difference between humans and non-humans, let alone between verdant, dry or concrete jungles, is not always clear. Less often (but not never), 'regarding the pain of others'[3] can kill the viewer too. Rubber-necking a car crash may not always be done with impunity.

In 1996, a song by the Welsh band Manic Street Preachers, titled 'Kevin Carter', reached number nine on the UK Singles Chart. The subject of the lyrics was the eponymous Pulitzer Prize-winning photographer, who in 1994 was awarded the Prize for Feature Photography for his image, *The Vulture and the Little Girl*, taken in what is now South Sudan during the notorious 1993 famine. The image showed a small child crawling on the ground with a vulture loitering close by. Carter was a South African photographer and member of The Bang-Bang Club, a group of four conflict photographers active within the townships of South Africa between 1990 and 1994.

---

2 See Davis, 2016; Goodley, 2024; Hall, 2015; Yu, 2025; and the *Disability Studies Quarterly* journal.
3 Sontag, 2004.

Fig. I.1 Kevin Carter, *The Vulture and the Little Girl* (1993), Wikipedia, https://en.wikipedia.org/wiki/File:Kevin-Carter-Child-Vulture-Sudan.jpg

http://hdl.handle.net/20.500.12434/3e75498e

He was shocked by what he had just photographed and chased the vulture away, but then boarded a small UN plane and left the child behind. The photograph first appeared on 26 March 1993 in the *New York Times*[4] and was syndicated worldwide. Many people contacted the newspaper to ask about the fate of the child. The paper replied that according to Carter, 'she recovered enough to resume her trek after the vulture was chased away' but that it was unknown whether she had reached the nearest UN food centre. In 2011, the child's father revealed the child was actually a boy, Kong Nyong, who had in fact reached the aid station but had died in 2007, of unspecified 'fevers'.

Carter was reportedly troubled by the conflict between his professional responsibilities (photographic reportage) and moral considerations (intervening in what he was photographing). Four months after winning the Pulitzer he killed himself by carbon monoxide poisoning, aged thirty-three. His suicide note read as follows:

> I'm really, really sorry. The pain of life overrides the joy to the point that joy does not exist… I am haunted by the vivid memories of killings & corpses & anger & pain… of starving or wounded children, of trigger-happy madmen, often police, of killer executioners…[5]

Or, as the Manic Street Preachers would put it:

> Hi, Time Magazine, hi, Pulitzer Prize
> Tribal scars in Technicolor
> Bang-bang club, AK-47 hour
> Kevin Carter
> Hi, Time Magazine, hi, Pulitzer Prize
> Vulture stalked white piped lie forever
> Wasted your life in black and white
>   Kevin Carter. (Manic Street Preachers, 1996)

The permutations of life as a phenomenon that is nasty, brutish and short has been the subject of cultural artifacts ever since humanity began to decorate its caves.

---

4 See further https://en.wikipedia.org/wiki/The_Vulture_and_the_Little_Girl
5 See https://www.lehigh.edu/~jl0d/J246-02/carter.html

It is one of the never-ending preoccupations of literature, music and art. This volume will gather together essays that focus on literary and visual works from Brazil and Portugal, from the eighteenth century to the present, created under the malignancy of disease, both physical and mental, as well as the impact of the shortcomings in societies' care for their un-fittest.

Kermit the frog memorably lamented that it wasn't easy being green when everything around one was green too: 'It seems you blend in with so many other ordinary things'. But he re-thought his position, and in a moment worthy of the Portuguese poet Alberto Caeiro's[6] philosophical laid-backed posture, he ruminates that:

> When green is all there is to be
> It could make you wonder why
> But why wonder why wonder
> I am green, and it'll do fine
> It's beautiful, and I think it's what I want to be. (Raposo, 1970)

> I like everything to be real and for everything to be correct.
> And I like it because it would be so even if I didn't like it.
> Therefore, if I die now, I will die happy,
> Because everything is real and everything is right.
>   (Caeiro, 1946 [1993], p. 87)

The physical and emotional/mental cripples of the world would agree. Being whole(some) and unremarkable is 'beautiful, and I think it's what I want to be'. But there again, where would the Arts be without life's damaged goods? God may have made 'all things bright and beautiful' (which, however, as the Epicurean paradox rightly points out, begs the question 'if so, where did the rest come from?') but his Son was less picky: he purportedly loved all things, bright *and* ugly.

The biographical circumstances of the subject of Chapter 1—race, illegitimacy and deformity—and the fact that Antônio Francisco Lisboa's life was to be both *defined* and *unconfined* by them, offers the blueprint for how we may approach the ontological drive in the chapters that follow, behind broken minds in Camilo Castelo Branco's Marta, Clarice Lispector's Macabéia and Laura, and broken bodies in Victor Willing, Paula Rego and Ana Palma. He becomes the scaffolding for thinking about their works.

Chapter 1 considers the life and work of the Brazilian eighteenth-century architect and carver, Antônio Francisco Lisboa, also known as 'o

---

6   See Chapter 4 in this volume.

Aleijadinho' ('the Little Cripple'). Lisboa was best-known as the creator of churches and religious statuary in the state of Minas Gerais. He was a key representative of the Baroque movement not only in Brazil but in the whole of South America. The chapter will highlight his achievement in view of profound disability that for a considerable part of his life deprived him of the use of his feet, and at a later stage, most of his fingers.

Chapter 2 discusses *A brasileira de Prazins*, a nineteenth-century novel by the Portuguese author Camilo Castelo Branco, in which, breaking from his customary High Romantic style, he uses the trope of the mental illness of the eponymous heroine as a means of commenting on the political decline of the nation in the aftermath of the loss of its empires in South Asia and Brazil.

Chapter 3 considers two texts by Clarice Lispector, a twentieth-century Brazilian descendent of Ukrainian Jewish refugees whose work became iconic amongst French Feminist theoreticians such as Hélène Cixous. The two texts considered here, a short story ('A imitação da rosa') and a novel (*A hora da estrela*) focus on Lispector's signature concern with mental and physical entrapment as the result of gender and poverty expressed through the means of verbal embattlement.

Chapter 4 looks at the work of the twentieth-century artist, Victor Willing (Portuguese by marriage and sometime-resident in Portugal), the second phase of whose paintings were defined by his disability, caused by multiple sclerosis.

Chapter 5 analyses the use of physical trauma in the visual works of Paula Rego, inflicted by medical factors (illness, abortion, female genital mutilation) as well as social and political violence.

Chapter 6 considers the visual works of London-based Portuguese artist Ana Palma and analogies with Paula Rego, in a series of paintings, drawings, watercolours and sketches inspired by the physical and mental effects of amenorrhea (absence of menstruation in women of child-bearing age).

The book closes with interviews and recollections: an interview with Lila Nunes, Paula Rego's main female model over many decades, one with Ana Palma and an *in memoriam* by her old friend, Helder Macedo are also included.

Works Cited

Caeiro, Alberto, 1946 [1993], 'When Spring Comes', in 'Poemas Inconjuntos', in Fernando Pessoa, *Poemas de Alberto Caeiro,* 10th ed. (Lisbon: Ática), p. 87.

Davis, Lennard J. (ed.), 2016, *The Disability Studies Reader* (London: Routledge).

Goodley, Dan, 2024, *Disability Studies: An Interdisciplinary Introduction* (London, New York, Dehli and Singapore: SAGE Publications).

Hall, Alice, 2015, *Literature and Disability* (London: Routledge).

Manic Street Preachers, 1996, 'Kevin Carter' (*Everything Must Go*).

Raposo, Joe, 1970, 'Bein' Green' (*The Muppet Show*).

Showalter, Elaine, 1987, *The Female Malady: Women, Madness and English Culture, 1830-1980* (London: Virago).

Sontag, Susan, 2004, *Regarding the Pain of Others* (London: Penguin).

Tolstoy, Leo, 2003, *Anna Karenina* (London: Penguin Classics).

Yu, Tiffany, 2025, *The Anti-Ableist Manifesto: How to Build a Disability-Inclusive World* (Guildford: Souvenir Press).

1. Little Cripples: Antônio Francisco Lisboa ('O Aleijadinho')

> Cavalhadas, Luminárias.
> Sinos, procissões, promessas.
> Anjos e santos nascendo
> em mãos de gangrena e lepra
> Finas músicas broslando
> as alfaias das capelas.
> Todos os sonhos barrocos
> deslizando em pedra.
>
> Cecília Meireles, referring to Antônio Francisco Lisboa, 'Romance XXI ou das Idéias', in *Romanceiro da Inconfidência*[1]

> Ah gits weary
> An' sick of tryin'
> Ah'm tired of livin'
> An' skeered of dyin'.
>
> William Warfield, 'Ol' Man River'

Introduction

This chapter focuses on the life and work of the Brazilian eighteenth-century artist, architect and carver Antônio Francisco Lisboa, against

---

1 Oak carvings, illuminations.
   Bells, processions, promises.
   Angels and saints born
   in hands of gangrene and leprosy. Fine music embellishing
   the altarpieces of the chapels.
   All the baroque dreams
   sliding on stone. (Cecília Meireles, referring to Antônio Francisco Lisboa, 'Romance XXI ou das Idéias', in *Romanceiro da Inconfidência*).

the background of severe disability in a society where his status as the mixed-race son of a slave and of a Portugues migrant did not prevent him from becoming a key proponent of the Baroque style in South America, as well as a major influence on the Brazilian Modernist movement, one-and-a-half centuries later.

***

The Aleijadinho: The Man, His Body and His Work

The life of Antônio Francisco Lisboa is inextricably linked to any consideration of his work both as sculptor and carver, the nature of the work itself being in fact almost entirely determined by the tastes and interests of the financial entities that commissioned it (mainly the Roman Catholic Church in Brazil at the height of the Baroque movement in the eighteenth century). Were it not, therefore, for the extraordinary adversity of his circumstances (race, disability), the *homem* behind the *obra* might have remained as anonymous as those behind many of the great architectural and design monuments of that period, or indeed any other period anywhere. There are exceptions, of course (Michelangelo, Christopher Wren, Antoni Gaudi, Le Corbusier, Frank Lloyd Wright, Norman Foster), but in general does anyone, other than architectural art historians, know the names of those responsible for the conception of King's College Chapel in Cambridge, the Monastery of the Jerónimos in Lisbon or even Versailles? We may know which kings, governments or entities commissioned famous buildings; their architects, sculptors, carvers and builders, however, tend not to be household names, and many are not known at all. Not so, however, in the case of 'Aleijadinho' (the 'Little Cripple'). Even more so than in the case of the writers and artists that will be discussed in the chapters that follow, in this instance, the legend and the life *are* of the essence regarding the work, determined by a combination of biographical factors which throw light on the 'texts' (I use the term 'texts' advisedly, albeit possibly anachronistically), but which also exceed them in terms of the interest they aroused. We know about the Church of Saint Francis of Assisi in São João del-Rei (Fig. 1.1) and the Church of the Good Lord of Matosinhos and the Twelve Prophets (Fig. 1.7) *because* they are the work of Aleijadinho.

Fig. 1.1 Antônio Francisco Lisboa, *Church of Saint Francis of Assisi (1749–1809) São João del Rei*, Congonhas, Brazil. Photo by Marinelson Almeida (2014), Wikimedia Commons, CC BY 2.0, https://commons.wikimedia.org/wiki/File:Igreja_de_S%C3%A3o_Francisco_de_Assis._A_joia_rara_de_S%C3%A3o_Jo%C3%A3o_Del_Rei_-_MG_(15277299478).jpg

Plato, 'like all heroic Greeks, a cunt'[2] (paraphrasing Jorge de Sena, who knew a thing or two about diversity) did not approve of anything that was not perfection. The ugly and the sick, for example, had no place in his utopian republic. Neither did artists or playwrights, as it happens, which would leave the artist to be discussed here very much in the doghouse for being what he was (deformed) and doing what he did (art). Or worse than the doghouse, since in *The Republic* the Greek praises dogs for being true philosophers *as well as/or because* they were xenophobic in the most literal sense of the word (lovers of the familiar, who distinguished the face of a friend or an enemy purely on the criterion of knowing and not knowing them) (Plato, 2018, p. 60).

We will return to this. But perhaps Pierre Bourdieu's lament that 'every established order tends to produce the naturalization of its own arbitrariness' had a point, then and now (Bourdieu, 1977, p. 115). For Bourdieu the body is a generator of social divisions which it mirrors. It carries symbolic value imprinted on particular bodily forms. De(form)ities? And Bordo (not Bourdieu), albeit with a focus on gender (but it

---

[2] 'In Crete with the Minotaur'; see https://ruadaspretas.blogspot.com/2008/11/jorge-de-sena-em-creta-com-o-minotauro.html for the original text.

applies to other areas of marginalization such as disability) debates the ways in which body ideals serve as mechanisms of social power and control.

In 'The Body Beautiful: Symbolism and Agency in the Social World', Erica Reischer and Kathryn S. Koo draw on Bourdieu and Foucault to debate how the body has become of interest to social theory which, rather than considering it through a 'naturalistic approach [...] as a biological given', redefined it as a 'sociocultural and historical phenomenon': 'the body as a conduit of social meaning' (Reischer and Koo, 2004, p. 298). Mary Douglas (1970) memorably defined it as a text or script upon which social meanings are inscribed; and albeit from the specific perspective of the female body under patriarchy (but it will have relevance here too), Bordo sees body ideals not simply as harmless symbols of social values but also as mechanisms of social power and control, body size and shape signifying the moral state of the individual. Plato would have agreed.

The way we look determines how society engages with us, and for Maurice Merleau-Ponty (1958), the reverse is also true.

> The living body [...] could not escape the determinations which alone made the object into an object and without which it would have had no place in the system of experience. (Merleau-Ponty, 1958, p. 63)

> The human body [is] the outward manifestation of a certain manner of being-in-the-world. (Merleau-Ponty, 1958, p. 64)

> Sense experience, thus detached from the affective and motor functions, became the mere reception of a quality, and physiologists thought they could follow, from the point of reception to the nervous centres, the projection of the external world in the living body. The latter, thus transformed, ceased to be my body, the visible expression of a concrete Ego, and became one object among all others. Conversely, the body of another person could not appear to me as encasing another Ego. It was merely a machine, and the perception of the other could not really be *of the other*. (Merleau-Ponty, 1958, p. 64)

In the end, however, if the body is a vehicle for the imposition of social, political and economic forces onto individuals and groups, it must also be seen as the instrument of resistance to those forces. It 'can never be a struggle-free zone' and has the ability to challenge them (Comaroff, 1985, p. 40).

Antônio Francisco Lisboa (born in either 1730 or 1738, died 18 November 1814, Fig. 1.2), better known as Aleijadinho, was a sculptor, carver and architect in colonial Brazil, noted for his works on various churches as well as religious art, statuary, reliefs and carvings (Fig. 1.3). He is considered the greatest representative of the Baroque movement in the Americas. Almost all of his work was carried out in the state of Minas Gerais, especially in the cities of Ouro Preto (formerly Vila Rica), Sabará, São João del-Rei and Congonhas. Practically all the information about his life is derived from a biography written in 1858 by Rodrigo José Ferreira Bretas, forty-four years after his death, and allegedly based on documents and testimonies of individuals who had known the artist personally: *Traços biográficos relativos ao finado Antônio Francisco Lisboa, distinto escultor mineiro, mais conhecido pelo apelido de Aleijadinho* [*Biographical Notes Regarding the Deceased Antônio Francisco Lisboa, Distinguished Sculptor from Minas Gerais, better known as The Little Cripple*][3] in which he reproduced excerpts from the original document, that were later lost. Recent criticism has tended to consider this biography unreliable but it cannot be entirely discarded, since it is the oldest and most substantial evidential text, most of the later accounts being to a greater or lesser extent based on it. Critical studies carried out by the Brazilian Modernists in the first half of the twentieth century also put forward unverified interpretations of his life and work, which added to the legend that surrounded him and is perpetuated to this day in the popular imagination, both by critics and by tourism interests in the cities where he worked. Aleijadinho was described by Bretas in the following terms:

> He was dark brown, had a strong voice, a passionate speech, and an angry temper: his stature was short, his body was full and poorly shaped, his face and head were round, and his forehead was voluminous, his hair was black and curly, that of his beard [was] bushy and broad, broad forehead, regular and somewhat pointed nose, thick lips, large ears, and short neck.[4]

---

3   Available at https://aleijadinho.com.br/o-aleijadinho/
4   Ibid.

Fig. 1.2 *Supposed Portrait of Aleijadinho.* Artist unknown (early nineteenth century), oil on parchment. Image size approx. 39.6 × 41.7 cm. Museu de Congonhas. Photo by Janine Moraes/Ministério da Cultura (2015), Wikimedia Commons, CC BY 2.0, https://commons.wikimedia.org/wiki/File:Inaugura%C3%A7%C3%A3o_do_Museu_de_Congonhas_(23425316429).jpg

Antônio Francisco Lisboa was the illegitimate son of a respected Portuguese master builder and architect, Manuel Francisco Lisboa (whose surname suggests he may have been a crypto-Jew on the run to Brazil from the Portuguese Inquisition) and his African slave, Isabel. He was manumitted by his father on the occasion of his birth. The birth certificate does not specify a date and there is credible evidence that he was in fact born not in 1730, as sometimes thought, but in 1738, a date accepted by the Aleijadinho Museum and recorded on his death certificate.

In 1738, his father married Maria Antónia de São Pedro, a Portuguese migrant from Azores, with whom he had four children. The artist grew up with them. He was never legitimized, but according to Bretas, his knowledge of drawing, architecture and sculpture was acquired from his father, for whom he worked as an apprentice.

From 1750 to 1759, he boarded at the Seminary of the Franciscan Donatos of the Hospice of the Holy Land, in Ouro Preto, where he learned grammar, Latin, mathematics and religion, at the same time assisting his father in the work the latter carried out at the Church of

Antônio Dias and the House of Stories (Casa dos Contos, Fig. 1.3). His first individual project dates back to 1752: a design for the fountain in the courtyard of the Governors Palace in Ouro Preto.

Fig. 1.3 Antônio Francisco Lisboa, *Museum Casa dos Contos* (1782–84), Ouro Preto, Brazil. Photo by Cecioka (2019), Wikimedia Commons, CC BY-SA 4.0, https://commons.wikimedia.org/wiki/File:Museu_Casa_dos_Contos_2019_26.jpg

In 1756, it is thought that he travelled to Rio de Janeiro accompanying Friar Lucas de Santa Clara, in charge of gold and diamonds to be shipped to Lisbon, and while there he may have been influenced by local artists. Two years later, it is thought that he created a soapstone fountain for the Holy Land Hospice and soon after that he became self-employed. Being of mixed race, however, he was often forced to accept contracts as a day labourer rather than as a master builder, and was paid accordingly, at a much lower rate.

From the 1760s until close to his death, Aleijadinho produced a large number of works, but in the absence of supporting documentation, several are only considered attributions. Upon his father's death in 1767, Aleijadinho, as an illegitimate son, was not included in his father's will, but back in Ouro Preto, he began to receive important commissions, including the design of the façade of the Church of Our Lady of Carmel (Fig. 1.4).

Fig. 1.4 Antônio Francisco Lisboa, *Church of Our Lady of Carmel* (1767–80), Ouro Preto, Brazil. Photo by Joedison Rocha (2019), Wikimedia Commons, CC BY-SA 4.0, https://commons.wikimedia.org/wiki/File:Igreja_de_Nossa_Senhora_do_Carmo,_Ouro_Preto-MG.jpg

Around 1770 he organized his workshop, which in 1772 was regulated and recognized by the Chamber of Ouro Preto. Still in 1772, on 5 August, he was received as a Brother in the Brotherhood of São José de Ouro Preto. John Bury (2006) argues that he role of the Brotherhoods (Guilds) in the social life of Minas Gerais served mainly mixed-race artisans (*mulattos*)[5] and attracted carpenters. They were organizations that sponsored the arts, fostered the spirit of Christian living, created a network of mutual assistance for their members, and dedicated themselves to caring for the poor. The Brotherhoods also had a political role, acting in the promotion of social consciousness in an environment otherwise dominated by the white Portuguese elite. Aleijadinho became a member of the Brotherhood of São José, at a time when Minas Gerais was in a state of political and social agitation, being pressured by the Portuguese Crown to increase the productivity of gold mines, a problem that gave rise to the Minas Gerais Conspiracy (*Inconfidência Mineira*). Aleijadinho may have had dealings with one of the conspirators, Cláudio Manuel da Costa.

Bretas reports that around 1777 he began to show signs of a degenerative condition which in due course earned him the nickname *Aleijadinho*, i.e. 'Little Cripple'. The exact nature of his illness remains unclear, but possible

---

5   The term, as used at the time, will be used here too.

diagnoses have included leprosy (an unlikely suggestion, however, since he was never excluded from social contact), deforming rheumatism, 'cardine' intoxication, syphilis, scurvy, physical trauma from a fall, rheumatoid arthritis, poliomyelitis or porphyria (the latter being a disease that causes photo-sensitivity—which would explain the fact that in later years he worked at night or protected by an awning).

He always worked by commission, earning half an eighth of gold a day, and kept three slaves: a main helper with whom he shared his earnings, a carving assistant, and one who guided the donkey he used to move around.

As the disease progressed, his body became greatly deformed, and he endured constant pain. He lost several fingers, leaving only the index and thumb of one hand, as well as part of his feet, which forced him to drag himself on his knees. In order to work, he had to have chisels tied to the stumps of his hands, and in the most advanced stage of the disease he had to be carried. His features were also damaged, lending it a grotesque appearance. In order to hide his condition he supposedly wore loose-fitting clothes and large hats that concealed his face.

Even with increasing difficulty, however, Aleijadinho continued to work. In 1796, he received an important commission: the realization of the sculptures of the *Via Sacra* for the *Sanctuary of Bom Jesus and the Twelve Prophets* of Matosinhos, in Congonhas (Fig. 9), now considered to be his masterpiece.

Between 1807 and 1809, with his illness at an advanced stage, he closed his workshop, but continued to work. From 1812 onwards, his health deteriorated further. By this time, he was nearly blind and he died on 18 November 1814. He was buried in the Mother Church of Antônio Dias, in a tomb next to the altar of Our Lady of the Good Death.

Bretas praised Aleijadinho's achievements against a hostile environment and overwhelming illness in quasi-hagiographical terms, and at the beginning of the twentieth century (1922, the centenary of Brazil's independence from Portugal in 1822), the Modernist movement adopted his work as part of their agenda to define a Brazilian (i.e. non-European) cultural and ethnic identity, seeking to transform the nation's Portuguese heritage into something original and geographically specific. Aleijadinho's illness became and continues to be an important element in the endeavour to exalt the monumental (pun intended) effort of his work.

Monstrously Unwell: Illness, Badness and Deformity

> But I am a blasted tree; the bolt has entered my soul; and I felt then that I should survive to exhibit, what I shall soon cease to be—a miserable spectacle of wrecked humanity, pitiable to others, and intolerable to myself.
>
> <div align="right">Mary Shelley, <i>Frankenstein</i></div>

Nobody loves a freak, but historically we certainly seem to have enjoyed ogling them. For a large part of his life, Aleijadinho endured the illness that deformed his limbs, face and body and ultimately turned him into a miscreation. What links him to Frankenstein's monster, Quasimodo, the Phantom of the Opera, Richard III, the Elephant Man and the bearded lady at the circus was physical deformity, which traditionally has been considered both to cause and reflect moral abjection (according to Bretas, as his condition worsened, Aleijadinho became aggressive and paranoid).[6] We may have our own voyeuristic propensities and cruelty in part to blame for that, going back at least as far as Plato's Diotima[7] (although the former may have been merely observing what myth and legend had taught him to be true). The Sphinx, the Basilisk, the Chimera, the Manticore, the Hydra, the Medusa and the Sirens (to name but a few) all suggest that whilst the good are supposedly beautiful in a cause-and-effect confederacy, the same logic applies to ugliness and viciousness. Handsome is as handsome does. And again, vice versa, 'vice' being the operative word.

In Act I, Scene I of Shakespeare's *Richard III*, following the famous 'winter of our discontent' opening, Richard elaborates on how in effect the Plantagenet 'glorious sun' of York is a red herring, glimpsed briefly before darkness descends again in all its hideousness: ugliness that is physical but, more to the point, moral:

> *But I, that am not shaped for sportive tricks,*
> *Nor made to court an amorous looking-glass;*
> *I, that am rudely stamp'd,* and want love's majesty
> To strut before a wanton ambling nymph;
> *I, that am curtail'd of this fair proportion,*

---

6   Ibid.
7   Plato, 1993, Section 10: 210a–212c.

> Cheated of feature by dissembling nature,
> Deformed, unfinish'd, sent before my time
> Into this breathing world, scarce half made up,
> And that so lamely and unfashionable
> That dogs bark at me as I halt by them;
> Why, I, in this weak piping time of peace,
> Have no delight to pass away the time,
> Unless to spy my shadow in the sun
> *And descant on mine own deformity:*
> *And therefore, since I cannot prove a lover,*
> To entertain these fair well-spoken days,
> *I am determined to prove a villain.* (Shakespeare, italics added)

Richard, according to himself, is evil because he cannot help being ugly. The rest is history, in the form of two princes murdered and buried in the Tower of London (while Richard himself was ignominiously forgotten in what eventually became an urban car park in Leicester five-and-a-half centuries later).[8] Or it is so at least in the rendition by this tract of Tudor (i.e. anti-Plantagenet) propaganda. Richard's turpitude is both the cause and the reflex of his deformity, one becoming the objective correlative for the other, as often debated by critics (Zamir, 1998; Torrey, 2000).

Across time, geography, genre and media, critics have tended to agree that disease and deformity spoke about individual or collective failure in body and soul. Matthew Ancell, writing on the poet Luis de Góngora, maintains that the 'poetics of disfiguration addresses epistemological problems precipitated by the sceptical crisis. [...] What is at play in Góngora, then, is an aesthetic expression of sceptical arguments that increasingly found purchase as conventional knowledge came under attack. By the late sixteenth century, a concatenation of factors—religious conflict, the discovery of the New World, an increasingly educated public, scientific discoveries and technologies, as well as economic, political, and legal changes—challenged world views and promoted a growing epistemological doubt that found confirmation in ancient Greek scepticism' (Ancell, 2011, p. 549). Claire Catenaccio, on the subject of Sophocles' *Oedipus Tyrannus*, suggests that 'the king's flawed feet are intimately connected with his flawed understanding of himself. They are the visible, dramatic representation of his spiritual defect'

---

8 See Kennedy, 2017.

(Catenaccio, 2012, p. 102) which in turn brings plague upon the city. In a different context, Randall Griffin, on the subject of Andrew Wyeth's iconic painting *Christina's World* (1948)[9] states that the image 'provides insights into how the diseased body is socially inscribed. It serves as a reminder that the "abnormal" body is often inextricably bound to notions of femininity and poverty. Furthermore, the incongruities of Christina's body raise unsettling questions about the way selfhood is eroded and fragmented when the body becomes assaulted by disease' (Griffin, 2010, p. 45).

Elena Lazzarini maintains that 'even in moments of great splendour, beauty and order', the human body is accompanied by its 'indispensable counterparts, ugliness and disorder' (Lazzarini, 2011, p. 415), and that, drawing upon Aristotle, 'the ambivalent depiction of monsters means that they are vehicles of both pleasure and horror' (Lazzarini, 2011, p. 418). And for Sarah Covington, 'the wounded body has long provoked writers to explore the associated stigma and pain, but also the manner in which individuals transform bodily traumas into a new sense of being in the world' (Covington, 2008, p. 14).

In a society (Brazil in the eighteenth-century)—a country that, having been colonized by the Portuguese in 1500, became Spanish in 1580, Portuguese again in 1640, and in which the indigenous population had become nearly extinct whilst black people and mixed-race groups were slaves—anyone who wasn't white, prosperous and preferably male was in effect flawed in body, mind and soul. They were deemed to be existentially (or later, one would say, Darwinianly) *aleijados* (cripples), even if their body was intact, which in the case of the *Aleijadinho* it was not: whether his malady was one that carried stigma (leprosy) or an undiagnosed one that merely evoked pity.

All This and Black Too: The Question of Race

The notion of Brazil as a racial democracy has never been anywhere even close to the truth. Its population may be extraordinarily mixed, but certain rules of thumb apply now as they did from the time of European contact, and even after independence from Portugal, little changed. It

---

9   See https://www.moma.org/collection/works/78455

was the last country in the Western hemisphere to abolish slavery (in 1888), and even when it did, no measures were taken to cater to the subsistence needs of freed slaves.[10]

The term 'mongrel complex' ('complexo de vira-lata', a 'vira-lata' being an ownerless dog of indeterminate breed) coined by the Brazilian writer Nelson Rodrigues in the 1950s,[11] was a derogatory expression, usually used by nationalists to refer to a supposed 'collective inferiority complex' purportedly felt by many Brazilians when comparing Brazil and its culture to other parts of the world, primarily the developed world. The term carries associations with racism and ultra-nationalism.

The idea that the Brazilian people were inferior to others or 'degenerate' can be officially traced back to the nineteenth century, when Arthur de Gobineau visited Rio de Janeiro in 1845 and described the city's residents as 'unbelievably ugly monkeys'.[12] Gobineau's race theories gained currency in Brazil in the 1920s and 1930s, when sociologists such as Raimundo Nina Rodrigues, Francisco José de Oliveira Viana and José Bento Renato Monteiro Lobato proclaimed that the white race was superior to others and miscegenation was the root of all of Brazilians' problems:

> Brazil, son of inferior parents—destitute of these strongest characters that imprint an unmistakable stamp in certain individuals, such as it happens to the German and the English, grew up sadly—resulting in a worthless kind, incapable of continuing to self-develop without the vivifying assistance of the blood of some original race. (Lobato, 1959, p. 1903)

What was formulated in the nineteenth century, must of course, be traced back to the earliest beginnings of Brazil post-contact with Europe (Portugal) in 1500.[13] In 'Race and Identity: Sílvio Romero, Science, and Social Thought in Late 19th Century Brazil', Marshall C. Eakin (1985) offers an incisive summary of the views of cultural analysts whose work had untold effect on the way Brazil saw itself from its earliest days as a colony. Although what follows is the result of a phenomenon that post-dated the life and work of Aleijadinho, it arguably builds upon the

---

10 See https://brazillab.princeton.edu/research/racialized_frontiers
11 See https://pt.wikipedia.org/wiki/Complexo_de_vira-lata
12 See https://en.wikipedia.org/wiki/Mongrel_complex#cite_note-5
13 See Lisboa, 2023.

reality of the century that preceded it, and his lived experience.[14]

In the second half of the nineteenth century, Sílvio Romero was one of the great 'influencers' (using current terminology), whose open racism against mixed-race groups (*mulattos*) had no repercussions on the high regard in which his work was and still is widely held (*História da literatura brasileira* and other works). Romero believed that the literary critic must examine the social basis of literary production. Literature, he argued, is a manifestation of man's interaction with other men and of his social relations. This view went beyond literature as textual criticism to explore its social roots. This critical approach led Romero to believe that Brazil had reached a crucial juncture in its historical development that ought to set the agenda for future analysis and action. Looking back at Brazilian culture, he saw four centuries of cultural sterility relieved by very few writers or intellectuals of true quality. Only in the last half of the eighteenth century, and the first half of the nineteenth century, did he discern the beginnings of original Brazilian contributions to humankind's (*man*kind's) cultural progress. According to him, in order to contribute significantly to world-culture, Brazil had to repudiate the past and strikeout on a different course, drawing inspiration from new currents of thought and new philosophies. The time had come to 'reform the intellectual, literary, and scientific order of the country', and to bring about changes in the 'political and social orbit' of Brazil, in the fields of ideas, politics and society (Eakin, 1985, p. 12).

> Under the influence of Tobias Barreto, Romero became an ardent disciple of the 'scientific' world view, and this provided the foundation for his brand of literary and social analysis. 'The new generation reads the scientific writers,' Romero wrote, and 'there is no poet worthy of that name who is not at least slightly acquainted with the modern philosophers and naturalists. [...] Knowledge which is not generalized,' he wrote, 'remains unprofitable and sterile'. (Eakin, 1985, p. 13–15).
>
> Romero became one of the leading proponents of naturalism in Brazilian literature, and in doing so, he took an uncompromising positivist stance. The study of man, he maintained, demanded rigorous criticism, and this criticism required the aid of natural science. Here Romero expounded

---

14 A forerunner of Aleijadinho was Joaquim Maria Machado de Assis, Sílvio Romero's target of choice. Machado, like Aleijadinho, was a mixed-race man. Each man, a century apart, became the key figure in the art he practiced: architecture/sculpture and literature respectively.

the imperialism of the scientific world view at its extreme: science became the only valid and useful form of knowledge. (Eakin, 1985, p. 15)

Romero had acquired this typically nineteenth-century social evolutionist scheme from Herbert Spencer's belief in the inherent inequality of peoples, with race providing the key to his social thinking regarding human evolution. For Romero, three centuries of African slave trade and miscegenation had led to a multiracial Brazil with more black and mixed-raced people than white people. Romero and his contemporaries found themselves in an uncomfortable intellectual bind as they attempted to reconcile Brazil's ethnic reality with European theories that denigrated non-white and racially-mixed societies. Brazilian intellectuals who espoused these theories had to accept that their country was by definition inferior and on a path to further degeneration: a problem that led to intellectual anguish and social alienation. Nothing, according to them, could be done to alter the regressive tendencies of Brazil's racial mixture. Romero, like the notorious Raimundo Nina Rodrigues (1862–1906), stood out as the most pessimistic and fatalistic of the Brazilians who embraced 'scientific' race/racist theorists.

Romero believed that Brazil's history resulted from the encounter of white, black and indigenous peoples which created a fourth category: the *mestiço*. He recognized that miscegenation (between three entirely 'distinct' races: black, white and indigenous *Índios*) had played a central part in the formation of Brazilian society, something which a subsequent generation of Brazilian social scientists led by Gilberto Freyre after the First World War took to its logical conclusion. Freyre took Romero's concept of miscegenation as the Luso-tropical driving force in the evolution of Brazilian society, although unlike Romero, he emphasized its positive aspects. Freyre espoused a new vision of Brazil which recognized the role of racial mixture in his country's history. He provided a bridge from Romero's cultural contempt to a Luso-tropicalist sociology of hope. Freyre's utopian 'racial democracy', however, notoriously lent itself to the purposes of what proved to be mostly totalitarian propaganda, and the result continues to be that of a country recognized, by charities such as Oxfam, as one of the most unequal societies in the world in terms of indexes of race, sex, sexual preference and distribution of wealth.[15]

---

15   See https://www.oxfam.org/en/brazil-extreme-inequality-numbers

The impact of race on inequality is a determinant factor in what is, ironically, one of the most ethnically-mixed populations in the world, composed of indigenous *Índios*, Europeans of various provenance (but mainly Portuguese), and black people brought in under the slave trade from Africa. Slavery in what became Brazil had begun long before the first Portuguese settlement, but the Portuguese colonizers became heavily dependent on indigenous labour during the initial phases of settlement in order to maintain a subsistence economy. The enslavement of the indigenous populations quickly gave way to the importation of African slaves, which began in earnest half-way through the sixteenth century and continued until the stages of the 1871 Rio Branco Law/Law of the Free Womb (all children of slaves born after the law was passed were born free); the 1885 Saraiva-Cotegipe Law/Sexagenarian Law (all slaves over sixty years of age were freed); and the 1888 Lei Áurea/ Total Emancipation Law (the complete abolition of slavery). In cases of mixed-race children such as Aleijadinho, if the white parent was the father (which accounted for the vast majority of cases), the child could be manumitted either at birth or later in life.

The topic of race in Brazil has continued to inform social, political and cultural debate extending from Romero and Nina Rodrigues, through Freyre to Lília Moritz (1993); António Cândido (2006); Florestan Fernandes (2006, 2007 and 2008); Octávio Ianni (2004); and Eduardo França Paiva (2009). It continues, to this day, to signal just another way of being disabled.

The Baroque in Brazil

The Baroque movement, of which Aleijadinho became the foremost proponent in architecture, carving and painting in Brazil, originated in Italy at the turn of the sixteenth century, in the midst of the greatest spiritual crisis Europe had ever faced: the Protestant Reformation. It was a style of reaction against the Neo-Classicism of the Renaissance, whose foundations revolved around symmetry, proportionality, economics, rationality and formal equilibrium. Baroque aesthetics valued asymmetry, excess, expressiveness and irregularity: a culture that emphasized contrast, conflict, dynamism, drama, grandiloquence and the dissolution of boundaries, along with an accentuated taste for the opulence of shapes and materials, making it a perfect vehicle of expression for the Counter-Reformation Catholic Church and the rising absolutist monarchies. It also represented the attempt by Jesuits to appeal to popular taste, as an aggressive proselytizing campaign against Protestant austerity via the arts.

The Baroque in Brazil became the dominant artistic style during most of the colonial period, making its appearance in the country at the beginning of the seventeenth century. It was introduced by Jesuit missionaries and was shaped by a close association between the Church and the State. In a colony which did not boast a court that would serve as patron of the arts, the majority of the art and architecture of the Brazilian Baroque period was sacred art: statuary, painting and the work of carving for the decoration of churches and convents, or for private worship. The most typical characteristics of the Baroque were described as a dynamic, narrative, ornamental style, its purpose being decorative but also the transmission of Catholic doctrine. In the plastic arts, its greatest exponent was Aleijadinho, and it took root mainly in the Northeast Region of Brazil (*Nordeste*) and in Minas Gerais.

The Baroque appeared in Brazil about one hundred years after the beginning of the Portuguese colonization of Brazil. Slavery was a fundamental aspect of colonial Brazilian society, and was the infrastructure of its workforce. The movement was therefore associated with aspects of struggle and conquest, its artisans often including slaves of African descent, devoid of any education, let alone a classical one.

Although the threat of Protestantism was not a factor in colonial Brazil, the majority of its population were non-Christians (indigenous *Índios* and black Africans brought on slave ships) and the Baroque drew upon seductive motifs that aimed to attract and convert non-Christian populations. The Baroque Catholic mentality was prone to exaggeration and drama and involved a belief in miracles and in the value of relics and saints, combined with superstitions and practices learned from indigenous peoples and African slaves, and considered unorthodox by the church, which feared associations with the practice of witchcraft. Non-mainstream Christian mysticism tottered towards heresy, but sometimes made itself discernible even in Church-sponsored Baroque art. Having come about as a reaction against Protestant austerity, the Baroque placed emphasis on sensoriality, the richness of the materials and forms and hyperbolic visual language in carvings and paintings.

It privileged the most dramatic moments of sacred history, including Christ being flogged, graceful Madonnas and the baby Jesus, and, in the case of Aleijadinho, corporal and mental suffering (Figs. 1.5 and 1.6).

In 'Memento Mori in Baroque Rome', Corinna Ricasoli discusses an enormously influential anonymous pamphlet, printed in Cologne under the title *Ars bene moriendi. Tractatus brevis et valde utilis de arte et scientia bene moriendi*, intended as a manual for the sick and the dying. It belongs to a then-new genre in the *artes moriendi* that focused less on the terror of death and more on how to prepare devoutly for it (with an emphasis on the good death as a summation of a good life). Surprisingly, the Counter-Reformation and the Jesuits were leaders in this movement, something that reflected upon funerary art, with a focus on a peaceful eternal rest.

> A funerary monument might forestall oblivion by securing the memory of one's passage through this world [...]. In baroque Rome, death was acknowledged with resignation in everyday life, yet it never gained total and complete acceptance as the presence of funerary monuments standing as bulwarks against oblivion clearly suggest. (Ricasoli, 2015/16, p. 462)

Resignation is arguably less commonly found in the work of Aleijadinho, which is more oriented towards the darker aspects of the Christian narrative (Figs. 1.5 and 1.6).

Fig. 1.5 Antônio Francisco Lisboa, *The Ascent to Calgary* (1796–99), polychromed wood, life-size sculptures. Sanctuary of Congonhas da Campo, Brazil. Photo by Rosino (2011), Wikimedia Commons, public domain, https://commons.wikimedia.org/wiki/File:Aleijadinho_01.jpg

Fig. 1.6 Antônio Francisco Lisboa, *Jesus' Crucifixion* (1796–99), polychromed wood, life-size sculptures. Photo by Ricardo André Frantz (2015), Wikimedia Commons, CC BY 3.0, https://commons.wikimedia.org/wiki/File:A_crucifica%C3%A7%C3%A3o_de_Jesus_-_Aleijadinho_-_Congonhas.jpg

In the eighteenth century, Minas Gerais was an only-recently settled region. Its distance from the coastal metropoles permitted greater creative freedom, with a profusion of brand-new churches, and, when the region proved to be a rich source of gold and diamonds it flourished, its centre being the old Vila Rica (now Ouro Preto), founded in 1711.

As with other colonial artists, the conclusive attribution of Aleijadinho's works has proved difficult due both to the fact that artists of the period did not sign their works and to the scarcity of documentary sources. In general, documents such as contracts and receipts agreed between religious Brotherhoods and artists were the safest sources for determining authorship. Another aspect that must be taken into account is the prevalence of collective workshops in Minas Gerais at the time. With regard to Aleijadinho, there may be occasional uncertainty regarding the extent of his direct intervention in the execution of some of his works, including the documented ones. Often the master builders intervened in the original design of the churches but supervision of construction was carried out by teams linked to corporations associated with the civil and ecclesiastical powers, which also had directive power. An indeterminate number of assistant craftsmen also participated in the carving of altars and sculptures, who, whilst following the guidelines of the designer in charge of the commission, left their distinctive mark on the finished pieces. Aleijadinho's documented work is therefore limited to relatively few commissions (two of them including the large sculptural sets of Congonhas, the *Via Sacra and the Twelve Prophets*: Fig. 1.7), but the general catalogue published by Márcio Jardim in 2006 listed 425 pieces as his exclusive work. Aleijadinho's uncontested participation as a carver is also documented as designer and executor in at least four large altar pieces.

The final stage in the evolution of his style as a carver is illustrated by the altar pieces he created for the Church of Our Lady of Carmel in Ouro Preto, designed and executed by him between 1807 and 1809, these being the last ones he created before his illness forced him to supervise rather than execute his ideas.

Aleijadinho's greatest achievement in full-figure sculpture are the sets at the Sanctuary of Bom Jesus de Matosinhos, in Congonhas—the sixty-six statues of the *Via Sacra*, *Via Crucis* or *Passos da Paixão*, distributed in six independent chapels, and the *Twelve Prophets* in the churchyard. All the scenes on the *Via Sacra* (Fig. 8) were carved between 1796 and 1799.

Fig. 1.7 Antônio Francisco Lisboa, *Church of the Good Lord of Matosinhos and the Twelve Prophets* (1800–05), life-size soapstone statues. Photo by Silvia Schumacher (2014), Wikimedia Commons, CC BY-SA 4.0, https://commons.wikimedia.org/wiki/File:Conjunto_da_Bas%C3%ADlica_do_Senhor_Bom_Jesus_de_Matosinhos3.JPG

The twelve prophets have attracted the attention of many researchers, and several theories have been proposed to interpret them, including by Martin Dreher, who, in his book *A Igreja Latino-Americana no Contexto Mundial*, sees an association between them and the political situation of Minas Gerais, ach statue possibly representing one of the conspirators of the *Inconfidência Mineira*.

***

Conclusion

After a period of relative obscurity following his death, Aleijadinho re-emerged thanks to Bretas' biography of in 1858. Emperor Pedro II was an admirer of his work and later his importance was promoted by members of the Modernist movement (Tarsila do Amaral, Afonso Celso and Mário de Andrade).

His recognition against the formidable odds of race, social status and disability, endured and extends beyond Brazil. For many modern critics, Aleijadinho represents a unique moment in the evolution of Brazilian art, a meeting point for the social, ethnic, artistic and cultural roots that came to constitute the nation. Carlos Fuentes considered him the greatest 'poet' of colonial America (Fuentes, 1999, p. 201).

I Beg Your Pardon, I Never Promised You a Rose Garden

Aleijadinho's influence has been acknowledged by a number of Brazilian artists, including the Modernist Tarsila do Amaral (Fig. 1.8) and most recently Ana Maria Pacheco.[16]

Fig. 1.8 Tarsila do Amaral, *Workers* (1933).
© Artistic-Cultural Collection of the Governmental Palaces of the State of São Paulo. Wikipedia, https://pt.wikipedia.org/wiki/Ficheiro:Operarios.jpg#/media/Ficheiro:Operarios.jpg
http://hdl.handle.net/20.500.12434/d1054e2f

He left behind works that it would take an earthquake or an excavator to demolish. His busted body, however, was a different story. It is true

---

16 See https://prattcontemporaryart.co.uk/work/the-banquet/

that no one ever promised a rose garden to this man: someone born into slavery to a black woman[17] and to a possibly-exiled crypto-Jewish father. Turning the song around, in a rose garden, by rights, 'along with the rain, there's gotta be a little sunshine sometime'.[18] This, however, was eighteenth-century colonial Brazil. Independence, abolition and social reform were far in the future. Some would say that in some respects, even when they did come, little changed, and that all is still much the same today. In the land of carnival, beaches and football, sunshine, for many, is still at a premium.

> Racism in Brazil is well hidden, subtle, and unspoken, underestimated by the media. It is nevertheless extremely violent. (Joaquim Barbosa)[19]

> Father, take that chalice away from me
> Father, take that chalice away from me
> Father, take that chalice away from me
> Blood red wine.
> [...]
> How to drink this bitter drink
> Swallow the pain, swallow the toil
> Even with the mouth shut, the chest remains
> Silence in the city is not heard.
> [...]
> Maybe the world is not small
> Nor is life a fait accompli
> I want to invent my own sin
> I want to die of my own poison.
>   (Chico Buarque and Milton Nascimento, 'Chalice/Cálice', 1978)

---

17 For a discussion of the reality of being black in different periods in Brazil see, for example, Lisboa, 2023.
18 Joe South, 'Rose Garden' (1967); see https://en.wikipedia.org/wiki/Rose_Garden_(song)
19 See https://www.brainyquote.com/quotes/joaquim_barbosa_774421; original quotation: 'O racismo no Brazil é mascarado, sutil, expresso de maneira velada subestimado pela mídia. Mesmo assim é extremamente violento'. Weekend edition of *Le Monde* around 15–16 September 2012 (reported by Radio France Internacionale (RFI) on 17 September 2012 and by Brazilian media outlets, such as the Gelédes Institute's portal RFI, on 18 September 2012). Sincere thanks to Viktor Mendes for helping me to locate this statement at the speed of light.

Works Cited

Ancell, Matthew, 2011, 'Este . . . Cíclope: Góngora's Polifemo and the Poetics of Disfiguration', *Hispanic Review*, 79.4, 547–72, https://doi.org/10.1353/hir.2011.0047

Bordo, Susan, 1993, *Unbearable Weight: Feminism, Western Culture, and the Body* (Berkeley: University of California Press).

Bourdieu, Pierre, 1997, *Outline of a Theory of Practice* (Cambridge: Cambridge University Press).

Bury, John, 2006, *Arquitetura e arte no Brazil colonial* (Brasilia: MONUMENTA), https://archive.org/details/arquitetura-e-arte-no-brasil-colonial

Cândido, Antonio, 2006, 'A sociologia no Brasil', *Tempo Social: Revista de Sociologia da USP*, 18.1, 271–301.

Catenaccio, Claire, 2012, 'Oedipus Tyrannus: The Riddle of the Feet', *The Classical Outlook*, 89.4, 102–07.

Comaroff, J., 1985, *Body of Power, Spirit of Resistance* (Chicago: University of Chicago Press).

Covington, Sarah, 2008, 'Teaching the Wounded Body: Mutilation and Meaning in Western War and Religion', *Transformations: The Journal of Inclusive Scholarship and Pedagogy*, 19.2, 14–31.

Douglas, Mary, 1970, *Natural Symbols: Explorations in Cosmology* (New York: Pantheon Books).

Dreher, Martin, 1999, *A Igreja Latino-Americana no Contexto Mundial* (São Leopoldo: Editora Sinodal).

Eakin, Marshall C., 1985, 'Race and Identity: Silvio Romero, Science, and Social Thought in Late 19th Century Brazil', *Luso-Brazilian Review*, 22.2, 151–74.

Ricasoli, Corinna, 2015/16, 'Memento Mori in Baroque Rome', *An Irish Quarterly Review*, 104.416, 456–67.

Fernandes, Florestan, 2006, *A revolução burguesa no Brasil: ensaio de interpretação sociológica* (Rio de Janeiro: Globo).

Fernandes, Florestan, 2007, *O negro no mundo dos brancos*, 2nd ed. (São Paulo: Editora Global).

Fernandes, Florestan, 2008, *A integração do negro na sociedade de classes*, 5th ed. (São Paulo: Globo).

Foucault, Michel, 1979, *Discipline and Punish: The Birth of the Prison*, trans. A. Sheridan (Harmondsworth: Penguin).

Freyre, Gilberto, 2006, *Casa-Grande & Senzala: formação da família brasileira sob o regime da economia patriarcal*, 51st ed. (São Paulo: Editora Global).

Fuentes, Carlos, 1999, *The Buried Mirror: Reflections on Spain and the New World* (Houghton: Mifflin Harcourt).

Griffin, Randall C., 2010, '"Andrew Wyeth's *Christina's World*": Normalizing the Abnormal Body', *American Art*, 24.2, 30–49.

Ianni, Octavio, 2004, 'O preconceito racial no Brasil', *Estudos avançados*, 18.50), 6–20.

Lamb, John B, 1992, 'Mary Shelley's Frankenstein and Milton's Monstrous Myth', *Nineteenth-Century Literature*, 47.3, 303–19.

Lazzarini, Elena, 2011, 'Wonderful Creatures: Early Modern Perceptions of Deformed Bodies', *Oxford Art Journal*, 34.3, 415–31, https://doi.org/10.1093/oxartj/kcr038

Lobato, Monteiro, 1959, *A todo transe* (São Paulo: Brasiliense).

Kennedy, Maev, 2017, 'Leicester Car Park Where Richard III Was Buried Given Protected Status', The Guardian (21 December), https://www.theguardian.com/uk-news/2017/dec/21/leicester-car-park-richard-iii-buried-given-protected-status

Lisboa, Maria Manuel, 2023, 'A Muted Palette; or, the Importance of Not Being Black: José de Alencar and Bernardo Guimarães', *The Journal of Romance Studies*, 23.3, 269–99, https://doi.org/10.3828/jrs.2023.18

Merleau-Ponty, Maurice, 1958, *Phenomenology of Perception*, trans. Colin Smith (London and New York: Routledge and Kegan Paul).

Moritz, Lilia, 1993, *O espetáculo das raças: cientistas, instituições e questão racial no Brasil – 1870 – 1930* (São Paulo: Companhia das Letras).

Paiva, Eduardo França, 2009, *Escravos e libertos nas Minas Gerais do século XVIII: Estratégias de resistência através dos testamentos* (São Paulo: Annablume).

Plato, 1993, *The Symposium*, trans. and ed. Christopher Gill (London: Penguin Classics).

Plato, 2018, *The Republic*, ed. G. R. F. Ferrari, trans. Tom Griffith (Berkeley: University of California Press).

Reischer, Erica, and Kathryn S. Koo, 2004, 'The Body Beautiful: Symbolism and Agency in the Social World', *Annual Review of Anthropology*, 33, 297–317.

Ribeiro, Darcy, 2006, *O povo brasileiro: a formação e o sentido do Brasil* (São Paulo: Companhia das Letras).

Rodrigues, Raimundo Nina, 2011, *As raças humanas e a responsabilidade penal no Brasil* (Rio de Janeiro: Centro Edelstein de Pesquisa Social).

Torrey, Michael, 2000, '"The Plain Devil and Dissembling Looks": Ambivalent Physiognomy and Shakespeare's *Richard III*', *English Literary Renaissance*, 30.2, 123–53, https://doi.org/10.1111/j.1475-6757.2000.tb01167.x

Zamir, Tzachi, 1998, 'A Case of Unfair Proportions: Philosophy in Literature', *New Literary History*, 29.3, 501–20, https://doi.org/10.1146/annurev.anthro.33.070203.143754

2. Camilo Castelo Branco's *A brasileira de Prazins*: 'When in Danger or in Doubt, Run in Circles, Scream and Shout'[1]

A dream is not reality, but who's to say which is which?

Lewis Carroll, *Alice Through the Looking Glass*

Grecia, Roma, Cristandade,
Europa—os quatro se vão
Para onde vai toda idade.
Quem vem viver a verdade
Que morreu D. Sebastião?

Fernando Pessoa, 'Quinto império'[2]

Felizes os que podem ver de longe a pátria nas garras do abutre.

Camilo Castelo Branco, *Mistérios de Lisboa*[3]

I will talk no more of books or the long war
But walk by the dry thorn until I have found
Some beggar sheltering from the wind, and there
Manage the talk until her name come round.

---

1 Herman Wouk, *The Caine Mutiny*.
2 'Greece, Rome. Christianity, Europe
   All four fade
   Where age decrees.
   Who will acknowledge the truth
   That Don Sebastião is dead' (Fernando Pessoa, 'Fifth Empire').
3 'Happy they who can glimpse the motherland in the claws of the vulture from afar' (Camilo Castelo Branco, *Lisbon Mysteries*).

> If there be rags enough he will know her name
> And be well pleased remembering it, for in the old days,
> Though she had young men's praise and old men's blame,
> Among the poor both old and young gave her praise.
>
> W. B. Yeats, 'Her Praise'

Introduction

Camilo Castelo Branco lived his life at a time during which the personal and the political were at times uncomfortably entangled. He was imprisoned for a period for adultery, but was also involved in politics at a time of profound national upheaval, marked by the loss of the empire in Brazil and a civil war at home. Personal and political instability are mirrored in the vicissitudes of the characters in this novel, *A brasileira de Prazins* [*The Brazilian Woman from Prazins*], published at the end of a long and turbulent career. Over the years, the author found himself on the wrong side of political events, was knighted, transitioned from the status of prime figure in the Romantic movement to proto-realist, and ultimately died by suicide.

***

'Always historicize' (Jameson, 1981, p. 9). Frederic Jameson's rallying cry is at the very heart of the New Historicist (Cultural Materialist) approach to culture, raising the question as to whether knowledge of the historical/social/political background can elucidate our understanding of a literary text and vice versa. Does History shape the way a text is written? Or, on the other side of the argument, can literature throw light on our understanding of History? Can it act as a historical document? At the (Postmodernist) extreme of the spectrum, is there even such a thing as History or is there only textual interpretation of would-be documented facts?

These questions inform the approach to be adopted here. The answer to them, both from conventional historiography and from Postmodernist relativism would be a resounding no. And with enemies like these who needs to be right?

Conventional historiography accepts nothing other than sourced and verified documentation as the fitting tool for historical inquiry. The postmodern position, on the other hand, argues that text is separated both from a reference to the real world and from its author. For the latter, no existing language single-handedly maps the world accurately. For Jacques Derrida (1976, p. 201), famously, there is nothing outside of the text and for Jean-François Lyotard, 'it is therefore impossible to judge the existence or validity of narrative knowledge on the basis of scientific knowledge and vice-versa: the relevant criteria are different. All we can do is gaze in wonder at the diversity of discursive species, just as we do at the diversity of plant or animal species' (Lyotard, 1984, p. 26).

As ever, reason may be found somewhere in the unexciting middle, in the field of what became the discipline of New Historicism, which itself has its roots in political theory that branched out into fields such as Marxist theory, feminist theory and postcolonial theory, to name but a few.

In *On Literature and Art*, Karl Marx and Frederick Engels defined great literature as that which has its finger on the pulse of the period it is considering, irrespective of ideological positioning. When examining literature and art, they focused their attention on the merits of Realism: in their view, the tool to access the most accurate depiction of reality in an artistic work. Realism, as a trend in literature and as a method of artistic creation was regarded as the supreme achievement of art. Engels formulated what is generally recognized as the standard definition of it. 'Realism, to my mind', he wrote, 'implies, besides truth of detail, the truthful reproduction of typical characters under typical circumstances' (Engels, 1888, n.p.). Realist representation, he and Marx emphasized, is by no means a mere copy of reality, but a way of penetrating into the very essence of a phenomenon, a method of artistic generalization that makes it possible to disclose the typical traits of a particular age. This is what they valued in the work of the great realist writers (amongst whom they included not just Gustave Flaubert, Honoré Balzac and Alexander Pushkin but also, more controversially, Miguel de Cervantes, William Shakespeare and Johann Wolfgang von Goethe). Marx described the English realists of the nineteenth century—Charles Dickens, William Thackeray, the Brontë sisters and Elizabeth Gaskell—as novelists 'whose graphic and eloquent pages have issued to the world more political and social truths than have been uttered by all the professional politicians, publicists and moralists put together. [...] I have learned more [from Balzac] than from all the professed historians, economists and statisticians of the period together' (Marx, 1854, n.p.).

In *Writing Degree Zero*, Roland Barthes wrote as follows:

> Art binds the writer to society. Writing, free in its beginnings, is finally the bond which links the writer to a History which is itself in chains: society stamps upon him the unmistakable signs of art so as to draw him along the more inescapably in its own process of alienation. (Barthes, 1967, p. 40)

And Antonio Gramsci maintained that:

> The starting point of critical elaboration is the consciousness of what one really is, and it is 'knowing thyself' as a product of the historical process to date which has deposited in you an infinity of traces, without the help of an inventory. (Gramsci, 1971, p. 324)

New Historicism: A Context beyond the Text

Peter Weir's film of 1989, *Dead Poets' Society*, is often described as a coming-of-age narrative in which an inspirational teacher of English Literature uses unconventional methods to encourage his students to ask new questions from old shibboleths. At its most literal, this involves encouraging the boys (of course, they are all boys), students of a privileged school (of course it is) to jump on their desks so as to see the world 'from a different point of view'. The outcome is the suicide of Neil, the brightest amongst them, but it needn't have ended that way. Had he but known it, what Neil was attempting was not so different to what his autocratic father (had *he* but known it) encouraged: namely, the contemplation of life, the universe and everything *de haut en bas*. Given time, the handsome Neil would almost certainly have followed the path assigned to him by his elders, increased his family's considerable fortune and lived prosperously (and only somewhat unhappily) ever after. So far, so Henry James/Edith Wharton/*Age of Innocence*.

The questions raised are important, but more or less limited, and entirely defined by who asks them. The radical teacher in *Dead Poets' Society* is, after all, the Cambridge-educated Mr. John Keating. The martyr to thespian ambitions is Neil Perry—rich, tall and handsome— and his appalled, ultimately come-of-age sidekick is Todd Anderson, whose flashback narrative frames the story. It is sad, even tragic, but, for those of a more cynical disposition, hardly earth-shattering: everyone is male, rich, handsome, appealing, clever, and, with the one exemplary exception, able to learn a salutary lesson. How many of those boys, or indeed their eccentric teacher, would have thought to ask whether the greatest slaughter of humanity had been provoked by wars or by doctors not washing their hands prior to attending a woman in childbirth. Or whether the great democratic equalizer that was the Black Death in the fourteenth century had not done more towards freeing surviving serfs from their chains than any middle-class-led revolution in history. Deborah Lipstadt (*Denying the Holocaust*) reasonably argues for 'the uncircumventable phantom of history; Slavery happened; so did the Black Plague and the Holocaust' (Lipstadt, 1994, p. 21). And Saul Friedlander, in *Probing the Limits of Representation: Nazism and the Final Solution*, states that there is 'something irreducible which, for better or worse, I would still call reality' (Friedlander, 1992, p. 20).

The pertinent questions asked by New Historicists inconvenience both old-fashioned historians (the truth isn't necessarily confined to libraries and archives) or sharp-elbowed postmodern relativists (yes, historical truth does exist and may be accessible through positive practice). Who gets to tell the story? Is there a story in this class? Whose point of view endures? Is there anything more fluid than a point of view? Who decides what is important? Echoing a weary Pontius Pilate, what is truth? In the end, whatever may be the (relative) case, it is true is that master plots do erase the marginalized (women, children, subalterns, colonized objects, the sick and the (conveniently) dead). Catherine Gallagher and Stephen Greenblatt discuss 'the ability of art either to contain or unleash the potentially disruptive energies of history' (Gallagher and Greenblatt, 2000, p. 81):

> To mainstream historians, gender relations had appeared too stable and universal for historical analysis. [...] The feminist historian denied its naturalness by subjecting it to historical analysis [...] to show that gender relations, despite the endurance of male domination, only appear to stand outside of the historical processes. [...] Feminist counterhistorians raised a metahistorical question: What was it that made phenomena 'historical', and why did so much 'culture' fail to qualify? (Gallagher and Greenblatt, 2000, p. 59)

And closer to the Iberian homeland, Adriana Alves de Paula Martins argues powerfully as follows:

> I will propose a typology of postmodern historical fiction through which I will show how the different fictional representations of historical events and characters [...], while promoting the dialogue between fiction and historical discourse, suggest the notion that literary and historical representation are both political constructions whose logic is challenged by the literary text itself. (Alves de Paula Martins, 2016, p. 50)
>
> Focusing our attention on postmodern fiction, we identify two great trends resulting from the same need, namely, the need to investigate empirical reality and the ways in which it is interpreted and represented. [...] It is important to note that fiction and history were regarded for a long time as completely separate domains, on the premise that fictional discourse dealt with so-called imaginary referents whereas historical discourse dealt with supposedly real referents. This conferred a status of truth on the latter type of discourse alone, even when the former made explicit reference to chronologically precise historical periods reconstructed with the utmost accuracy. [...] In other word, it was as if only history could be deemed certain in relation to empirical reality, while fiction was relegated to the domain of fortune, that is, to the realm of the merely possible. (Alves de Paula Martins, 2016, pp. 50–51)

Invoking Hayden White, she argues that historiography, rather than claiming a document-based neutral status as truth should accept the ideological implications of the ontological and epistemic choices it involves. And finally, Jeremy Hawthorn writes as follows:

> The particular reading strategies with which I am concerned are those which can be loosely termed 'historicist', those that are committed to the belief that literary works are most fruitfully read in the illuminating contexts of the historical forces which contributed to their birth and the historically conditioned, and changing circumstances of their subsequent life. (Hawthorn, 1996, p. 3)

Auto-national Psychography

A brasileira de Prazins, Camilo Castelo Branco's 1882 novel, a late work in his vast body of writings, may be read as the psychography of Portugal as a nation from the sixteenth century to the time of the novel's creation, but also, paraphrasing Fernando Pessoa[4] (born six years after its publication), the autopsychography of its author. The narrative charts a path that takes the nation and some of its characters from promising early dreams to the realization that dreams are just that: at best, something that has no verifiable connection to reality; and at worst, a staging post to madness and/or death. Camilo's blindness, linked to syphilis, offers a curiously literal embodiment of the self-destruction of a nation that had overstayed its welcome for over four centuries (in what another crypto-Jew exile called the land of others ('o país dos outros'[5]), but ultimately found insalubrious). Montezuma's revenge took many forms beyond Latin America, though in Brazil, too, a kind of black magic was at work, contributing to the imperial nation's eventual downfall. The novel's depiction of revived Sebastianic desire for unwarranted power draws an uncomfortable link between the life of its author and that of the nation over five centuries.

Camilo Ferreira Botelho Castelo Branco, born in Lisbon in 1825, in later life first Viscount of Correia Botelho, a member of the minor aristocracy and descendant of Jews, twice married, former jail bird by reason of adultery, father of unstable sons, promiscuous, syphilitic, blind in his last years and dead by his own hand in 1890 (the latter a disastrous affair, the gun shot being so misdirected that it took him several hours to die), was a novelist, critic, playwright, poet, historian and translator. Both his father and his mother had died by the time he was ten, and he was brought up in turn by an older sister and by an aunt. He had an erratic education in adolescence, later studying first medicine and then law at the university of Porto, but completing neither degree. Like his contemporary, Eça de Queirós, his birth certificate registers him as the son of an unknown mother,[6] although his father, like Eça's, acknowledged paternity (David Frier, 1996).

He was one of a small number of writers who earned his living almost exclusively from his prodigious literary output. His turbulent life spanned one of the most agitated periods in national history and to a lesser extent in literary history too, the latter encompassing the paradigm shift from Romanticism to Realism. In his later works he

---

4   Pessoa, 1942 [1995].
5   Knopfli, 1959.
6   See https://querobolsa.com.br/enem/biografias/camilo-castelo-branco

acknowledged that his writing, although generally regarded as inscribed within the tenets of Romanticism, did share common ground with the emerging realist movement (in this respect, see Macedo, 1992). His life was directly affected by the extraordinarily unstable circumstances that defined Portugal's history in the nineteenth century. Neither his personal experiences nor his works—specifically the novel that concerns us here, *A brasileira de Prazins*—can be disconnected from the life of the nation.

It's a Mad, Mad World

The nineteenth century in Portugal was a period of acute political turmoil. In November 1807, the Napoleonic armies under the command of General Jean-Andoche Junot invaded. The royal family and the court escaped to Brazil, with Rio de Janeiro becoming the capital of the empire. In 1820, following the defeat of Napoleon and the end of the British Protectorate under William Beresford, the king, Don João VI, was summoned back to Portugal by the new liberal government that became known as the *Vintistas* (from 'vinte', ie. 'eighteen-twenty'). He left behind in Brazil his eldest son, Pedro, who, in 1822, rebelled against his father and declared Brazil independent with himself as emperor.

Vintismo was replaced by *Setembrismo* (1822–23), a movement that broadly followed the liberal principles of *Vintismo*. In 1823, however, the absolutist faction in parliament succeeded in wresting power from the liberal regime. In that year, the Holy Alliance (the coalition of the powers of Austria, Prussia and Russia formed at the behest of Tsar Alexander I after the final defeat of Napoleon) had authorised a French invasion of Spain, intended to bring down the liberal government in Madrid and restore King Ferdinand VII (a reactionary monarch who had been deposed and imprisoned by Napoleon). This encouraged a copycat uprising led by the Count of Amarante in the north of Portugal, representing the absolutist party of the Queen, Dona Carlota Joaquina and her second son, Don Miguel. The latter considered his father and the latter's supporters guilty of supporting liberal ideas and Freemasonry[7] (Marques, 1990; Ventura, 2020). On 23 May 1823 Miguel travelled to Vila

---

7   The Grand Orient of Lusitania, founded in 1802, is part of the liberal or continental Freemasonry tradition, proclaiming the absolute liberty of conscience and freedom from dogmatism.

Franca de Xira, near Lisbon, where he was joined by the 23rd Regiment of Infantry. This rebellion became known as the *Vilafrancada*. With the Queen and Don Miguel preparing to force him to abdicate, the king was compelled by his younger son to surrender, and Miguel returned to Lisbon in triumph. The king had succeeded in preventing the ultra-reactionary faction from coming to power, but Miguel, supported by the Queen's party, continued his manoeuvres, and less than a year later a new absolutist rebellion broke out: the April Revolt of 1824 (*Abrilada*), which however culminated in defeat for the absolutist faction and with Miguel going into exile until 1827.

Meanwhile, in Brazil, on 10 March 1826, D. Pedro, self-proclaimed emperor of the former colony, received word that his father had died, and that he himself had acceded to the Portuguese throne as Don Pedro IV. Pedro briefly became king of Portugal before abdicating in favour of his daughter, Dona Maria II and agreeing that his brother would rise to the throne on condition that he marry Maria (an echo of the avuncular marriage to be discussed in *A brasileira de Prazins*). During his short reign, Pedro oversaw the ratification of the *Carta Constitucional* (Constitutional Charter) of 1826.[8]

In 1827, Don Miguel feigned compliance with Pedro's wishes and returned from exile. Soon after being proclaimed regent in early 1828, however, he abrogated the Constitution. Supported by those in favour of absolutism (including his mother), he was acclaimed as King on 23 June 1828, but failed to honour the agreement to marry his niece. Meanwhile, back in Brazil, in early 1829 Don Pedro began to consider returning to Portugal. On 7 April 1831 he abdicated as emperor in favour of his son Don Pedro II, and sailed for Europe, landing in the Atlantic archipelago of Azores, the only Portuguese territory that had remained loyal to his daughter, Dona Maria. After a few months of preparation he embarked for mainland Portugal. On 8 July 1832, a fleet of sixty ships landed in Mindelo, in the north of the country, and on 9 July entered the city of Porto unopposed. His brother's troops moved to encircle the city, beginning a siege that lasted for more than a year but was not breached, leading to Porto becoming known as *a cidade invicta* ('the unconquered city'). This was the beginning of a two-year long civil

---

8   This was called a Charter because it was signed by the King (Pedro) rather than the elected Cortes (Parliament).

war known as the *Guerra dos Dois Irmãos* (the War of the Two Brothers). In August 1834, Don Miguel was defeated and exiled to Bavaria and in December 1834 the Courts banished him and all his descendants from Portugal upon pain of death were he to return. The Constitution of 1838 categorically excluded the collateral *Miguelista* line from the throne and he died in exile in 1866.

Don Pedro I had died of tuberculosis on 24 September 1834, just a few months after he and the liberal faction had emerged victorious. He was hailed by both contemporaries and posterity as a key figure in enshrining the ideals of liberalism that subsequently allowed both Brazil and Portugal to move from absolutist regimes to representative forms of Parliamentarian government. His daughter succeeded him to the throne as Dona Maria II. The constitutional monarchy was restored and so, provisionally, was the 1822 Constitution. Dona Maria II, however, favoured the less liberal *Cartista* faction (from *Carta Constitucional*: a constitution approved by the monarch rather than by parliament) and between 1834 and 1836 she appointed a series of conservative-leaning ministers. By 1840, the liberal *Setembristas* had largely lost influence and the Queen appointed António Bernardo de Costa Cabral as Minister of Justice within a conservative cabinet, following which, in January 1842, a coup brought Costa Cabral to power as Prime Minister. The period between 1842 and 1846 became known as *Cabralismo*. Costa Cabral embarked upon a programme of massive public expenditure. The resulting deficit and dissatisfaction with his dictatorial rule, however, would be one of the factors in his eventual downfall. In 1846 the Queen reluctantly dismissed him but a palace coup known as the *Emboscada* (ambush) replaced him with another conservative, the Duke of Saldanha. The liberal Setembristas set up a parallel rebel government in Porto and another civil war began. The war ended in a clear *Cartista* victory, with the support of foreign powers (the Holy Alliance mentioned above).

After the end of the second civil war, Portuguese politics entered a period of political stability, with *Cartistas* (now the *Partido Regenerador*: Regeneration Party) and non-Cartistas (the *Partido Histórico*: Historic Party) alternating in power as centrist factions (centre-right and centre-left, respectively). Both were led by politicians loyal to the monarchy, to economic reconstruction and to the resolution of the deepening financial crisis. By 1870, insurmountable financial difficulties, turmoil in the streets and in Parliament, and a succession of incompetent governments once again led the Prime Minister, the Duke of Saldanha, to implement a brief dictatorship (25 May–29 August) which was soon toppled, leading to the rise of the Marquis of Sá de Bandeira, leader of the liberal Reformist Party (Mattoso, 1993–94; Marques, 1990, 1991; Saraiva, 2001, 2005).

On the cultural side, radical changes were introduced in the last quarter of the nineteenth century by the *Geração de Setenta* [the Generation of (Eighteen-)Seventy]. The realist movement—which, with the exception of its liberal sympathies, ran counter to its immediate predecessor: Romanticism—was ceremoniously inaugurated in Lisbon during the *Conferências do Casino* [the Casino Conferences] (an event intended to take place between 22 March and 26 June 1871) under the initiative of writers, intellectuals and historians such as José Maria Eça de Queirós, Antero de Quental and Joaquim Pedro de Oliveira Martins. Its tenets, which at that point would have been profoundly antipathetic to Camilo, pronounced the death of Romanticism and the new order of Realism/Positivism/Determinism (Saraiva, 2001, 2005). Politically, the Realists associated themselves with secular and scientific parameters and with the principles of democracy, liberalism, republicanism and (Proudhonian) socialism that had dominated European thought for a large part of the nineteenth century. The *Conferências*, however, were suspended by the authorities after the first six lectures, for running counter to the institutions of Church and State.

Gabriel Paquette (2015) rightly argues that Iberian liberalism engaged intellectually with literary Romanticism (the former shared liberal political sympathies with the realist movement that superseded it), offering the examples of João Baptista da Silva Leitão de Almeida Garrett and Alexandre Herculano. Camilo was a key figure in the Romantic movement, but unlike Garrett and Herculano, his largely right-leaning, conservative tendencies (he was loyal to Don Miguel, fought on the side of the *Miguelista* faction and was involved in the creation of the Royal Order of São Miguel da Ala, whose key role was the suppression of Freemasonry's promotion of liberalism)[9] may account for *A brasileira*'s satire against impostor would-be monarchs. Although it has been suggested that in 1846 he was inducted into the northern Freemasons,

---

9   See Ventura, 2020.

this is unlikely, seeing as in the same year, he took part in the *Maria da Fonte* uprising on the side of the *Miguelistas*. In general, moreover, notwithstanding his unorthodox life story and his interest in some of the marginalized of society (the illegitimate; the sick; the disenfranchised; the mentally ill; Jews; dissenters), he tended to side with the old guard in political debate. An example of this was his attack against his fellow writer and historian, Alexandre Herculano, whose invective against the Roman Catholic Church ('Eu e o Clero' ['The Clergy and I']) Camilo contested in 'O Clero e o Sr. Alexandre Herculano' ['The Clergy and Mr. Alexandre Herculano'].

His entrenched *Miguelista* sympathies may partly explain the satire of the phony Don Miguel in *A brasileira de Prazins*. In a world that was rapidly changing regarding both political and cultural matters, the inclination to depict new phenomena as false ('fake news'?) and the desire to revive the integrity of what had been deemed outmoded, may not have been entirely unexpected. Then, as now, moreover, uncertainty created the desire for the exposure of fraud and the restoration of what had been (the revival of real 'strong' kings and the ousting of their impersonators), if not in reality, at least in his own fiction, 'por virtude do muito imaginar' ['by virtue of much imagining'] (Luís de Camões, 1864, p. 568): 'literature [is] not [...] an "inert" discourse, but [...] a totality that lives because of the praxis which has produced it' (Swingewood, 1973, p. 176).

An Ideal Home for Lunatics: *A brasileira de Prazins*

This late novel, published in 1879, in the last decade of Camilo's life, is far removed, both in style and emotional preoccupation, from his better-known Romantic novels, of which the most famous was *Amor de perdição* [Ill-Fated Love]: the latter, more than any other of his works, having helped coin the common phrase *drama camiliano* [Camilian drama], commonly applied to melodramatic events in fiction and in real life.

A brasileira, however, was in many respects the picaresque antithesis of both the conventional *drama camiliano* or *dramalhão romântico* [Romantic hyperdrama] and of the nineteenth-century historical novel focusing on heroic past events. Its eponymous heroine notwithstanding, the greater part of the short novel concerns itself not with a standard narrative of ill-fated love—although it does involve a dead young lover—but with his star-crossed beloved married to another man and mother to his many children (not everyone dies for love: Dante's Beatrice, if it was really she, married a banker and bore him six children). More to the point, it includes a number of anti-heroes active within the turbulent political events described above. Specifically, it details the supposed return from exile not of a *desejado* Don Sebastião/Don Miguel, but of a charlatan posing as the latter: himself, moreover, a reactionary, illiberal prince, traitor to his father, his elder brother and his niece/fiancée (but supported by Camilo). Both national history and love tragedies are here writ small, reducing both public and private concerns to lampoon-style versions of the past. A historical contextualization of the novel can be found in Veríssimo 1994–95.

The plot of *A brasileira* dovetails into two separate narratives linked by shared characters, foremost of which are Marta and her rejected *Sebastianista/Miguelista* suitor, Zeferino das Lamelas. The latter is the local stonemason: the deluded enabler of a fraudulent would-be Don Miguel supposedly returned to Portugal from exile to reclaim the throne.

The narrative is set in Prazins, a village in Minho, in northernmost Portugal. As is common in Romantic novels, the love plot is introduced by the device of letters exchanged in the past between a pair of sundered lovers. The narrator explains that he had found a note inside a book that led him to discover the story which he proceeds to narrate. The eponymous character is Marta, daughter of Simeão. Marta's cognomen of 'brasileira' comes from her marriage to her uncle, recently returned from Brazil where he had accumulated a fortune prior to returning to Portugal. The early love plot involves Marta's passion for José Dias, the son of Joaquim de Vilalva, a rich farmer who, like his wife, Genoveva, refuses to approve his son's marriage to a lowly-born young woman to whom, moreover, other objections also attached.

José's mother had a horror of hereditary illnesses. Marta's mother, of dubious morals, had eloped from the marital home with a renegade friar from Santo Tirso. Thought to be possessed by the devil, she eventually becomes mad and commits suicide by drowning. Following the logic that the apple doesn't fall far from the tree, José's family opposes the union between Marta and their son. The two young people become lovers on the assumption that José's pious mother, faced with the *fait accompli*, would agree to the marriage. Instead, José Dias dies a consumptive death. Marta, counter to every tenet of High Romanticism, marries her uncle, and although she goes mad herself, has many children and lives to an insensible old age.

The vicissitudes of sentimental life in this novel are intertwined with the socio-political events discussed above. The struggle for power between Don Pedro and his brother Don Miguel presents itself in the novel as a guerrilla-type conflict that occupies a large part of the narrative. José Dias and his father are persecuted by a group of fanatics led by Zeferino, followers of Don Miguel (or, in this instance, his impersonator). Zeferino has not merely a political reason for his actions: he is also José Dias' rival for the love of Marta, who had been promised to him in marriage by her father, a promise subsequently broken in favour of Simeão's own brother. The latter, Feliciano, Marta's uncle, aged forty, bachelor and nouveau-millionaire, arrives from Brazil where he had made his fortune. He aspires to Marta's hand and becomes his brother's (her father's) favoured prospective son-in-law. Faced with this, Zeferino swears a vendetta against all who stand in the way of his passion. José Dias, in true romantic hero fashion, contracts galloping tuberculosis and dies. Following his death, Marta tries to commit suicide like her mother, but is prevented from doing so, and in due course marries her uncle, leaving Zeferino still with unabated dreams of revenge.

All at Sea

In an article that considers the phenomenon of the *'brasileiros'*, the Portuguese men that historically emigrated to Brazil in times of economic hardship, made their fortune and returned to Portugal, Maria Beatriz Rocha-Trindade discusses 'a ferocidade dos retratos camilianos' ['the ferocity of Camilo's depictions'] regarding this socioeconomic group (Rocha-Trindade, 1986, p. 149). She refers, moreover, to the 'malefícios da emigração para o Brasil' ['the evils of migration to Brazil'] (Rocha-Trindade, 1986, p. 150), a phenomenon that left the nation, in particular in rural regions, despoiled of manpower for the purposes of agriculture, fishing and other economic pursuits:

> The importance and evidence of the figure of the 'Brazilian' in Portuguese society in the last quarter of the nineteenth century still seems to gain

new strength through the insistence with which the most prolific of our romantic novelists, Camilo Castelo Branco, made him appear in his plots or in the atmospheric social situations that he so vividly knew how to describe. [...] He is a sad figure on whom Camilo seems to focus all his disdain and malevolence. (Rocha-Trindade, 1986, p. 150)

The 'brasileiro' in Portugal is one version of a historical fact in the nation's identity as a sea-borne empire from the fifteenth century to the twentieth: namely the phenomenon of those who left the European motherland in search of better prospects overseas and were often not welcome when they returned. Camilo had already explored this theme in other works, albeit with some modifications, including, most famously, in the figure of the contemptible Bento Montealegre in *Eusébio Macário* of 1879. Historically, the phenomenon of the *retornado* ['returnee': a term, strictly speaking only much later applied to those who left the African colonies after the latter gained independence from Portugal in 1975] is used here to refer to 'brasileiros' but also to economic migrants to south Asia, Africa and Europe (France, Germany and the UK, pre- and post- the creation of the European Union). They figure across the centuries in the work of writers such as Gil Vicente, Camões, Almeida Garrett, José Maria Ferreira de Castro, Olga Gonçalves and Miguel Torga; and also, in this novel, with its allusions to Don Pedro (the quintessential *retornado* 'brasileiro'), Don Miguel and, by implication, Don Sebastião himself, that counterproductive non-returned *desejado* ['desired one'] of a misguided nation.

In the novel, an incident follows the uncle's return that becomes decisive in bringing about Marta's marriage. Zeferino, eager for revenge, tries to murder her father. Seriously wounded and in danger of his life (although, contrary to Ultra-Romantic expectations, he recovers to drink, have fun and debauch another day), Simeão extracts from his daughter the deathbed promise that she will marry her uncle. Marta accordingly marries Feliciano, although as a result, the signs of her illness, which had been feared to be hereditary, do indeed worsen: in addition to epileptic seizures (epilepsy at the time carrying the stigma of an illness thought to affect the offspring of alcoholics and syphilitics or, more exotically—a reference to her own mother—those possessed by malignant spirits),[10]

---

10   For a review of the historical stigma of epilepsy, consult https://pmc.ncbi.nlm.nih. gov/articles/PMC8051941/

she begins to show symptoms of progressive psychopathy, marked by an obsession with romantic love (a latter-day show of cynicism by the erstwhile Ultra-Romantic author of *Amor de Perdição*: in *A brasileira*, only the insane love forever). She marries her uncle, with whom she goes on to have five children in seven years, but this alliance never goes beyond the physical plane, leaving her emotionally attached to the phantom of the deceased José Dias. On him are concentrated all her dreams and affections. It is to the memory of José Dias that she continually returns in what becomes a hallucinatory half-life of withdrawal from conscious agency. The narrative ends with the husband, already adapted to the circumstances of this strange conjugal life, concerning himself, above all, with the further acquisition of wealth. Marta remains oblivious to reality and lives to old age in a state of semi-conscious reverie, waiting for the return of her dead beloved who (like the equally deluded nation bereft of Don Sebastião/Don Miguel) she believes will one day return to her.

Louc[a] porque quis grandeza...[11]

'...qual a sorte a não dá' ['such as fate forbids'] (Fernando Pessoa, 1972, p. 42). Marta's doomed longing for her lost lover (not unlike that of the Portuguese for the mythical Don Sebastião—all of them 'cadáver[es] adiado]s] que procria[m]' ['postponed corpses that procreate'] (ibid.)—mirrors that of the supposedly sane characters in the novel, whose actions, however, are also determined by an irrational belief that the dead/defeated can return: Don Sebastião from North Africa; José Dias from his untimely grave; and Don Miguel (or an impostor posing as him) from exile, to claim the throne. As the narrative itself makes clear, this would-be nineteenth-century rendition of the history of Don Sebastião (who died in battle in north Africa in 1578, leaving the country to fall under the dominion of Spain) is a degraded version of the myth of *Sebastianismo*: that of the once-and-future-king that supposedly did not in fact die and would return one day to save the country and restore it to imperial glory. The ensuing damage done by the persistent nostalgia (*saudade*) that arguably exacerbated the nation's tendency to live in the past (the golden age of empire) is reflected in the outcome of the novel's

---

11   'Mad, because I sought greatness...'

personal and historical motifs. And indeed, Marta's deluded conviction in the return of José Dias, like Zeferino's belief in the return of Don Miguel, are merely anthropomorphic depictions of a nation's fixation on a disastrous monarch in the sixteenth century and on imperial dreams stubbornly indulged thereafter.

This *moebius* strip of a narrative begins with Zeferino's primarily personal motivations. His frustrated love for Marta sets him on the path of political activities that involve his support for the would-be Don Miguel, but eventually returns him to the starting point of personal revenge (though still masquerading as political conflict). His belief in the impostor king mirrors the national longing for Sebastião as well as Marta's deluded belief in the return of her dead sweetheart. Personal tragedy is adumbrated by national disaster: the bride of a dead youth married to an unwanted husband; two men fighting over a girl; two sister nations—Spain and Portugal—embroiled in an increasingly acrimonious union in the sixteenth and seventeenth centuries under the Spanish Philippine 'uncles'; two royal brothers unleashing civil war against each other in the nineteenth; and a nation fixated on the impossible recovery of a variety of kings (Sebastião from Alcácer Quibir/Ksar-el-Kebir; Pedro from Brazil; and Miguel from two periods of political exile: first in Vienna and later, for the remainder of his life, in the Grand Duchy of Baden).

With regard to the longing for reinstated imperial glory, the outcome, as was the case in Portugal at the end of the nineteenth century, was apparent action (the project of the Pink Map which nearly led to war with Britain and to the humiliation of the 1890 Ultimatum)[12] followed by prolonged stagnation. And in the novel, at the end, lovers are dead, impostors are in prison, rebels are tamed, and when we last glimpse Marta, she is living the life-in-death of a somnambulist. The failed suicide attempt that had mirrored her own mother's supposedly situates her within what, at the time of the novel's creation was the intellectual formula not of deterministic heredity to which Camilo, as the paladin of Romanticism officially did not subscribe, but that of adverse fate to which, as a former High Romantic, he did. But the fog of mental imbalance that leaves Marta living a long life of apparent orthodoxy (upper middle-

---

12   For more information, see https://en.wikipedia.org/wiki/Pink_Map

class wealth and prolific maternity), rather than dissipating to reveal her true love and the bereaved nation's Don Sebastião, becomes the opposite of Romanticism's penchant for black-and-white resolutions, upholding instead Realism's reliance on non-metaphysical explanations. Marta may be mad because her mother was too, but her body is fully functional for the purposes of reproduction, the continuity of the male blood line and the transmission of property within the family (doubly so, since her husband is her father's brother and the great-uncle of his own children). With regards to the future, for this family and for a nation forever fixated on Don Sebastião—a collective folly that was revived as late as the twentieth century by Salazar, presented by the Estado Novo's propaganda machinery as the reincarnation of the lost king[13]—the prospects were not promising. Instead, they lent credence to the notion that one definition of madness (made more likely at the level of the family by consanguineous marriages and by the nation's short-sighted jingoism) is the repetition of past mistakes in the expectation of a different outcome.

What's What?

We know Marta is mad, but to the onlooker she is not. We know José Dias is dead, but to the deluded Marta he is still with her. We know Don Sebastião died in battle, but to a grieving nation he will return. We know that historically at least four fraudsters claimed to be the lost king, but we suppose they were not.[14] We know Don Miguel was a bad son, a bad brother, a bad uncle and a bad king who tore the nation apart not once (like Sebastião) but twice, although many longed for his/their return. As a nation the Portuguese thought that the Sebastianic dream of empire was the right path to follow, but many, including Camilo's predecessors (Gil Vicente, Camões), his contemporaries (Alexandre Herculano, Antero de Quental, Oliveira Martins, Eça de Queirós) and his successors (Fernando Pessoa, Miguel Torga, Almeida Faria, Lidia

---

13 See António Ferro's highly successful propaganda campaign, which cast Salazar as a quasi-Sebastianic figure, emerging from the ashes of political instability to restore Portuguese colonial power in the African colonies.

14 Since Sebastião's body was never identified after his death, various impostors claimed to be him in 1584, 1585, 1595 and 1598 (see Belo, 2023, and https://pt.wikipedia.org/wiki/Sebastianismo).

Jorge, Margarida Cardoso) begged to differ. And the narrative of an empire that had once, temporarily, made Portugal powerful, in the long term proved to be misguided in the case of a country that might have been better advised to follow the example of medieval monarchs (Don Afonso III; Don Dinis; Don Afonso IV) and stayed home cultivating peace with Spain (or, as 'the patriarch Voltaire', Castelo Branco, 1984, p. 262 would have it, fruitfulness in their own garden).

Crazy Love *Oitocentista*-Style: Amor de Alucinação

In Camilo, both Zeferino and Marta are driven mad by love, but while Marta's condition leaves the status quo untouched, Zeferino's mania carries wider repercussions (the support for impostor kings and resulting civil strife). The novel is haunted by a series of unproductive returns: counterfeits of Don Miguel/Don Sebastião as icons of a lost dream; Feliciano back home from Brazil; the hallucination of a living José Dias experienced by Marta; and not Don Miguel but an inveterate liar called 'Veríssimo' (a real name which translates as 'Most Truthful'): pernicious simulacra one and all.

> This is precisely what was feared by the Iconoclasts [...]. Their rage to destroy images rose precisely because they sensed this omnipotence of simulacra, this facility they have of erasing God from the consciousness of people [...]. It can be seen that the iconoclasts, who are often accused of despising and denying images, were in fact the ones who accorded them their actual worth, unlike the iconolaters, who [...] were content to venerate God at one remove. But the converse can also be said, namely that the iconolaters possessed the most modern and adventurous minds, since, underneath the idea of the apparition of God in the mirror of images, they already enacted his death and his disappearance in the epiphany of his representations. (Baudrillard, 1988, pp. 166–84)

In this short but complex narrative, the key national concepts of God, motherland and family are brought forth as central to our understanding of individual and collective outcomes, only to be comprehensively undone in all that they might have had to offer within personal and political narratives. Many strands are interwoven within it: the debates between Romanticism and Realism/Naturalism/Determinism; myth and history (real and false monarchs and messiahs); love and lust; progress and decadence; reality and madness; Peninsularism and empire; life and postponed death. And, above all, truth (reality) and untruth (delusion, deceit, insanity). What is left is uncertainty without any dimension of grandiosity: those that die do so to no purpose and those that do not die live to old age as mockeries of meaningful existence. Nothing is what it seems or ought to be.

> Myth is constituted by the loss of the historical quality of things: in it, things lose the memory that of which they once were made. [...] It has turned reality inside out, it has emptied it of history [...]. Myth deprives the object of which it speaks of all History. In it, history evaporates. [...] Nothing is produced, nothing is chosen. (Barthes, 1984, pp. 142–43)

Honest to God

Camilo's priests, God's ambassadors on Earth and representatives *par excellence* of the iconolatry that underpins Roman Catholicism (with its vast array of saints and images), are often corrupt and pawns of political interests. Some might be sincere:

> Father Osório made his stain-free cassock respectable. It seems like he doesn't have them in his life either. He passes for being a sad old man, who had no youth, nor the ambitions that supply the sweet affections of the heart mutilated by calculation or frozen by temperament. (Castelo Branco, 1984, p. 9)

But misguided:

> The priests of Minho, at that time, did not tax their memory; they were ordained so indifferent to the demands of the soul that [...] they read the psalms from the breviary with great uncertainty. (Castelo Branco, 1984, p. 14)

More often than not, however, they are downright mendacious and willing instruments in the exploitation of the credulous:

> Father Cosimo de Tagilde had been ordained so as to inherit some property from a blessed relative who hated the troops. [...] Father Silvestre da Azenha, [...] explained to the women what the group of incubus demons was. He told stories of some who became pregnant by these lewd people. (Castelo Branco, 1984, pp. 226–29)

Mostly, however, they and their associates in one way or another turn out to be tricksters. Reality acquires the form of farce whereby a crook, experimenting with various possible identities including that of priest (in this case a seducer of women) and dentist (the latter, more often than not, a role performed by barbers wielding handy pliers), eventually settles for passing himself as the exiled Don Miguel returned to reclaim his throne. And at the level of the personal, lost lovers are preserved in a state of phantasmic delusion that endures in parallel with a semblance of real life:

> Marta, without awareness of her organic life, has five children, as if she had wrenched out the ignoble portion of herself and withdrawn it from her husband's sensual exigencies, saving her soul from that unconscious materiality. (Castelo Branco, 1984, p. 262)

Tragic *perdição* is replaced by satire without *amor* and national history gives way to farce.

> The reader may ask:—What is the scientific, disciplinary, modern purpose of this novel? What proof does it offer? What is useful here as an element that reorganizes the individual or the species? I answer: Nothing, by my word, nothing. My novel does not intend to reorganize anything. And the author of this sterile work asserts, in the name of the patriarch Voltaire, that we will leave this foolish and evil world, just as it was when we began it. (Castelo Branco, 1984, p. 262)

Eça de Queirós, Camilo's contemporary but unlike him fully committed to the practice of Realism, was widely condemned as being unable or unwilling to take tragedy to its highest pitch, cutting it short with inappropriate laughter. Camilo, however, it transpires, could and possibly did teach Eça a lesson in the genre of pantomime: 'Oh yes, I am the king!' 'Oh no, you're not!' Regardless of the literary movement each officially endorsed, the means and the end may have been the same:

> What do we want [...]? To paint the picture of the modern world, in the ways in which it is bad, for persisting in educating itself 'according to the past'; we want to take a photograph, I would almost say the caricature of the old bourgeois world, sentimental, devout, Catholic, exploitative, aristocratic, etc.; and exposing it to scorn, laughter, the contempt of the modern and democratic world—to prepare its ruin. (Queirós quoted in Sacramento, 1945, p. 219)

And the resulting ridicule, unexpectedly, is as savage in the erstwhile Ultra-Romantic Camilo as in the cynical Realist that was Eça.[15] The status quo that the latter parodied and the former rejected with a bullet in the head was a desperate one where priests fomented immorality, the Sebastianic/Messianic/*Miguelista* hope for a Second Coming turns to farce, and mothers like Marta fulfil their assigned role (childbearing) in a state of obliviousness, in a home, family and nation whose heart they are supposed to be, but where instead there is a vacuum.

The conjuncture wherein the woman's question meets up with nationalism raises a number of fundamental questions about the very meaning of the term 'politics'.

> Why is it that the advent of the politics of nationalism signals the subordination if not the demise of women's politics? [...]. By what natural or ideological imperative or historical exigency does the politics of nationalism become the binding and overarching umbr.ella that subsumes other and different political temporalities. (Radhakrishnan, 1992, p. 186)

***

Conclusion

Eça trod in Camilo's footsteps when in *O crime do padre Amaro* [*The Crime of Padre Amaro*] he created the eponymous protagonist (a corrupt priest), S. Joaneira (an ineffectual mother) and Amélia (a dead one); in *Os Maias* [*The Maias*] Maria Monforte (a destructive progenitor); in *A tragédia da Rua das Flores* [*The Tragedy of the Street of Flowers*] an incestuous suicidal one; and in *A relíquia* [*The Relic*] a phony King of the Jews whose shroud is in fact the night gown of a prostitute (not even a redeemed Magdalene/Mary of Egypt but merely an unrepentant Maricoquinhas). António Sérgio summed it up in his essay 'Interpretação não-romântica do sebastianismo' [Unromantic Interpretation of Sebastianism]:

> In short, the hypothesis I propose to you is the following: Portuguese messianism (of which Sebastianism is a phase) originated, not from a psychology of race [...] but [...] from social conditions similar to those of the Jews, reinforced by the ideas of Jewish messianism [...]. These

---

15 For a discussion of this see Macedo (1992).

conditions come to be summarized, to speak to you as theologians do, in a consciousness of 'Fall', accompanied by a lack of true independence; [...] Hope in a Messiah, in a Desired One, in a Redeemer, is common to all races; but the social and mental situation of the Jews and the Portuguese intensified in these two peoples the tendency common to all. First, the ideological (or educational, in the broadest sense of this word) of the New Christians and the Bible [...] spread messianic thought throughout our country, and the special conditions of the Jew in Portugal naturally reinforced the aspiration to a Messiah. The catastrophe of Álcacer Quibir and the disappearance of the monarch; then, the preaching of the religious orders [...]; and with this, to this day, the fact that national circumstances do not satisfy patriotic pride—explain why the old dream lasts in the souls of people little accustomed to initiative and self-government. (Sérgio, 1976, p. 249)

If to lose an empire (India) was a misfortune and to lose two (Brazil) was carelessness, what do we call the loss of a third (Africa, in the twentieth century, by Salazar, the would-be returned Sebastião)? Unforgivable? Or unforgiven? To date, the punishment continues, as does arguably, the delusion. Is the dream of imperial Portugal to be forever doomed to remain what António Lobo Antunes cruelly (and crudely) called 'os cus de Judas' ['the back of beyond', or literally 'the arsehole of Judas'].

The name Marta (Martha), Latin from the Ancient Greek Μάρθα (Mártha) and from Aramaic מרתא (Mārtā) means 'mistress' or 'lady', feminine for ('master'). In the Gospels (*Luke* 10: 25–37), Martha is a passive character who waits on Jesus hand and foot ('Marta, que ama e fia a seus pés!' ['Martha, who loves and weaves at his feet'] (Queirós, 2020b, p. 60)). Not a good role model for an effective heroine: and in Camilo, the descendent of crypto-Jews[16] and son of a *mãe desconhecida* [unknown mother], whither the mother, thither the nation:

> History has its truth, and so has legend. Legendary truth is of another nature than historical truth. Legendary truth is invention whose result is reality. Furthermore, history and legend have the same goal; to depict eternal man beneath momentary man. (Hugo, 1889, p. 34)

>> Ah, who will write the history of what might have been?
>> That will be, if someone writes it,
>> The true history of humanity. (Álvaro de Campos, 1944 [1993], p. 299)

---

16 Not all scholars acknowledge the Jewish factor as relevant to an understanding of Camilo.

Works Cited

Antunes, António Lobo, 1979, *Os cus de Judas* (Lisbon: Vega).

Barthes, Roland, 1967, *Writing Degree Zero*, trans. Annette Lavers and Colin Smith, preface by Susan Sontag (London: Jonathan Cape Ltd.).

Barthes, Roland, 1984, *Mythologies*, trans. Annette Lavers (London: Paladin).

Baudrillard, Jean, 1988, 'Simulacra and Simulations', in *Jean Baudrillard: Selected Writings*, ed. Mark Poster (Redwood, CA: Stanford University Press), pp. 166–84.

Belo, André, 2023, *Morte e ficção do rei dom Sebastião* (Lisbon: Tinta da China).

Bronfen, Elizabeth, 1992, *Over Her Dead Body: Death, Femininity and the Aesthetic* (Manchester: Manchester University Press).

Cabral, Alexandre, 1988, *Dicionário de Camilo Castelo Branco* (Lisbon: Caminho).

Camões, Luís Vaz de, 1964, *Obras* (Lisbon: Imprensa Nacional).

Camões, Luís Vaz de, 1980, *Os Lusíadas* (Porto: Porto Editora, 1980).

Campos, Álvaro de, 1944 [1993], 'Pecado original', in *Poesias de Álvaro de Campos/ Fernando Pessoa* (Lisbon: Ática), p. 299.

Castelo Branco, Camilo, 1850, *O Clero e o Sr. Alexandre Herculano* (Lisbon: Francisco Xavier de Sousa).

Castelo Branco, Camilo, 1984, *A Brasileira de Prazins* (Lisbon: Ulisseia).

Castelo Branco, Camilo, 1998, *Eusébio Macário: história natural e social de uma família no Tempo dos Cabrais* (Lisbon: Ulmeiro).

Chorão, João Bigote, 1989, *Camilo Castelo Branco: A Obra e o Homem* (Porto: Vega).

Derrida, Jacques, 1976, *Of Grammatology*, trans. Gayatri Chakravorti Spivak (Baltimore and London: Johns Hopkins University Press).

Eça de Queirós, José Maria, 1981, *A tragédia da Rua das Flores* (Lisbon : Livros do Brasil).

Eça de Queirós, José Maria, 2011, *Os Maias* (Lisbon: Livros do Brasil).

Eça de Queirós, José Maria, 2020a, *A relíquia* (Lisbon: Livros do Brasil).

Eça de Queirós, José Maria, 2020b, *O crime do padre Amaro* (Lisbon: Livros do Brasil).

Engels, Frederick, 1888, 'Letter to Margaret Harkness London', April, transcribed by Dougal McNeill, 2000, https://www.marxists.org/archive/marx/works/1888/letters/88_04_15.htm

Ferro, António, 1939, *Salazar: Portugal and her leader*, trans. H. de Barros Gomes and John Gibbons, with a preface by Sir Austen Chamberlain, K. G., and foreword by António de Oliveira Salazar (London: Faber and Faber).

Friedlander, Saul (ed.), 1992, *Probing the Limits of Representation: Nazism and the Final Solution* (Cambridge, MA, and London: Harvard University Press).

Frier, David G., 1996, *Visions of the Self in the Novels of Camilo Castelo Branco (1850–1870)* (Lewiston: Edwin Mellen Press, 1996).

Gallagher, Catherine, and Stephen Greenblatt, Stephen, 2000, *Practicing New Historicism* (Chicago: Chicago University Press).

Garcia, José Luís Lima, 1993, 'Miguelismo e Messianismo n'A Brasileira de Prazins', *Tellus*, 20, 62–68.

Garcia, José Luís Lima, 1991, 'A Brasileira de Prazins e o Mito do Eterno Retorno', in *Camilo Castelo Branco: Perspectivas — Actas de las Jornadas Internacionales sobre Camilo, ed.* Ángel Marcos de Dios (Salamanca: Universidad de Salamanca), pp. 35–50.

Gramsci, Antonio, 1971, *Selections from the Prison Notebooks*, trans. and ed. Quintin Hoare and G. Nowell Smith (New York: International Publishers).

Habermas Jürgen, 1986, *Knowledge and Human Interests* (London: Polity).

Hatcher, John, 2008, *The Black Death* (London: Orion).

Hawthorn, Jeremy, 1996, *Cunning Passages: New Historicism, Cultural Materialism and Marxism in the Contemporary Literary Debate* (London: Hodder Education).

Herculano, Alexandre, 1850, *Eu e o Clero: Carta ao Exmo. Cardeal Patriarca* (Lisbon: Imprensa Nacional).

Hugo, Victor, 1889, *Ninety-Three* (London, New York: George Routledge and Sons).

Jameson, Frederic, 1981, *The Political Unconscious: Narrative as a Socially Symbolic Act* (London: Methuen).

Kiernan, Ryan (ed.), 1996, *New Historicism and Cultural Materialism: A Reader* (London: Bloomsbury Academic).

Knopfli, Rui, 1959, *O País dos Outros*. Lourenço Marques: Minerva Central.

Lipstadt, Deborah, 1994, *Denying the Holocaust* (New York: Plume Books).

Lobo Antunes, António, 2004, *Os cus de Judas* (Lisbon: Dom Quixote).

Lyotard, Jean-François, 1984, *The Postmodern Condition: A Report on Knowledge*, Trans. Geoff Bennington and Brian Massumi, foreword by Fredric Jameson (Manchester: Manchester University Press).

Macedo, Helder, 1992, '*A Brazileira de Prazins*: Fragmentação e Unidade', *Colóquio Letras*, 125–26.

Marques, A. H. de Oliveira, *História da Maçonaria em Portugal* (Lisbon: Editorial Presença, 1990).

Marques, A. H. de Oliveira, *História de Portugal* (Lisbon: INCM—Imprensa Nacional Casa da Moeda, 1991).

Marx, Karl, 1854, 'The English Middle Class', *New-York Tribune*, 1 August 1854, transcribed by Andy Blunden, https://web.archive.org/web/20180303071731/ https://marxengels.public-archive.net/en/ME1912en.html

Marx, Karl, and Frederick Engels, 1976, *On Literature and Art* (Moscow: Progress Publishers), http://www.marxists.org/archive/marx/works/subject/art/preface.htm

Martins, Adriana Alves de Paula, 2016, 'José Saramago's Historical Fiction', *Portuguese Literary and Cultural Studies*, 6 (2016), 49–72, https://doi.org/10.62791/rc9pmr97

Mattoso, José, 1993–94, *História de Portugal, Volume V: O Liberalismo (1807–1890)*, ed. Luís Reis Torgal and João Lourenço Roque (Lisbon: Circulo de Leitores).

Paquette, Gabriel, 2015, 'Romantic Liberalism in Spain And Portugal, c. 1825–1850', *The Historical Journal*, 58.2, 481–511.

Pessoa, Fernando, 1972, 'D. Sebastião, Rei de Portugal', in *Mensagem* (Lisbon: Ática).

Pessoa, Fernando, 1942 [1995], 'Autopsicografia', in *Poesias* (Lisboa: Ática), http://arquivopessoa.net/textos/4234

Prado Coelho, Joaquim, 2001, *Introdução ao Estudo da Novela Camiliana*, 3rd edition (Lisbon: Imprensa Nacional Casa da Moeda - INCM, 2001).

Radhakrishnan, Rajagopalan, 1992, 'Nationalism, Gender, and the Narrative of Identity', in *Nationalisms and Sexualities*, ed. Andrew Parker, Mary Russo, Doris Sommer and Patricia Yaeger (London: Routledge), pp. 77–95.

Rocha-Trindade, Maria Beatriz, 1986, 'Refluxos culturais da emigração portuguesa para o Brasil', *Análise Social: Terceira Série*, 22.90, 139–56.

Sacramento, Mário, 1945, *Eça de Queirós: Uma Estética da Ironia* (Coimbra: Coimbra Editora).

Santos, João Camilo dos (ed.), 1995, *Camilo Castelo Branco no centenário da morte. Colloquium of Santa Barbara* (Santa Barbara: Centre for Portuguese Studies, University of California).

Saraiva, José Hermano, 2001, *História de Portugal* (Lisbon: Europa-América).

Saraiva, António José, 2005, *História da Literatura Portuguesa*, 17th edition (Porto: Porto Editora).

Sérgio, António, 1976, 'Interpretação Não Romântica do Sebastianismo', in *Ensaios* (Lisbon: Livraria Sá da Costa Editora).

Swingewood, Alan, 1973, 'Literature and Praxis: A Sociological Commentary', *New Literary History: What Is Literature?*, 5.1 (1973), 169–76.

Veeser, H. Aram (ed.), 2013, *The New Historicism* (London: Routledge).

Ventura, António, 2020, *Uma História da Maçonaria em Portugal (1727–1986)* (Lisbon: Temas e Debates).

Veríssimo Serrão, 1994–95, *História de Portugal* (Lisbon: Verbo).

3. 'I Know Where You Were Last Night'[1]: Clarice Lispector or When Stars Become Supernovas

> 'Wild roses,' I said to them one morning.
> 'Do you have the answers? And if you do, would you tell me?'
> The roses laughed softly. 'Forgive us,' they said. 'But as you can see, we are just now entirely busy being roses.'
>
> Mary Oliver, 'Felicity'

> Para ganhar sentido o teu tormento
> Meu tormento terá que ser igual
> Daí toda esta ausência de total
> No apertar dos ferros. E sustento
> Que só candura esfibro em cada vento
> Onde perpassa a dor de ter-te igual
> Ao que sempre sugeres ser teu mal
> Sem que o mal meu se iguale ao nosso alento.
> Mais que querer-te é de ódio que sustento
> O seguido acicate e a dor de ouvir-te
> Sob o ferro gemer ao leve ordenho
> Em que recolho o medo de ferir-te.
> Tendo que dar-te a morte mal sustenho
> O fero ferro onde é amor mentir-te.
>
> João Pedro Grabato Dias, 'O berdugo vondoso'[2]

---

1   Lispector, 1999.
2   'For your torment to make sense,
    My torment must be its equal.
    Hence this total absence

And even today the notion of a structure lacking any centre represents the unthinkable itself.

Jacques Derrida, 'Structure, Sign, and Play in the Discourse of the Human Sciences'

Introduction

For Clarice Lispector—that gifted purveyor of the ever-delayed, ever-playful transcendental signified, and author of 'A menor mulher do mundo' ['The Smallest Woman in the World']—size and status, in the most literal possible sense, did not matter, at least not as far as women were concerned. What a (free) player she was! And in her hands, the law of diminishing returns becomes an un-circumventable problem for the patriarchy. Or, to mix metaphors, in worlds in which men and women exist in parallel universes, the vanishing point of infinity becomes just that: as two trains move along on parallel tracks, each gets smaller to the naked eye although, the laws of physics notwithstanding, outside the field of vision there may after all be a crash. Anything multiplied by infinity is zero (i.e. nothing, which, as we know, is what sound and fury signify). In a world of nothingness, are we/they all mad?

***

The Games She Played

Considered one of the major writers in the Portuguese language, Clarice Lispector continues to defy pigeonholing within categories of genre.

> In the tightening of the chains. And I maintain
> That I only shed candour in every wind
> Where the pain of having you my equal
> To what you always suggest is your evil
> Without my evil equalling our breath.
> More than loving you, it is hatred that I sustain
> The constant spur and the pain of hearing you
> Under the iron moan at the light milking
> In which I gather the fear of hurting you.
> Having to give you death, I can hardly sustain
> The fierce iron where it is love to lie to you' (João Pedro Grabato Dias, 'The Kindly Torturer').

Blending stream-of-consciousness with a uniquely individual style, her work provokes the reader with unanswered questions regarding the meaning of existence (what Olga de Sá described as 'to exist while narrating', Sá, 1979, p. 63) and blurs both the boundaries of the ego and of ontological adventure (the nature of subjectivity, Yannuzzi, 1997, pp. 484–86) within the parameters of sex, language and social power.

She wrote in the genres of the short story, novel, chronicle, journalism, literature for children and translation. Born in Tchetchelnik, Ukraine, in 1920, she was a two-month old baby when her family migrated from Europe to Brazil at the tail-end of the flu pandemic, not long after the end of World War I: first to the impoverished Northeast and later to Rio de Janeiro. In 1943, she graduated from Law School and married a fellow student whose diplomatic career would take them abroad before she left her husband and returned to Brazil in 1959.

From the second decade of the twentieth century onwards, a new reality demanded cultural articulation. The difficulties inherent in this process, earlier confronted by the European Modernists—and to a lesser extent the Brazilians—related to the ruins of the old world in the aftermath of the calamities of World War I, the flu pandemic, the 1928 Wall Street crash and the uncharted problems that followed. It is within this global context that Lispector's writing must be understood, but personal factors played a significant role too. Lispector, after all, lived many of her intellectually formative years in Europe, and her origin was that of European Jewish trauma: prior to their departure for Brazil her mother, Mania, had been raped by a gang of Russian soldiers during a pogrom in Ukraine, sometime in 1919 or 1920. As a result, she contracted syphilis, for which she received no effective treatment, dying of the disease when her daughter was around eight.[3] Lispector's own peripatetic married life made her—as British right-wing discourse has decried almost one hundred years later—a citizen of nowhere: the Wandering Jew (ish apple *no escuro*) that, however, never falls very far from the postlapsarian Judaeo-Christian Tree (of knowledge/epistemology). It is in light of this existential turbulence that the fundamental importance in her writing of language itself ought to be emphasized, as that which must be struggled against and drawn upon in the abstract formulation of that new reality.

---

3   See Katz, 2009.

In Lispector's lifetime, moreover, Brazil underwent a long stretch of political turbulence that plunged it into two periods of dictatorship. In 1930, a military coup d'état, saw the rise of Getúlio Vargas as President. Between 1937 and 1945, Vargas instigated a regime of full dictatorship. In 1946, democracy was reinstated under General Eurico Gaspar Dutra. Five years later, in 1950, Vargas was democratically returned to power but in 1954 he committed suicide. In 1964, the then-President, João Goulart was deposed by a military coup and by 1968 the country again underwent dictatorship under the rule of General Humberto de Alencar Castello Branco. Due to a period of extraordinary economic growth known as the 'economic miracle', however, the regime gained a significant level of popularity. In 1974, General Ernesto Geisel began his project of re-democratization and in 1985 democracy was fully restored under José Sarney.

Lispector, therefore, lived to see the country returned to democracy, an event that, however, did not change the fact that Brazil, then as now, was ranked by a number of international bodies as one of the most unequal countries in the world.[4] And, as ever, in circumstances of political instability, women find themselves at the bottom of any given pile.

For Lispector, as Sá (1979, p. 119) would argue, justice—and, more to the point, we would suggest now, *in*justice—was such an obvious 'goes-without-saying' concern that it never surprised her and therefore she did not always address it directly in her writing. Except of course when she did. At the heart of that consciousness of injustice, be it as victim, perpetrator, interested or indifferent spectator, there was almost always a woman.

What Wo(men) Want

There can certainly be no doubt that Lispector's work has been enormously influential on Cixous's literary and critical development. What is striking about the above assessments, however, stems from their not-so-subtle reversal of this intertextual relationship, Lispector becoming in effect more 'Cixousian' than Cixous herself has been 'Lispectorian'. (Klobucka, 1994, p. 44)

---

4   See Gradín, 2020; Pereira, 2016; and Oxfam's report on the same topic (https://www.oxfam.org/en/even-it-brazil/brazil-extreme-inequality-numbers), as well as Statista's report on income inequality in Brazil (https://www.statista.com/statistics/751758/income-distribution-monthly-gross-income-brazil/).

Recent re-thinking on Jacques Derrida, Michel Foucault and Gilles Deleuze by the likes of Rosi Braidotti, Lois McNay, Sally Robinson, Patricia O'Brien and Alice Jardine has resulted in challenging aspects of theory that, one might argue, yet again confirm that, in the words of Anna Klobucka, one of Lispector's most theoretically-sophisticated readers, the Brazilian writer got there first (Klobucka, 1994, p. 44). Derrida and others in fact articulate what Lispector's writing had always practiced. Which of course is what theory does, anyway.

Bringing theory straight back into the realm of 'real' alienation, Braidotti's self-declared monist concept of the posthuman, outlined in her book *Transpositions: On Nomadic Ethics*, and elaborated upon in an interview with Cosetta Veronese, argues as follows:

> The great emancipatory movements of postmodernity [including feminism] are driven and fuelled by the resurgent 'others': They inevitably mark the crisis of the former humanist 'centre' or dominant subject-position and are not merely anti-humanist, but move, beyond it to an altogether novel project. These social and political movements are simultaneously the symptom of the crisis of the subject, and for conservatives even its 'cause' and also the expression of positive, pro-active alternatives. [...] They express both the crisis of the majority and the patterns of becoming of the minorities. (Braidotti, quoted in Veronese, 2016, p. 98)

And Karin Sellberg, engaging with Braidotti, argues that '[her] notion of ethics is a process that has nothing to do with either dominant morality or relativism: Rather it contains clearly set limits that are activated by careful negotiations' (Sellberg, 2006, p. 139). She argues that 'to accept differential boundaries does not condemn us to relativism, but to the necessity to negotiate each passage' (Sellberg, 2006, p. 139). It is in their eyeball-to-eyeball engagement with Foucault and Derrida that McNay, O'Brien and Jardine also raise questions that, one might argue, were implicitly raised *avant la lettre* by Lispector.

For O'Brien, in *Discipline and Punish* Foucault fails to differentiate sufficiently between the treatment of female and male prisoners (O'Brien, 1978, pp. 514–18) and McNay concurs that for Foucault the female body has no specificity apart from the male norm:

> It must be recognized that the trade-off has not simply been one way. Feminists have also drawn attention to certain inadequacies in Foucault's

treatment of gender issues. One predominant criticism has been that Foucault's analysis does not pay enough attention to the gendered nature of disciplinary techniques on the body and that this oversight perpetuates a 'gender blindness' that has always predominated in social theory. Sandra Bartky (1988) argues that, in the final analysis, Foucault treats the body as an undifferentiated or neutral gender and, consequently, he fails to explain how it is that men and women relate differently to the institutions of modern life. (McNay, 1991, p. 131)

Macabéa, Laura and Pequena Flor could have told (or at least *shown*) them as much. For Clarice's women, praxis, not theory, was always the only thing there was.

An Apple a Day

In *A maçã no escuro* [*The Apple in the Dark*] (1961), Martim, the male protagonist, perceives the world as an apple, which, as we know, is both a wholesome fruit and, in *Genesis*, the instrument of temptation leading to the first apocalypse in the Western imagination: the Fall. And of course we know who was primarily to blame for that: *cherchez la femme*. When in *A paixão segundo G.H.* [*The Passion According to G.H.*] of 1964, G.H. encounters a cockroach (echoes of the beetle of that other Eastern European Jew?) and eats it, she engages in an act that clearly anticipates by two decades Julia Kristeva's trope of the abject,[5] rendering *herself* abject and therefore Other. That, we would argue now, may be a *midrashic* pursuit (Lispector was after all the child of diaspora Jews) but one which ultimately fails to provide answers to hitherto unformulated questions. In 'Coming to Writing' and *L'Heure de Clarice Lispector* [*The Hour of Clarice Lispector*], Hélène Cixous argues that Lispector goes beyond binaries which, as we know, are the shortcut to fixed meaning.

When in 1943, aged seventeen, Lispector published her first novel, *Perto do coração selvagem* [*Close to the Wild Heart*], the critical establishment hailed it as a turning point in Brazilian fiction, heralding, as it did, the advent to Brazil of the technique of stream-of-consciousness writing first attempted in Europe by figures such as Virginia Woolf and James Joyce. The significance of the assimilation of this formal innovation to Brazilian literature encompassed (as had been the case with its

---

5   Kristeva, 1982.

European precursors) implications of an import much greater than the purely stylistic, gesturing as it did—in the case of Brazil three decades later than in Europe—towards the articulation of a crisis of modernity which, in that country, however, given the euphoric boom of the 1920s, would only be felt much later (and only in the cultural centres of São Paulo and Rio de Janeiro: the *Nordeste* [Northeast] is always a different matter).

In Clarice, it is discourse, itself, and the brutal authoritarianism of a language rendered all-powerful in the face of the protagonists' existential difficulties, that determines the narratives: discourse as the demiurge of self and other; discourse as the source and definer of the narrative world; discourse as a linguistic creator; and discourse as the articulator, classifier and omnipotent decision-maker concerning character, time and place in these universes of fiction. It is discourse, in the end, that triggers moments of unreliable epiphany, by means of which the protagonists (even if not quite the readers), attain moments of admittedly slippery understanding. The answer to life, the universe and everything may after all be 42 (Adams, 1979), even if that only makes sense to the eccentric/insane few. And eccentricity/insanity, after all, are what define Lispector's universe, even if her fools are also wise ones, whose epistemological activity is impenetrable to many/most. Her/their quotidian is the stuff of our oneiric rantings, but on the other hand, everyone dreams occasionally.

Something which is, as we shall see, profoundly of the essence in the case of Rodrigo S. M. in *A hora da Estrela* [*The Hour of the Star*], even if the end result for him is implied death at the phantasmic hands of someone he had earlier killed. Whether dealing with first-, second- (interpelative) or third-person narratives, therefore, it is language itself as the instrument of gnosis that beckons to character and reader with the promise of understanding, only immediately to shatter that possibility. And it is the focus on that moment of fragmentation—the moment that separates the time when knowledge, truth and understanding seemed to be still possible, from the non-linearity and disconnection of awkward space/time dimensions following the moment of breakage—that is the hallmark of Lispector's writing. She dwells repeatedly throughout her novels and short stories, on the process whereby the everyday, the ordinary and the intelligible are set adrift, stripped of cohesion and abandoned as the residues of a previous system of signification, now obsolete. In this new reality, the focus of narrative concern is the unfolding and broken/breaking subjectivity of the protagonists, of the world seen through their eyes, and of the act of gazing upon an erstwhile ordinary reality now rendered imponderable. In the process, too, in the face of the abrupt defamiliarization of the quotidian and its subsequent destruction, the concept of 'ordinary reality' becomes itself questionable or even nonsensical. *Ostranenie* rules and everyone is affected: the protagonists themselves, the support actors, and the readers too.

Lispector's reader signs a contract that rescinds all entitlement to linear meaning. Reading her, therefore, requires the acceptance of loss on the part of the spectator: loss of old terms of reference; of the readers' right to understanding; of logic; of received wisdom; and of expectation. What replaces them is the tacit readerly agreement to go with the flow (of language) in the text and to surrender to the disorder that this language carries in its wake: now putting it to a use that is not the fixation of meaning, but rather its postponement or even its abolition.

In considering Lispector's writing, the cognitive/existential/emotional quicksand of her protagonists' subjectivity forces us to question their participation or exclusion from reality, and the tenability of previous definitions of normality (reliable consciousness), of linearity of time, of circumscription of space and of the possibility of signification. And in doing so, this non-Aristotelean reality forces also the confrontation of their (the characters') dilemmas: a position from which we, as consumers of text, are forced to entertain the hypothesis that logic, language and meaning are not monopolies of a single (or as Derrida would *not* have it) transcendental origin but are rather defined by dispersal. And that being the case, it becomes apparent that preexisting transcendental meaning may not be available to the audience, emerging instead as an unstable phenomenon.

It is the disruption of reader-expectation, the refusal of the reader's entitlement to digestible meaning, which is required of Lispector's public, as is her refusal to provide plot or clear-cut character outlines. This also forces the reader to posit the likelihood that here, indeed, we have a new language focused (or not: who's claiming the right to teleology here?) on a new reality, not just an old one put to relatively new usage. Language, in Lispector, is of the essence (or, nodding to

Derrida, *not* of the *essence*), and abdicates unambiguous meaning: it is both life-giving and life-draining. It is the workings of language itself which we witness in these narratives, allowing us as readers to view its backstage scaffolding: and in doing so discarding, also, the need for (or even the possibility of) suspension of disbelief. Instead, what replaces it is an exhibition of language in action, at play (sometimes sadistic play) in the new worlds it invented, rather than language as a transparent mirror held up to a reliable reality.

Lispector's writing is peppered with moments of epiphany, but not epiphany as the revelation of privileged meaning, only the realization that any meaning is likely to be so transitory, so dispersed as to relinquish the right to what the word itself entails. In terms of plot parameters or character identifiability as such, in works such as *A hora da estrela*, 'Amor' ['Love'] or 'A imitação da rosa' ['The Imitation of the Rose'], this realization potentially leads to a temporary (or indefinite) suspension of sanity, or to the affirmation of madness. If, as is the case with Laura in the latter narrative, her madness allows us a glimpse of her immersion into a different reality, it is a reality that our language, circumscribed by the constraints of logic and reason, cannot convey, being reduced instead to underpinning it through the rules of crazed incoherence. Madness, which becomes simply an alternative state of consciousness following its severance from everyday logic, is a *leitmotif* in this writer's work. Another recurring trope is the relinquishing of social or political activism in favour of prioritizing philosophical abstraction or random subjectivity. But in any case, in a country where patriarchal and economic power rule ok (Brazil is, to this day, one of the most unequal countries in the world on all indexes: economic, gender, race, sexual preference/identity, wealth distribution and mental health),[6] madness and subjectivity may be all that is left to women, people of colour, the poor and many other Others. And showing it, however obliquely, may itself be a form of activism. 'Everything's got a moral, if only you can find it', said the hideous Duchess to Alice in *Alice in Wonderland* (Carroll, 2000, p. 131). One doesn't have to be male/beautiful/mainstream/empowered/sane to be right or good, even if, according to Plato (2003),

---

6   See https://www.oxfam.org/en/brazil-extreme-inequality-numbers; https://www.unesco.org/en/fieldoffice/brasilia/expertise/gender-equality; and https://www.statista.com/topics/10060/mental-health-in-brazil/#topicOverview

at least the first two certainly helped.

Madness and subjectivity (though not masculinity or beauty), elicit a question to be addressed presently when discussing both 'A imitação da rosa' and *A hora da Estrela*, namely that of whether there is a significant social and political as well as a philosophical dimension to Lispector's work. The question may be asked, but it might be inconsequential, if we agree that the cognitive is always political anyway, and that it may or may not involve skin colour/gender/class/education/wealth (see for example 'A menor mulher do mundo'). In Brazil, that most unequal of tropical paradises (although every visitor is told with some insistence, 'Brazil is a marvelous country'), all these interests sing from the same hymn sheet. Disenfranchisement comes in different modalities, but they all share common endpoints in a world in which arguably *it*, not *they*, is defined by an insanity that needs articulating:

> Language is not speech, it is a full circle from word to sound, to perception, to understanding, to feeling, to memorizing, to acting and back to the word about the act thus achieved. And before the listener can become a listener, something has to happen: he or she must expect. (Rosenstock-Huessy, 1983, p. 145)

A Rose by Any Other Name Would Be as Mad

The world is full of mad women who sometimes, however, live to tell the/a tale. The mad wife is the epitome of the enemy within, the fifth columnist, the pantomime villain: she's behind you...! But who is her victim? It is a well-known fact that murder, like charity, begins at home. So we are told (warned) by the paradigmatic tales and true-crime narratives of our culture.

Statistics show that a woman is more likely to be attacked and/or killed by a man she knows, often intimately, than by a stranger. But what if the boot switches to the other foot? Female murder/escape fantasies have informed writing by women from early on (Susan Glaspell, 'A Jury of her Peers;' Charlotte Perkins Gilman, *The Yellow Wallpaper*; Kate Chopin, *The Awakening*, to name but a few). Sometimes, for example, these reversals appear in unexpected forms, such as in the medieval *Cantigas de amigo* [*Songs of Friendship*], in which the male poet speaks in a female voice (a girl, her mother, the girl's girlfriend); in which the male is erased (contrary to Jane Austen's lament, in this case the pen is not officially in his hand); and in which she does not even need to dispose of him (kill him). He simply writes himself out from a narrative which he may accessorize but neither controls nor defines, merely assist(er)ing in the self-erasure.

Indeed—and that will be the core of the argument that follows regarding both 'A imitação da rosa' and *A hora da estrela*—on the whole the male voice is not necessary as a means of self-destruction (although if the man helps, that is fine too), because often, as it turns out, the Sisters are perfectly capable of doing that for him (and on each other's behalf). And the madwoman in the attic often does not even need to escape from her confinement in order to wreak havoc on the order of things: she can stay home and, with or without a little help from her friends, she contrives to compel the hapless would-be patriarch into a vortex of his own creation. If, as has been persuasively argued (Gilbert and Gubar, 2020; Auerbach, 1984), behind every languishing damsel there lurks a madwoman, monster woman or whore waiting to do her worst, the means to that particular end, rather than turning the tables, may consist in an invitation for the gentleman to join the cannibal's party as the dish of the day (chef's special). Ladies' literary salons come in many different shapes and forms.

Ellen Douglass's (1988) reading of Lispector's 'A imitação da rosa' engages with Marta de Senna's take on the story as a narrative of quest (for self) and follows an Existentialist (Sartrean) path that sees Laura's trajectory towards the finding of the self through self-absenting from being into nothingness. And for Earl E. Fitz, 'all of Lispector's now famous themes [...] derive directly from an underlying preoccupation with what we do and how we verbalize it, with the uncertain relationship between words (signs) and reality (experience)' (Fitz, 1980, p. 51).

In her study of the same short story, Marta de Senna (1986) considers the spiral of madness that links Laura to the bouquet of roses to which she lays claim in her struggle to keep a grip on reality. But for Joshua Alma Enslen, for example, 'Laura's downward spiral into insanity is not depicted as a typical 'descent' [but instead] alludes to both Zarathustra's rise to overman and Christ's transfiguration on the Mount of Olives' (Enslen, 2014, p. 69). Enslen concludes that all that makes Laura unfit for purpose (her barrenness, her lethargy, her madness) become the definition of her individuality, her resistance to the temptation of normality. In the current reading, however, we would go one step further than these critics. Douglass (1988), for example, sees Laura as attaining a state of 'absolute independence' through madness, annihilation being the price of achieving a space for the self in an alternative reality. On this side of that choice, for Douglass, there still remains a husband who is part of the commonweal of normality, still waving, not drowning: or in other words, diminished but still paddling. But a closer look at the last lines of Lispector's narrative, we now maintain, is less forgiving. Armando, at the end, may find that his wife's alternative reality may have after all drawn him into a state of non-being of *her* creation, but that consumes *him* too:

> She was sitting in her little house dress. He knew she had done her best not to become luminous and unattainable. With *shyness and respect*, he looked at her. Looking older than his age, tired, curious. But he didn't have a single word to say. Through the open door he could see his wife who was sitting on the sofa, straight-backed, alert and calm again, like someone on a train. That had already left the station. (Lispector, 1991b, p. 69, italics added)

In that new world of Laura's, he, his friends and his world no longer exist. They may not be dead, but to her they don't figure. They don't *signify*. And surely, from her point of view, *her* world is all that is the case.[7] If, moreover, she was their defining Other, what's to become of them now?

Barren or *grávida de futuro*[8]? Macabéa and the Stars

In *A hora da estrela* (Lispector, 1990) following an authorial preamble and a list of possible titles (a hint of uncertainty on the part of an otherwise demagogic male first-person narrator), the text gives us a deceptively decisive opening: 'Everything in the world began with a "yes"' (ibid., p. 25). Deception, however is the order of the day, and the seeming affirmativeness immediately gives way first to dissonance ('a strident, staccato tune' (ibid., p. 21)); then to nothing more than limp

---

7   Wittgenstein, 2002, p. 5.
8   'Pregnant with a future'.

acquiescence ('one molecule said yes to another molecule and life was born. But before prehistory there was the prehistory of prehistory and there was the never and there was the yes. There always has been. I don't know what' (ibid., p. 25)); and finally to absolute negativity ('I know the universe had no beginning' (ibid., p. 25); 'it is obvious that history is true, albeit made up' (ibid., p. 26)). Not so much a case of unpromising beginnings, as of no beginning at all. Faced with which, the baffled reader, thrown in at the deep end, is entitled to list a number of questions that mirror the indecisiveness of that inaugural list of possible titles:

>THE FAULT IS MINE
>OR
>THE HOUR OF THE STAR
>OR
>LET HER LOOK AFTER HERSELF
>OR
>THE RIGHT TO SHOUT AT THE FUTURE
>OR
>A BLUE'S LAMENT
>OR
>SHE DOESN'T KNOW HOW TO SCREAM
>OR
>WHISTLING IN THE DARK
>OR
>THERE'S NOTHING I CAN DO
>OR
>RECORD OF FOREGONE FACTS
>OR
>THREE-HANKY PULP FICTION. (ibid., p. 23)

All listed in capitals, admittedly, but that is just a way of shouting in order to say nothing conclusive, including the last possible option (that moreover, just to complicate matters further, suggests the possibility of a furtive escape to yet another idea, however undetermined and unteleogical: 'UNOBTRUSIVE EXIT THROUGH THE BACK DOOR' (ibid., p. 23)). What are we talking about here? Do you know? If not, IT IS NOT MY FAULT.

Faced with such sneakiness, the critic may be forgiven for offering not a reading but a reciprocal list of questions. And since 'amor com amor se paga' [you give as good as you get] and one is entitled to 'pagar um mal com o seu igual' [heal with the hair of the dog that bit you] (because opposites sometimes are the same, and never more so than in Clarice), questions may not lead to answers. We can all play at that same game. Tit for tat. An eye for an eye. Like for like. *Quid pro quo*. Something for something.

Or something for nothing. We can all play the fool.

So let us start, though not with 'yes' (and she didn't, not really) but with an inadequate summary followed by a list of question (marks). The novel begins with the narrator, Rodrigo S. M., discussing what it means to write a story. He breaches the fourth wall, addresses the reader directly and ponders the philosophical beliefs that guide him. The narrative itself, when he finally begins, centres on Macabéa, an impoverished nineteen-year old *nordestina* 'so young but already rusty' (ibid., p. 40) (the *nordeste*, of course, being the signifier in Brazil of dispossession) but now living in Rio de Janeiro. Ie. displaced to the power(lessness) of a million.

For a number of critics (Naomi Lindstrom, Lúcia Helena, Clarisse Fukelman, Regina Dalcastagné) the temptation to anchor this slippery writer to a tangible socio-political interpretation has proved too powerful. We would argue, however, that of them all, Dalcastagné's approach is the least reductive, emphasizing, as it does, the gender/articulacy components in the context of a binary definition of self and other:

> In short, the existence of a northeastern migrant—according to Rodrigo S. M.—must be described objectively and clearly, focusing on the facts; and that's a man's job. Between the lines of this discourse are prejudices against women and women's writing, but also, in a way, against the poor and their presence in literature. [...] Rodrigo S. M.—Macabéa's secret creator and narrator of himself—and doubly suspect. First, because he is an intellectual talking about a working-class woman (and reaffirming his prejudice); then, because he uses the misery of his protagonist (who becomes even more pitiful in his writing) so as not to seem so miserable himself. (Dalcastagné, 2000, pp. 85–86)

Macabéa leads a difficult life, but seems to be largely unaware of this fact. A clear case of 'learned helplessness'[9] (or possibly stoical acceptance),

---

9   See Lawrenz, 2024.

her reaction to adversity is always calm, including, in a defining moment, apologizing to her boss for the inconvenience of his having to fire her. In due course she acquires a violent boyfriend called Olímpico (of course: spot the binary), who mistreats her and eventually betrays her with her co-worker, Glória (of course: nothing is ever new). Feeling guilty about stealing her friend's boyfriend, Glória recommends that Macabéa visit a fortune teller who predicts that her life will improve dramatically, and that she will become rich, happy, and married to a foreigner called Hans (white? German? Aryan? Nazi?). Instead, upon leaving the fortune teller's house 'pregnant with her own future', Macabéa is run over by a man in a yellow Mercedes (a German car, indicative of wealth) and dies (Lispector, 1990, p. 98). In the battle between Macabéa and the (male) world, it would appear that it is game, set and match to the world that is defined by masculinity, property and racial privilege (in the latter instance, industrialized Northern Europe vs underdeveloped Global South). But is that necessarily so?

'Killing Must Feel Good to God. He Does It All the Time'[10]

'And are we not created in his image?'[11] At the heart of the novella sits the uneasy relationship between Macabéa and the world: a world that encompasses power (which requires powerlessness in order to define itself), adequately-remunerated work (whose *sine qua non* is exploitation), and voice (as opposed to silence). And representing those parameters are two men—the narrator, Rodrigo S. M. (sado-masochist?) and Olímpico (a murderous God avatar?)—who control her life and death, but whose existence, we will find out, may become impossible if she ceases to exist, because she is their/society's Other, without whom they too, cease to have substance: which is another definition of personal apocalypse. The narrative, written in the first person, affirms two things with some insistence: first, the narrator's sex (male: Rodrigo S. M.); and second, his ultra-macho ontological power, which, however,

---

10 Quote from Hannibal Lecter, *Hannibal* (TV Series), 'Amuse-Bouche' (Season 1, Episode 2).
11 Ibid.

affirms itself, oddly, in language that sometimes seems to adopt the lexicon of *écriture feminine*: 'This story makes me more aware every day, and I understand that each day represents borrowed time. I am not an intellectual, *I write with my body*') (Lispector, 1990, p. 30, italics added).

Already in the prologue, as indicated earlier, certainty is denied, since the author (an unreliable narrator?) may be after all 'truly Clarice Lispector' (ibid., p. 21). Which might explain why such a stereotypical macho male writes 'with his body'. As he will eventually find out at his own cost, his *übermensch* narratorial status notwithstanding (are you still there, Hans? Was that your car that ran her over?), he may after all be no more than the dupe of two women; Macabéa, without whom after all he does not exist, and the narrator ('truly Clarice Lispector', ibid., p. 21), who in the end destroys *him* and immortalizes *her*.

Rodrigo, Power and Language: 'The Things that You're Liable to Read in the Bible'

'... it ain't necessarily so'. Right until the end (although, as we shall see, not *at* the end), Macabéa, quasi-eponymous status notwithstanding, appears tenuous in all respects: 'But the person to whom you refer has barely a body to sell, nobody wants her, she is a virgin and harmless, nobody needs her' (ibid., pp. 27–28). But 'the things that you're liable to read in the Bible [or elsewhere], it ain't necessarily so'.[12] For Rodrigo, writer/first-person narrator and monologic demiurge (can a demiurge or first-person narrator ever be truly dialogic? The stakes are always weighted in favour of a single voice), language is not necessarily power, merely the attempt to run away:

> As for me, I can only escape from being incidental because I write, an act which is a fact. (ibid., p. 52)

Writing is tantamount to affirming himself to be alive, as it is for the nameless *Autor* in *Um sopro de vida* [*A Breath of Life*], Lispector's last novel (how typical: though her death was precipitous – a few weeks from diagnosis to death – did she foresee her own last breath?).

---

12 George Gershwin and Ira Gershwin, 'It Ain't Necessarily So', *Porgy and Bess* (1935).

> There's one thing of which I am certain: this narrative will disturb something fragile: the invention of a whole human being which is definitely as alive as I am. (Lispector, 1991c, p. 33)

That acknowledgement, however, implies a recognition on the part of Rodrigo S. M. of responsibility and possibly guilt:

> The fact is that I have a destiny in my hands and yet I do not feel I have the power freely to invent it: I follow an occult and deadly trajectory. (Lispector, 1990, p. 35)
>
> Why do I feel guilty?' (ibid., p. 38)

The answer to this question, which he gives (and he does after all have a monopoly over discourse in his capacity as first-person narrator: just like Bento, jury/judge/executioner in Machado de Assis' *Dom Casmurro*: we have been here before) is Macabéa's vulnerability. Her origin, flawed as it is, of course must come from himself, her exegetist (however much he might try to pass responsibility to an unspecified outside agency):

> She had been born with bad genes and now looked like the child of a nobody who was apologetic about taking up space. (ibid., p. 42)

The Double-edged Blade of Language

In archetypal *nordestino* understanding, language is power and silence is death—and there are no better exponents of this than her (Clarice's? Macabéa's) fellow *nordestino* writers.[13] But what is Rodrigo's relationship to language? Demiurgic, surely? He is, after all, the first-person narrator. As regards Macabéa, however, the opposite may apply. Opposites, here, of course, being of the essence, or, if we choose to acknowledge Derrida's wink (surely we must), are of the non-essence. In a first-person narrative (Machado de Assis's *casmurro* Bentinho knew it better than none;[14] so did João Cabral de Melo Neto's Severino, in his life-affirming monologue culminating in disappearance),[15] the power of life itself is in the hands of he who speaks, and defines (s)he who does not:

---

13 The absence of language is a key trope in Graciliano Ramos' *Vidas Secas* (2021).
14 Joaquim Maria Machado de Assis, *Dom Casmurro* (1962).
15 João Cabral de Melo Neto, *Morte e vida severina* (2017).

> It seems like I'm changing the way I write. But as it happens I only write what I want, I'm not a professional—and I need to talk about this northeastern woman otherwise I'll suffocate. She blames me and the way to defend myself is to write about her. (ibid., p. 31)

I speak therefore I am, and you do not, therefore you exist only *if* and *how* I decide:

> The plot of this narrative will result in my transfiguration into someone else and, finally, my material transformation into object. (ibid., p. 35)

Existence is at the discretion of the articulator. As the monologue progresses, however, the urgency of erasing Macabéa becomes ever more accentuated:

> She lived in a technological society where she was a spare nail (ibid., p. 44).

At the end, of course, we might ask ourselves whether he protests too much.

Identifying with Her: A Pathological Co-dependency?

She isn't, therefore I am: as Rodrigo's voice progresses to an end which neither we nor he (first-person narrator though he is) can fathom, his ontological reality exhibits a binary dependency on Macabéa's non-being, which he asserts with ever more insistent desperation:

> I need to talk about this northeastern woman or I'll suffocate. She accuses me and the way to defend myself is to write about her. I write in vivid, rough painterly strokes. (ibid., p. 31)

Nothing, however, may be what it seems, and even early on – let alone later—discursive and existential control are always in question, and subsequently reneged outright:

> I swear this book is written without words. It's a silent photograph. This book is a silence. This book is a question (ibid., p. 31)

Moving from a political/social hermeneutics to what she calls the philosophical aspects of the narrative, Fukelman (1990) correctly engages with the existential considerations forced upon the reader and upon Rodrigo S. M. by his own position as narrator. Macabéa is a product of Rodrigo S. M.'s need for an Other against which to define himself: he living, she fading; he present, she evanescent; he discursive, she inarticulate:

> Although I have nothing to do with the girl I shall have to describe myself through her to my great surprise. (ibid., p. 39)

Letting Go: Dis-identifying from Her

As the monologue progresses, Rodrigo S. M. describes with growing contempt Macabéa's quasi-illiteracy. Strangely, however, in thinking about her, he begins a process of self-transformation that makes him more like her: 'The plot of this narrative will result in my transfiguration into someone else and, finally, my material transformation into object' (ibid., p. 35). And as will be argued at the end of this chapter, Rodrigo ultimately enunciates the negative capability that undermines the all-powerful position of the first-person narrator by self-destructing: the unwitting entanglement of the Self with its Other means that in the end, the narratorial decision to excise Macabéa from himself leads to the disappearance of his own *raison d'être*. In the most literal possible way, *ni avec toi, ni sans toi*. 'I, who don't amount even to being her, I feel that there is no point in my existence. I am pointless' (ibid., p. 48).

The moment Macabéa is declared tubercular, the narrator declares himself in love with her. She, however may be his necessary Other, but her absolute disappearance, rather than emphasizing his presence, will destroy him too. When Macabéa takes her life out of his control (encouraged by one woman, Glória, she goes to another—the fortune teller—to chart out a different life for herself) he is forced to eliminate her. Her death becomes murder at the hands of her creator (Why do I feel guilty?), (ibid., p. 38), but without the defining Other, the Self ceases to be viable:

> Macabéa killed me. She was finally free from herself and from us. Don't be scared, dying is an instant, it passes quickly, I know because I just died with the girl. (ibid., p. 105)

Visible Women: So Who Has the Power Now?

> I must say that this girl is not aware of me, if she was she would have someone to pray to and it would be salvation. But I am fully aware of her: through this young woman I give my cry of horror at life. At life that I love so much. (ibid., p. 49)

Even early on, Macabéa had exhibited some measure of power in creating a universe of her own (and overtaking his):

> It seemed to him that he had committed a crime and that he had eaten an angel [...] and, because he believed in them, they existed. (ibid., pp. 55–56)

In *A paixão segundo G.H.*, the eponymous heroine knows that it is important *not* to make sense:

> I'm afraid to start composing so that I can be understood by someone imaginary, I'm afraid to start 'sense', with the same gentle madness that until yesterday was my healthy way of fitting into a system. (Lispector, 1964, p. 18)

So who is the demiurge now?

Sim ou Não?[16] 'That of Which We Cannot Speak, We Must Pass over in Silence'[17]

Early on in the narrative, Rodrigo predicts the triumph of a (film) star's death (hers) that however, as we will learn later, will also eliminate him:

> No one [...] would teach [Macabéa] how to die one day: she would certainly die one day as if she had previously learned by heart how to play the role of a star. Because at the time of death a person becomes a brilliant film star, it is the moment of glory for each one and it is when, as in a chorus, high-pitched sibilants can be heard. (Lispector, 1990, p. 44)

In the end, however, she performs an act of inverted possession of her author. As the bond becomes closer to what one might call love, the creator begins to lose the possibility of his own individual existence.

---

16 'Yes or no?'
17 Wittgenstein, 2002.

Writing (about her) defines his own ontological possibility ('If I'm am still writing it is because I have nothing to do whilst I wait to die', ibid., p. 88); and even that possibility begins to slip away: 'In the past three days, alone, bereft of fictional characters, I depersonalize myself and cast myself off as one discards one's clothes' (ibid., pp. 88–89).

Macabéa, the nobody who is the counterpoint to others' reality, metamorphoses from a creature with 'ovaries bruised like boiled mushrooms' into a significant Other (ibid., p. 98). In 'A menor mulher do mundo', Pequena Flor—insignificant like Macabéa, 'pregnant' like Macabéa, a *matryoshka*-like entity (a tiny body enclosing an even a tinier body)—plunges the explorer, Marcel Pretre, as Macabéa does Rodrigo S. M., headlong into the search for salvation through language. Both men seek to retain a grasp over life by writing:

> Marcel Pretre had several difficult moments trying to understand himself. But at least he took the time to take notes more notes. Those who didn't take notes had to make do as best they could. (Lispector, 1991a, p. 96)
>
> I seem to be changing the way I write. But as it happens, I only write what I want, I'm not a professional—and I need to talk about this northeastern woman otherwise I'll suffocate. She accuses me and the way to defend myself is to write about her. (Lispector, 1990, p. 31)

Antoine de Saint-Exupéri's Little Prince affirmed, with some irritation (triggered by an annoying, vain, peevish little flower) that:

> Flowers have been growing thorns for millions of years. For millions of years, sheep have been eating them. And you think that it's not serious to try to understand why flowers go to so much trouble to grow thorns that are never used for anything? Is the war between the sheep and the flowers not important? (Saint-Exupéri, 2018, pp. 32–33)

In Lispector's wars between the sexes (sheep and flowers?), counterintuitively, men/sheep mostly fail (their mouths are torn by flowers). At the end, Macabéa shines like a star, Laura 'did her best not to become luminous and unreachable' (Lispector, 1990, p. 69) but still is, and Pequena Flor laughs like a fool (but who is the real fool here?).

In her essay 'Defamiliarization and Déjà Vu', Cláudia Pazos Alonso argues that in this writer men do not 'remain complacently locked into conventional parameters of masculinity, all the more so since these are shown to be on the brink of collapse [...]. If they do, they risk being left behind, in a truly undesirable reversal of subject positions' (Alonso, 2002, p. 88).

In Lispector, all the men (Marcel Pretre, Martim, Rodrigo S. M., Olímpico, Armando) on the other hand, in effect cease to signify: 'I feel that there is no point in my existence. I am pointless' (Lispector, 1990, p. 48). It is the end of one universe and the beginning of another. In the beginning was a word: 'yes'. But at the end? When a star (a supernova) explodes, what follows is both *fiat lux* and *horror vacui*. The destroyer is also destroyed. In the end, as we might expect if we even partly understand what she is up to, Lispector leaves us with nothing but questions, and not an answer in sight. What is the significance of madness/alienation in these stories? Do they carry a socio-political dimension or are these narratives purely a meditation on the fragmentation of the self, in modernity and in general? Are those fundamentally the same thing? Are the protagonists seeking a greater participation in reality, *or* escaping from it, *or* concluding that escape is impossible, *or* finding new ways in which it might be possible?

Yes and no to all.

What do alternating states of consciousness, and the breakdown of normal patterns of cause and effect say about 'ordinary reality' as we know it? Is there such a thing? Why do stars shine brightly when in fact by the time their light reaches us they are already dead?

In her reflection, 'Misappropriations of the "Feminine"', Sally Robinson, engaging with Braidotti, focuses on Derrida's *Spurs* and *Glas* and argues that Derrida's 'inscription of women in the texts of modernity [is] a "decoy"', 'a paranoid reaction that reproduces a certain castration scenario in relation to the death of the paternal metaphor' (Robinson, 1989, p. 48). At the end of *Glas*, Derrida confesses that he might be jealous of the mother who was able to change the phallus to infinity (Derrida, 1986, p. 261). Rodrigo S. M. must have known exactly how he felt. Alice Jardine's concept of *Gynesis* engages with the phenomenon of the enlisting of 'woman' in the work of Derrida, Lacan and Deleuze as a defensive reaction to that self-same idea (the deconstruction of the paternal metaphor) in a manoeuvre best summarized in the tactic 'if you can't beat them, join them'. 'Join them', however, as a pre-emptive means of ultimately annulling them. Lispector got there first, and ensured that in her own writing, at least, that specific masculinist enterprise was doomed to fail.

A supernova is a powerful stellar explosion. It occurs during the last evolutionary stages of a massive star (its final 'hora'). The original object, called the *progenitor*, either collapses into a black hole or is completely destroyed. When Macabéa's bright star bursts, Rodrigo S. M., her progenitor/creator/narrator, collapses too, into the non-matter of a black hole ('Macabéa killed me', Lispector, 1990, p. 105).

We and he had always known that that had been a possibility from the very start: 'Yes' has always inherent in it the possibility of 'No'. And when 'No' becomes the reality of a first-person narrator, the latter ceases to exist. No wonder Clarice chose a male narrator. That may have been what she always intended from the start. Braidotti notwithstanding, maybe society is not yet ready to transpose the binaries of *übermensch/untermensch*, let alone human/posthuman. The concept of the posthuman (Braidotti) is plagued by severe limitations, and her terminology of posthumanity ('posthuman theory contests the arrogance of anthropocentrism and the "exceptionalism" of the Human as a transcendental category', Braidotti in Veronese, 2016, p. 100) is itself open to an obvious deconstructive gambit, because we, humans, are still there: still calling the shots. It is a truth universally acknowledged that when we write about posthumanity, we still assume humans remain the prime performers (not unlike Hollywood science fiction, in which visiting aliens all speak English). No one, not even Braidotti, is suggesting global voluntary euthanasia by humanity for the sake of the planet's survival. Because if it did, who would be left to read her?

On the other hand, *relative* (rather than *radical*) difference is possible, and as J. R. R. Tolkien advised, 'not all who wander are lost' (Tolkien, 2010, p. 170). Furthermore, after a supernova explodes, there is nothing, and we need *something*, lest ontology become itself a non-concept, which would be literally the end of the world as we know it. Macabéa was not crazy: she could see things clearly although her reality was different from that of the sado-masochistic—and ultimately defeated/deleted—narrator. And as for us, the readers, if we are hermeneutically lucky, we will understand. Partly.

Conclusion

In *The Silence of the Lambs* (Harris, 1991), a famous psychopathic cannibal (who *was* crazy but also profoundly knowledgeable) says to another Clarice (Clarice *Star*ling: she who truly grasped the horror and allure-incarnate that is Hannibal L*ecter*—not Lis*pector*, but homophonously close; and Lithuanian, not Ukrainian, but like Lispector, a child escapee from pogroms): 'Orion is above the horizon now, and near it Jupiter, brighter than it will ever be [...] But I expect you can see it too. Some of our stars are the same, Clarice' (Harris, 1991, p. 533).

It takes one to know one.

In 1977, not long after the publication of *A hora da estrela*, in which Macabéa dies not *of* but *with* ovaries that resemble boiled mushrooms, Lispector was diagnosed with inoperable ovarian cancer and died within weeks, exhaling her last 'sopro de vida'. In her volume of chronicles, 'Where Did You Go Last Night?' (Lispector, 1974), she confronts us with disturbing tales of mystery disguised as reality. And in a chronicle with the same title, Lygia Fagundes Telles, Clarice's sister-writer and sidekick in mischief/fearlessness/daring, tells of an occasion during a conference in the town of Marília, when, in the early hours, while it was still dark, she woke up in her hotel room to find a swallow (definitely not a nocturnal species) trapped inside. The bird struggled for some time, then calmed down and perched for a few minutes at the foot of the bed looking at its human companion, who in a soft voice encouraged it to leave. Eventually it found the open window, pirouetted outside for a bit and then, as dawn was breaking, it flew away into the sky. Later that morning, still in the hotel, Telles was informed of Lispector's death: she sobbed: 'I already knew' (Telles, 2002, p. 22).

Their reality was different from ours. Their Jerusalem was built on a land often green but not always pleasant. Many of the stars they shared were the same.

Works Cited

Adams, Douglas, 1979, *The Hitchhiker's Guide to the Galaxy* (London: Pan Books).

Alonso, Cláudia Pazos, 2002, 'Defamiliarisation And Déjà Vu in Laços de Família', in *Closer to the Wild Heart: Essays on Clarice Lispector* (Oxford: Legenda), pp. 73–88.

Auerbach, Nina, 1984, *Woman and the Demon: The Life of a Victorian Myth* (Cambridge, MA: Harvard University Press).

Beckett, Samuel, 1983, *Worstward Ho* (New York: Grove Press, Inc.).

Braidotti, Rosi, 2002, *Metamorphoses: Towards a Feminist Theory of Becoming* (Cambridge: Polity Press).

Braidotti, Rosi, 2006, *Transpositions*: *On Nomadic Ethics* (Cambridge: Polity Press).

Carroll, Lewis, 2000, *Alice's Adventures in Wonderland* (Chicago: VolumeOne Publishing).

Chopin, Kate, 1984, *The Awakening and Selected Stories* (London: Penguin).

Cixous, Hélène, 1989, *L'Heure de Clarice Lispector* (Paris: Des femmes).

Cixous, Hélène, 1992, 'Coming to Writing', in *Coming to Writing and Other Essays*, ed. Deborah Jenson and Susan Rubin Suleiman (Cambridge, MA: Harvard University Press), pp. 1–58.

Dalcastagné, Regina, 2000, 'Contas a prestar: O intelectual e a massa em "A hora da estrela" de Clarice Lispector', *Revista de Crítica Literaria Latinoamericana*, 26.51, 83–98.

Derrida, Jacques, 1978, *Writing and Difference,* trans. and additional notes by Alan Bass (Chicago: The University of Chicago Press).

Derrida, Jacques, 1986, *Glas*, trans. John P. Leavy, Jr. and Richard Rand (Lincoln, NE: University of Nebraska Press, 1986), https://monoskop.org/File:Derrida_Jacques_Glas_1986.pdf

Douglass, Ellen H., 1988, 'Myth and Gender in Clarice Lispector: Quest as a Feminist Statement in "A imitação da rosa"', *Luso-Brazilian Review*, 25.2, 15–32.

Enslen, Joshua Alma, 2014, 'Between Tijuca and Mars: Maddening Intertextualities in Clarice Lispector's "A imitação da rosa"', *Luso-Brazilian Review*, 51.2, 68–79.

Fitz, Earl E., 1980, 'Freedom and Self-Realization: Feminist Characterization in the Fiction of Clarice Lispector', *Modern Language Studies*, 10.3, 51–61.

Fukelman, Clarisse, 1990, 'Escrever estrelas (ora direis): Introductory Essay to Lispector, Clarice', in *A hora da estrela* (Rio de Janeiro: Francisco Alves Editora), pp. 5–20.

Gilbert, Sandra, and Susan Gubar, 2020, *The Madwoman in the Attic: The Woman Writer and the Nineteenth-Century Literary Imagination* (New Haven, CT: Yale University Press).

Gilman, Charlotte Perkins, 2009, *The Yellow Wallpaper* (London: Penguin).

Glaspell, Susan, 1917, 'A Jury of her Peers', *Every Week Magazine* (5 March).

Gradín, Carlos, 2010, 'Race and Income Distribution: Evidence from the US, Brazil and South Africa', paper presented to the World Paper Series of the Society for the Study of Economic Inequality (ECINEQ).

Harris, Thomas, 1991, *The Silence of the Lambs & Red Dragon* (London: Peerage Books).

Helena, Lucia, 1990, 'Genre and Gender in Clarice Lispector's "The Imitation of the Rose"', *Style: Psychoanalysis, Gender, Genre*, 24.2, 215–27.

Helena, Lucia, 1992, 'A Problematização da Narrativa em Clarice Lispecto', *Hispania*, 75.5, 1164–73.

Jardine, Alice, 1985, *Gynesis: Configurations of Woman and Modernity* (Cornell, VA: Cornell University Press).

Katz, Lisa, 2009, 'The Lives of Others', *Haaretz* (5 December), https://www.haaretz.com/2009-12-05/ty-article/the-lives-of-others/0000017f-e822-df5f-a17f-fbfe65e10000

Klobucka, Anna, 1994, 'Hélène Cixous and the Hour of Clarice Lispector', *SubStance*, 23.1, 41–62.

Kristeva, Julia, 1982, *Powers of Horror: An Essay on Abjection* (New York: Columbia University Press).

Lawrenz, Lori, 2024, 'What is Learned Helplessness?', *Medical News Today* (9 December), https://www.medicalnewstoday.com/articles/325355

Lindstrom, Naomi, 1981, 'A Feminist Discourse Analysis of Clarice Lispector's "Daydreams of a Drunken Housewife"', *Latin American Literary Review*, 9.19, 7–16.

Lindstrom, Naomi, 1978, 'Clarice Lispector: Articulating Woman's Experience', *Chasqui*, 8.1, 43–52.

Lindstrom, Naomi, 1999, 'The Pattern of Allusions in Clarice Lispector', *Luso-Brazilian Review*, 36.1, 111–21.

Lispector, Clarice, 1943, Perto do coração selvagem (Rio de Janeiro: A Noite).

Lispector, Clarice, 1961, A maçã no escuro (Rio de Janeiro: Livraria Francisco Alves).

Lispector, Clarice, 1964, *A Paixão segundo G. H.* (Rio de Janeiro: Editora do Autor).

Lispector, Clarice, 1990, *A hora da estrela* (Rio de Janeiro: Francisco Alves Editora).

Lispector, Clarice, 1991a, 'A menor mulher do mundo', in *Laços de família* (Rio de Janeiro: Francisco Alves Editora), pp. 87–96.

Lispector, Clarice, 1991b, 'A imitação da rosa' in *Laços de família* (Rio de Janeiro: Francisco Alves Editora, 1991), pp. 47-69.

Lispector, Clarice, 1991c *Um Sopro de Vida: Pulsações* (Rio de Janeiro: Francisco Alves).

Lispector, Clarice, 1991d, 'Amor' in *Laços de família* (Rio de Janeiro: Francisco Alves Editora), pp. 29–41.

Lispector, Clarice, 1999, *Onde estiveste de noite?* (Rio de Janeiro: Rocco).

McNay, Lois, 1991, 'The Foucauldian Body and the Exclusion of Experience',

Hypatia: Feminism and the Body, 6.3, 125–39.

Machado de Assis, Joaquim Maria, 1962, *Dom Casmurro. Obra Completa*, Vol. I (Rio de Janeiro: Aguilar), pp. 805–942.

Marting, Diane E., 1993, *Clarice Lispector: A Bio-bibliography* (Westport, CO: Greenwood).

Neto, João Cabral de Melo, 2016, *Morte e vida severina: Auto de Natal pernambucano* (Rio de Janeiro: Alfaguara).

Nunes, Benedito, 1982, 'Clarice Lispector ou a Neuralgia da Introspecção', *Colóquio Letras*, 70, 13–22.

O'Brien, Patricia, 1978, 'Crime and Punishment as Historical Problem', *Journal of Social History*, 23, 508–20.

Pereira, Claudini, 2016, *Ethno-racial Poverty and Income Inequality in Brazil*, CEQ Working Paper 60, http://www.commitmentoequity.org/publications_files/Brazil/CEQ_WP60_Pereira_Nov23_2016.pdf

Plato, 2003, *The Symposium*, trans. Christopher Gill (London: Penguin).

Ramos, Graciliano, 2021, *Vidas Secas* (Rio de Janeiro: José Olympio).

Robinson, Sally, 1989, 'Misappropriations of the "Feminine"', *SubStance*, 18.2, 48–70.

Rosenstock-Huessy, Eugen, 1983, *Speech and Reality* (Eugene, OR: Wipf and Stock Publishers), https://www.erhfund.org/wp-content/uploads/589.pdf

Sá, Olga de, 1979, *A Escritura de Clarice Lispector* (Petrópolis: Editora Vozes).

Saint-Exupéri, Antoine de, 2018, *The Little Prince*, trans. Irene Testot-Ferry (London: Wordsworth Editions).

Schmidt, Rita Terezinha, 1989, 'Clarice Lispector: The Poetics of Transgression', *Luso-Brazilian Review*, 26.2, 103–15.

Sellberg, Karin, 2006, 'Review of Rosi Braidotti *Transpositions*: On Nomadic Ethics', *Deleuze Studies*, 2, 137–40. https://www.euppublishing.com/doi/full/10.3366/E1750224108000408

Senna, Marta de, 1986, 'A Imitação da Rosa' by Clarice Lispector: An Interpretation', *Portuguese Studies*, 2, 159–65.

Telles, Lygia Fagundes, 2002, 'Onde estiveste de noite?', in *Durante aquele estranho chá: Perdidos e achados* (Rio de Janeiro Rocco), pp. 15–22.

Tolkien, J. R. R., 2010, *The Lord of the Rings* (London: Harper Collins).

Veronese, Cosetta, 2016, '"Can the Humanities Become Post-human?" Interview with Rosi Braidotti', *Relations*, 4.1, 97–101, https://doi.org/10.7358/rela-2016-001-vero

Wittgenstein, Ludwig, 2002, *Tractatus Logico-Philosophicus* (London: Taylor & Francis), p. 5, https://www.gutenberg.org/files/5740/5740-pdf.pdf

Yannuzzi, Andrea, 1997, 'Clarice Lispector', in *Encyclopaedia of Latin American Literature*, ed. Verity Smith (Chicago: Fitzroy Dearborn Publishers), pp. 896–90.

4. Victor Willing: Being There

I once heard some idiot on the radio saying that all great art has suffering as its dominant theme, and that the greatest artists are only able to create because they suffer immensely in their own lives. What a bunch of bullshit. [...]. Suffering is only a single colour, and by itself it's boring.

Bart Yates, *Leave Myself Behind*

Life is short. Art long.

Hippocrates, *Aphorisms*

I remember a corridor, sometimes filled with crashing footsteps, sometimes so quiet that the only sounds were of my breathing [...] where the walls were hung with group photographs [...] to represent the passing of a year. [...] The significance was the date. This image of the corridor and of running the gauntlet of reproach long remained the "passage of time". Before, the amalgam of past and present seemed destined to continue endlessly, but [...] at that moment a languorous fatalism in face of the advancing blade was accompanied by a curious desire. If I had been asked then to define nostalgia I would have said it was a longing for a past time but this [...] seemed so much more that it was not apparent that *this* was nostalgia. [...] Our world is desire made concrete symbol. [...] When was now?

Victor Willing

Introduction

Victor Willing's life as an artist was a game of two halves: a precocious successful career as a young artist and an equally fascinating second-half with a prolonged break in between. What changed between the two was the diagnosis, onset and distraction wrought by multiple sclerosis, which, however, is arguably what made him into the great artist that he was by the time he died.

***

What's Left Behind?

Any student of Victor Willing's art but also of his captivating writings should consider the possibility that when he is smiling at something, it doesn't necessarily mean he thinks it is funny. In 1954, he wrote a part-humorous, part-serious text called *Travel by Bus: A Brief Manifesto*. In it he stated that 'no history can be independent of the present. It is by our definition of this relationship that we show our hand, indicating our direction' (Willing, 2000c, p. 15). It concludes with a series of bullet points of humorous recommendations which includes 'avoid becoming the victim of a dialectical situation'; and 'become like water'. The only solution to a dialectical situation, however, was a dead end: mostly not a good idea, either in life or art. And 'becoming like water' means you lose shape and flow away. The latter might be one aspect of what Nicholas Serota identified in his work when he wrote as follows:

> [His paintings] are not perceptions of the world, they're very much perceptions of the mind. [...] what he shows is invariably inanimate, but [his] paintings are about the most animated inanimate objects I have ever seen. There is something quite menacing about many of them. Everything is in a state of flux. You feel as though a murder has been recently committed [but also] an extraordinary sense of calm after the storm [...] to disclose a restless and tragic world. (Serota, 2000, pp. 17–21)

John McEwen, his friend and a perceptive commentator of his work, quotes Willing saying that 'we all have this problem—that we have an inner reality which only we can know. And this is the self we're inclined to forget about because there isn't very much use for it in the world—this real part of ourselves. [...] I think my painting is almost exclusively to do with that self which is normally neglected' (McEwen, 2000, p. 32).

In an essay called 'Masks' written in 1984, Willing wrote about a meeting with his friend Peter in 1955 during which the latter introduced him to his friend Sam, who had seen a reproduction of one of Vic's paintings in an art magazine and had expressed interest. Sensing the possibility of a sale, Vic, not long out of the Slade School of Fine Art and very short of cash, donned his one clean set of clothes and set off for what at the very least would be a free lunch. 'Peter' was Peter Snow, who at that time was designing sets and costumes for 'Sam's' new play (*Waiting for Godot*, directed by Peter Hall). Vic, a great reader but not a theatre buff was oblivious to the identity of his fellow lunch guest, concerning whom all he was told was that he 'wrote a play about two tramps'. The event proved to be awkward. Making not much headway with an uncommunicative 'Sam' who did not have much to say and [...] didn't respond to [Vic's] 'attempts to be interesting', Willing, with growing desperation, resorted to a rambling would-be philosophical monologue in the course of which he opined that 'even in the presence of others a monk's diminished ego is silent, while a prisoner's verbosity is his attempt to repair his. [...] We act and pretend, act to change the world, declare that we are there, and change ourselves. By pretending, we test possibilities, and discover ourselves among our disguises. This the painter does in solitude: the image is his drama' (Willing (b), 2000, pp. 46-47). The point of this partly hilarious and partly profound passage could be transmuted into a rendition of the famous stanza by Fernando Pessoa, a compatriot of Paula Rego, who was Vic's fellow artist, his lover and later his wife:

> The poet is a pretender
> And pretends so completely
> That he even pretends
> The pain he truly feels. (Pessoa, 1942 [1995], p. 235)

Pessoa, famously, was the creator of different poetic selves (Fig. 4.1). There are many ways of being a wandering Jew: one is to run away from oneself. Like Willing, Pessoa ('pessoa' means 'person' in Portuguese whilst his maternal surname, Nogueira, suggests crypto-Jewish ancestry) lived a peculiar life, albeit for different reasons. Also for different reasons, he attempted to escape the limitations of the self. Willing, as will be suggested in what follows, did so by rehearsing a future where he would no longer be around. Pessoa did it by dividing himself into 'heteronyms' who had never been around from the start (different selves, with different, biographies, different emotions, different problems, and, remarkably, entirely different poetic voices): a phenomenon he described as 'um drama em gente', 'a play made up of people', although with no narrative to go with them, both of them dis-embodied (Fig. 4.2). No person to see here.

Fig. 4.1 Photograph of *Fernando Pessoa* (1914). Wikimedia Commons, public domain, https://commons.wikimedia.org/wiki/File:Pessoa_chapeu.jpg

 Fig. 4.2 Victor Willing, *Rien* (1980, oil on canvas, 200 × 183 cm. ©The Estate of Victor Willing, https://www.tate.org.uk/art/artworks/willing-rien-t03187

http://hdl.handle.net/20.500.12434/4a5e0ac2

Nothing. 'Rien.'
 Or:

> I am nothing.
> I will never be anything.
> I can never want to be anything.
> Apart from that, I encompass within myself all the dreams in the world.
> (Campos (heteronym of Fernando Pessoa), 1944 [1993], p. 252)

Or as Beckett reportedly said when asked by a French journalist whether he was English: '*Au contraire*'.[1] And what about you, Mr. Willing? Are you present in these pictures? *Au contraire*.

In the end, the insights that emerged from the theatre of the absurd that was that lunch with 'Sam' turned out to be not in the slightest bit

---

1 See Baker, 2006.

comedic. In the last ten years of his life, Willing depersonalized his art and emptied it of all human presence. Were those empty spaces a means of pretending/performing the pain he truly felt? Were they representing in the most literal possible way his own nasty death foretold? In conversation with John McEwen, Willing refers to the empty spaces (of which much more later) in his second-phase work as follows:

> Willing described the spaces in his images as places in which 'something has happened or is about to happen but is not happening at the time depicted'. (Quoted in McEwen, 2019a, p. 36)

We will return to this in due course.

The Sound of Silence: *Quem Vive?*[2]

> And as imagination bodies forth
> The forms of things unknown, the poet's pen
> Turns them to shapes and gives to airy nothing
> A local habitation and a name.
>
> Willam Shakespeare, *Midsummer Night's Dream*

For those of us who believe with *silent* fervour that Wagner's *Götterdämmerung* (let alone the whole *Ring* cycle) amounts to a cruel, overlong exposure to sound and fury signifying not enough, the last six minutes or so may be a feeble attempt at saying sorry: still noisy, but at least the screeching and booming is merely instrumental. Small mercies; absence makes the heart grow relatively fonder; etc. In 'The Cognitive and Mimetic Function of Absence in Art, Music and Literature', Timothy Walsh argues as follows:

> Whenever we are confronted with a perceived absence, we typically become more intensely aware of our surroundings and more speculative in our thinking. [...] I would suggest that the aesthetic manipulation of absence and uncertainty can be productive and empowering [...]. The examples of absence I wish to examine are important and interesting precisely because there is something 'more missing' in them than in their relatively more stable surrounding context. (Walsh, 1992, p. 69)

---

2   'Who goes there?'

On the subject of the armless Venus of Milo, he maintains that 'we are all attuned in myriad ways to recognize significant absences. [...] Yet it is this very emptiness, this purely negative element, that seems to enhance our perception of the figure's beauty' (Walsh, 1992, p. 70). Referring to Walter Perry, Walsh argues:

> The evocative power of this particular work stems at least partly from the fact that it is incomplete, that it shades off suggestively into nothingness or, conversely, that it seems to take shape amidst a background of emptiness made more than usually palpable. (ibid., p. 72).

Walsh goes on to suggest that 'gaps and silence function as the principal means by which the limitations of human consciousness are encoded' (ibid., p. 77).

> Once an absence has been made conspicuous, once it has been 'implicated' in some fashion, we are forced to accommodate some degree of uncertainty in our interactions with hat larger entity of which the absence is a part. (ibid., p. 79)

In *The Production of Space*, Henri Lefebvre coined the concept of a conceptual triad of space: perceived space (the physical organization of space, such as daily routines and activities); conceived space (the space created and imagined by urban planners, architects, and other professionals); and lived space (the individual, subjective experience of space, shaped by symbols, images and personal emotions). With regard to lived space, he wrote that 'In the beginning was the Topos. Before—long before—the advent of the Logos, in the chiaroscuro realm of primitive life, lived experience already possessed its internal rationality; this experience was producing long before thought space, and spatial thought, began reproducing the projection, explosion, image and orientation of the body' (Lefebvre, 1984, p. 174). He also ponders the concept of a withdrawal into the self as a possible response to brutal reality. Which might encompass the brutal inevitability of confronting one's finiteness, sooner rather than later. *How are you?*

Aged thirty-eight, Victor Willing was diagnosed with multiple sclerosis, the disease that would inflict upon him a drawn-out and ugly death. Aged fifty-nine, he created a self-portrait of himself aged seventy (Fig. 4.3).

Fig. 4.3 Victor Willing, *Self-Portrait at 70* (1987), oil on canvas, 56 × 56 cm. Pallant House Gallery, Chichester. ©The Estate of Victor Willing. Photo by Mark Bridge (2006), https://www.flickr.com/photos/markbridge/179893540
http://hdl.handle.net/20.500.12434/7e2b0331

That turns out to have been optimistic: he died the following year, aged sixty. Following his diagnosis at a relatively young age, everything changed, not least his art. How does one depict pending nothingness? Not unlike the creators of 'scopic authority' in civic religious plays, such as those performed at York and Chester between the fourteenth and sixteenth centuries in which certain dramatic personae command 'scopic authority' or privileged attention 'without having to expend a large amount of energy on movement or vocalization' (Black, 2019, p. 239)? In these plays, Jesus contrasts with a loud, violent, angry Herod, commands intromissive properties and holds greater power over the playing space than those who shape their presence through dynamic movement and speech. Silence speaks louder than words, and it also achieves a state of partnership with an equally passive, non-participative audience who is also silent. Does one, as a spectator, feel closer to the self-effacing Jesus or to the blustering Herod on his throne and in all his pomp?

Which of the two, Jesus or Herod, achieved eternal glory and positive energy? When we look at the hauntingly de-populated yet welcoming spaces (chairs, swings, carriages, plants) in Willing's images, just like when we watch these plays, are we granted the privilege of what Richard Wollheim called the status of the internal spectator (being allowed in, even if only to look: from the inside, rather than entirely from the outside). The feeling evoked by Willing's paintings of the last phase are both akin to and unlike it. Where is he in those spaces devoid of human presence? *Where am I?* If nobody is there, where does the sound of weeping come from? What is the verdict of the Judge in Fig. 4.4: 'the balance of weighing the world made manifest'?[3]

---

3   Nick Willing, in correspondence, 6 April 2025.

 Fig. 4.4 Victor Willing, *Judge* (1982), oil on canvas, 250 × 200 cm. ©The Estate of Victor Willing, https://artuk.org/discover/artworks/judge-70485

http://hdl.handle.net/20.500.12434/1dac3bee

The Art of Not Being There

J'ai conservé de faux trésors dans des armoires vides.[4]

Paul Éluard, *Comme deux gouttes d'eau*

Victor Willing's circle of friends and neighbours in London included a group of well-known writers, artists and intellectuals. Amongst them were numbered Francis Bacon, a close friend, and Sylvia Plath, the latter knowing, as he himself learned all too young, that 'dying is an art, like everything else' and that you can either 'do it exceptionally well' or do it 'so it feels like hell' (Plath, 1981, p. 17). Or both. Willing did it both exceptionally well *and* so it felt like hell. And he painted us pictures so that we too might understand:

> They pulled me out of the sack,
> And they stuck me together with glue.
> And then I knew what to do.
> I made a model of you. (Plath, 1981, p. 56)

Or in his case, a model of himself. Victor Willing was born on 15 January 1928 in Alexandria, the son of a soldier. He studied at Guildford Art School (1948–49) and subsequently, after compulsory National Service, at the Slade School of Fine Art, University of London (1949–53). At the Slade he met Paula Rego (see Chapter 5), whom he married in 1959 and with whom he had three children.

Little survived of his student work, with the exception of six paintings: *Portrait of John Mills* (1951); *Girl on a Camp Bed* (1953); *Man Explaining* (1955); *Portrait of Rodrigo Moynihan* (1955); *Winter Machine* (1956); and *Runners* (1955). The painting he submitted for his diploma, *Act of Violence* (aka *Fighting Men*) is still with the University Art Collections, University College London. In 1955, he had a successful show at the Hanover Gallery, although no catalogue exists and very few

---

4   'I kept phoney treasures in empty cupboards'.

images survive (an exception being one bought by the Arts Council of Great Britain). Throughout his life, theft, accidental destruction, loss and the need to paint over canvases for lack of money to buy new ones meant that many of his works disappeared.

In 1957, pregnant by Willing who was then still married to his first wife, Paula Rego left the UK to live in the family's property in Ericeira near Lisbon in Portugal and he later joined her there. They were married in 1959. Few paintings produced during this period were preserved. The ones that remain include *Standing Nude* (Fig. 4.5).[5]

Fig. 4.5 Victor Willing, *Standing Nude* (1952–53), oil paint on hardboard. Support: 1538 × 1234 mm; frame: 1583 × 1286 × 75 mm. ©The Estate of Victor Willing, https://www.tate.org.uk/art/artworks/willing-standing-nude-t07126

http://hdl.handle.net/20.500.12434/a2d67180

In 1966, Willing was diagnosed with multiple sclerosis (MS) and in the mid-1970s the family, having lost all their money, returned to London. His condition, even while still in Portugal, had progressed quickly and he began to experience problems with mobility, as well as in using his arms and hands.

Back in London, standing only with difficulty, experiencing moments of intense pain and possibly as the result of sleeplessness and medication for MS, sometimes he just sat motionless and looked at the wall. During these periods of contemplation he had visions or 'reveries'[6] of an intense quality which he then drew or painted. These visions lasted four years.

> I found that I was very tired, tired but not sleepy,' he told the art critic Alistair Hicks in 1987. 'I would sit in an easy chair and look at the wall in front of me, resting. And I began to get the impression that the wall in front of me dissolved and an enormous hole, about the size of my canvases, appeared and I could see through the wall apparently to a room on the other side. (Willing quoted in Gleadell, 2022)

---

5   A number are included in the family's collection: *Nude Triptych – I, II and III* (1959); *Blue Nude I* (1958); *Blue Nude II* (1958); *Nude – Paula* (1957); *Precarious Drag* (1956); *Still Life with Model Boat* (1957); *Still Life* (1958); *Portrait of Caroline* (1958); *Portrait of Tia Narcissa* (1958); two large Untitled Paintings (1961); *Lech* (1957); *Manuela* 1(958); *No.13* (1959); several drawings.

6   Bachelard, 1992.

In 1978, he had a successful show at the AIR (Artist Information Registry) Gallery, followed, over the next ten years, by several exhibitions, including one at the Serpentine Gallery in London. In 1982, he was appointed Artist in Residence at Corpus Christi College and Kettle's Yard Art Gallery, both in Cambridge. His many drawings were also widely exhibited. He was involved in two group exhibitions at the Hayward Gallery Annual in London in 1982 and 1985 and he had a major retrospective at the Whitechapel Art Gallery in 1986 two years before he died. His work is included in important collections including Tate Gallery, the Arts Council and the Saatchi Collection.

This is the Devil that Rides Me

The life so short, the craft so long to learn.

Geoffrey Chaucer, *Parliament of Fowls*

Michelangelo suffered from either gout or osteoarthritis, or both. Francisco Goya suffered neurological problems (headaches, dizziness, hearing loss, visual problems and issues with his right arm) due to syphilis. Henri Matisse became a wheelchair user following surgery for cancer. Claude Monet lost his sight in his left eye and developed xanthopsia (yellow-coloured sight) as a side-effect of cataracts. Vincent Van Gogh suffered from temporal lobe epilepsy as well as bipolar disorder. Henri de Toulouse-Lautrec suffered from pycnodysostosis. Édouard Manet suffered from pain and partial paralysis in his legs (locomotor ataxia) as a side-effect of syphilis. Paul Klee contracted scleroderma. David Hockney has hereditary deafness and synaesthesia: a distinguished brotherhood of disabled artists for Victor Willing. And as Abigail Adams, wife of one of the he USA's founding fathers, urged her husband regarding basic human rights, 'remember the ladies, Sir'.[7] He didn't, but we can: Frida Kahlo (poliomyelitis leading to life-long complications such as pain and miscarriages); Billie Holiday (liver cirrhosis); Dorothea Lange (poliomyelitis); Christina Applegate (breast cancer and multiple sclerosis); Lady Gaga (chronic pain due to

---

7 See Letter from Abigail Adams to John Adams, 31 March–5 April 1776, https://www.masshist.org/digitaladams/archive/doc?id=L17760331aa

fibromyalgia). We tend to hear less about the women, though. According to one reviewer of his late work,

> Willing saw his terminal diagnosis as integral to his evolution as an artist. He believed it gave him the ability to look inward and develop his art, devoid of ego and pretence. [...] The sheer variety and scale of Willing's later paintings affirm this stoic ethos, their bold tenor defying the artist's severely debilitated physical state. A series of his sculptures (also on show as part of Visions) explores notions of sacred space and refuge, evoking a sense of quasi-religious speculation, perhaps indicative of one's quest for some sort of undetermined salvation. (Hastings Independent, 2019)

In Willing's case, as multiple sclerosis continued to affect his upper and lower limbs, the large paintings of the early 1980s sometimes, though not always, gave place to smaller works, but he continued to defy the physical problems involved in handling massive canvases. His last exhibition was at the Karsten Schubert Gallery in 1987 and towards the end of his life he also created some small sculptures (a possible throwback to his student days at the Guildford Art School). He died at home on 1 June 1988, aged sixty.

A documentary about his life and work involving his son was released in 2019: *Gallery Talk: Nick Willing & Scott McCracken on Victor Willing*.[8] Another one on Paula Rego, directed by Nick Willing (*Paula Rego, Secrets & Stories*),[9] which also discusses him, was broadcast on BBC2 in 2017. Willing's work of the last fifteen years of his life amounted to the chronicle of a death foretold. It shall be argued in what follows that in his paintings we witness the spectacle of a mind envisaging a reality in which he is no longer present, of spaces that he had already vacated.

In conversation with John McEwen, he remarked that 'MS made me take a rather more serious view of life than I might otherwise have done at forty. Forty is an age when you expect people to think seriously about things, but I think I might have gone on living a rather vain, egotistical sort of life if I had enjoyed good health. MS did make me more introspective—though I'd always been quite

---

8   See Turps, 'Gallery Talk: Nick Willing & Scott McCracken on Victor Willing', *YouTube* (2 December 2019), https://www.youtube.com/watch?v=dyU01sG2yVs
9   The documentary can be viewed at: https://archive.org/details/paula-rego-secrets-and-stories-2017-bbc

introspective—and less concerned with the notion I had of myself as a person in the world. [...] I have to try and recover from the fright I give myself when my imagination gets cracking' (Willing, quoted in McEwen, 2019b, pp. 122–23).

We Are the Dead

Because of all we've seen,
Because of all we've said
We are the dead.

David Bowie, 'We are the Dead'

Gérard Titus-Carmel's piece, *The Pocket-Size Tlingit Coffin* (1975–76) is a miniature coffin with a mirror lining, such that when looking down, one sees oneself lying in it.[10] Much has been written about this piece, including by Derrida in *The Truth in Painting* (2017). Natalie Kosoi discusses it in a text on Mark Rothko's work as labouring on the notion of nothingness/non-being. She reflects on the split between Sartre's concept of nothingness ('a negation of all things in the world that comes into "existence" through human consciousness') and Heidegger's principle that 'because any being is finite, nothingness forms beings and as such is pre-requisite of everything that is' (Kosoi, 2005, p. 21). Kosoi argues that Rothko's works 'are both on the verge of *being* nothing and represent nothingness' (Kosoi, 2005, p. 21). And Irving Sandler quotes Rothko's view that art should intimate mortality (Sandler, 1983, p. 11). Something which is not necessarily straightforward, at least if one shares the limitations of Damien Hirst's shark (Fig. 4.6). Sharks, however, may pre-date dinosaurs by two hundred million years, but notoriously, they are intellectually incurious (experience isn't everything, as Baby Boomers like Willing would readily quip): lack of curiosity was a fault which, however, no one ever attributed to him.

---

10 Gerard Titus-Carmel, *Plate 1, from The Pocket Size Tlingit Coffin* (1976), Centre Pompidou, Paris, 1 March–10 April 1978, https://www.artic.edu/artworks/227527/plate-1-from-the-pocket-size-tlingit-coffin

Fig. 4.6 Damien Hirst, *The Physical Impossibility of Death in the Mind of Someone Living* or *Death Denied* (2008), glass, steel, shark, acrylic and formaldehyde solution. Photo by Agent001 (2009), Wikimedia Commons, CC BY-SA 3.0, https://commons.wikimedia.org/wiki/File:Shark83.JPG

In *A Future for Astyanax*, Leo Bersani (1976) invites us to consider the possibility of life rather than death for Racine's Astyanax, the infant son of Hector and Andromache, who in Greek legend, epic and drama was thrown to his death from the top of the highest wall in Troy when the Greeks breached the city. For Bersani, playing with Jean Racine's hypothetical wishful thinking, the alternative was Andromache's compromise: she saves her son from the murderous victors of the Trojan war by consenting to marry Pyrrhus, the most violent of them all.

> Yet my son dies: he must be protected.
> Pyrrhus by wedding me will act for him.
> It is enough: I place my trust in him.
> I know this Pyrrhus.
> Violent, but sincere,
> Cephisa, he'll do what he promised here.
> I rely too on the Greeks' unreasoning anger:
> Their hate will grant Hector's son a father.
> I go then, since I must be sacrificed,
> To give to Pyrrhus what is left of life;
> I go to hear his vows at the altar,
> And bind him to my son all the deeper,
> But then my hand, fatal now to me,

> Will put an end to my disloyalty,
> And, to my honour, pay the debt I owe
> To Pyrrhus, son, self, and husband so.
> Here is my love is guiltless stratagem;
> Here is what my husband commands me then. (Racine, 1982, p. 52)

Bersani interprets this planned exchange of favours, had it come about, as an allegory for psychological liberation: in abandoning their former loyalties and the constraints of formulaic desire, Andromache and Pyrrhus would have assured 'a future for Astyanax'. Is the aesthetic rejection of death analogous to circumventing the elemental fear of it? Does it ever work, the charting tragedies from beginning to end in a few verses: from the rape of Leda by the swan/Zeus and the resulting conception of Helen and Clytemnestra, to Helen and Paris, to the fall of Troy, to Agamemnon's return to Greece and his murder by Clytemnestra as revenge for the sacrificial murder of Iphigenia, their daughter (for the sake of a favourable wind when sailing to Troy before it all began)?

> A sudden blow: the great wings beating still
> Above the staggering girl, her thighs caressed
> By the dark webs, [...]
> A shudder in the loins engenders there
> The broken wall, the burning roof and tower
> And Agamemnon dead. (Yeats, 1990, p. 241)

Racine was not the only poet or even the first one to reject the inevitability of Astyanax's death. In Pierre Ronsard's epic *The Franciade* (1572), the infant (Francio or Francus, Ronsard's alter ego for Astyanax) is saved by the divine intervention of Jupiter who replaces him with a decoy made of clouds. He survives and later, urged by Jupiter and Mercury, begins an epic journey which leads to him becoming the founder of a new realm across the Danube: the precursor of the kingdom of France. And even dating much further back, the link between the Franks and the escapees from Troy was often vented: in the seventh-century *Chronicle of Fredegar*; in the eighth-century *Historia Brittonum*, borrowing from the sixth-century Frankish Table of Nations; in the *Grandes Chroniques de*

France (thirteenth to fifteenth century); in Johannes Trithemius' *De origine gentis Francorum compendium* (1514); and in Jean Lemaire de Belges's *Illustrations de Gaule et Singularités de Troie* (1510–12). Of course everyone is allowed to fantasize, in the case of the Portuguese/ Lusitanians via Lusus, son or fellow reveller of Bacchus:

> Behold here Lusus, from whose fame.
> Our kingdom, Lusitania, draws its name. (Camões, 1980, p. 267)

Why Imagine the Inevitable? 'Reality Does Not Need Me'

> When Spring comes,
> If I am already dead,
> Flowers will bloom as usual
> And the trees will be no less green than last Spring.
> Reality does not need me.
>
> Alberto Caeiro, 'When Spring Comes'

Ronsard, Racine and Bersani may have rejected Homer's and Aeschylus' version of Astyanax's death. The latter were, after all, Greek and not exempt from vindictiveness even though they'd won, but the other three may have been forgiven for indulging in wishful thinking, rooting as they did for a contrary outcome (the survival of Astyanax/Francion). In *King Lear,* Edgar claimed that 'worse I may be yet: the worst is not so long as we can say, "This is the worst"' (*King Lear*, Act IV, Scene 1, lines 2279–80). It was easy for him to say so, but Mark Rothko, the son of secular intellectual Latvian Jews escaped from Russia in 1913 during the last days of Czarissm, had in his DNA the conviction that as a general rule, the worst almost certainly *does* happen. Furthermore, he may have been an abstractionist, but his death was the ultimate instance of performance art. He committed suicide and leaving nothing to chance he overdosed on barbiturates and severed an artery. Victor Willing's death was nothing like it. He died after an illness that took twenty-two years from diagnosis till death.

Fig. 4.7 Tribute, Mark Rothko Art Centre, Daugavpils (Latvia), October 2017. Photo by Traqueurdelumieres (2017), Wikimedia Commons, CC BY-SA 4.0, https://commons.wikimedia.org/wiki/File:Tribute,_Mark_Rothko_Art_Centre,_Daugavpils_(Latvia),_October_2017.jpg#/media/File:Tribute,_Mark_Rothko_Art_Centre,_Daugavpils_(Latvia),_October_2017.jpg

His paintings of those last twenty years, however, like Rothko's (Fig. 4.7), can be construed as a prolonged performance (staging) of the time when he would no longer be there. Curiously, they also evoke the same tranquillity at the thought of his future non-being as Rothko's (whose paintings' uncompromisingly matt quality in real life is betrayed by the glossy reproductions to be found in every other student room in university halls of residence in the 1980s), or as the placid poetry of Alberto Caeiro, the alter ego of the neurotic Fernando Pessoa. Pessoa was a compatriot of Willing's Portuguese wife (on Paula Rego, see Chapter 5), dead the year she was born. Caeiro, his heteronym, however, was the opposite of neurotic (and averse to Wagnerian twilights).

> I feel extremely happy
> When I think that my death doesn't matter at all
> If I knew that tomorrow I would die
> And that Spring was the day after tomorrow,
> I would die happy if it was the day after tomorrow
> I would die happy because it was the day after tomorrow.
> If that is the right time, when would death come other than when it is the right time?
>
> I like everything to be real and for everything to be correct.
> And I like it because it would be so even if I didn't like it.
> Therefore, if I die now, I will die happy,

Because everything is real and everything is right.

They can pray in Latin over my coffin, if they like.
If they like they can dance and sing around it.
I have no preferences regarding a time
when I will no longer be able to have preferences.
Whatever will be, when it is, is the thing that will be.
   (Caeiro, 1993, p. 87)[11]

Did he care what the world would look like after he was dead? Probably not, particularly since he didn't exist, but Willing, his compatriot-by-marriage, apparently did, although, like Caeiro, he too made the idea seemingly peaceful.

Disease Is an Art (Like Everything Else)

Death is a continuation of my life without me.

Jean-Paul Sartre

Not with a bang but a whimper.

T. S. Eliot, 'The Hollow Men'

Multiple sclerosis is an auto-immune disease. It can cause a plethora of symptoms, including loss of mobility and weakness in the arms and hands, loss of fine motor skills and extreme fatigue. As the condition progresses, one's body becomes an unreliable agent and the world an inimical environment in which even a minor rise in body temperature (for example, after eating) or environmental heat (a nice sunny day) can trigger visual difficulties and exacerbate other symptoms. Shelter from the sun becomes of vital importance. In Victor Willing's case, several of these symptoms manifested themselves, including, as regarded his activities as an artist, impaired gross and fine motor skills. In the end, however, he died of the MS patient's best friend: a respiratory infection. Did he go gently into that good night?

---

11 As mentioned in the Note on Texts and Translations, all Portuguese and Brazilian poems were translated by M. M. Lisboa. This one is available at https://cambridge.academia.edu/MariaManuelLisboa/Translations and https://www.academia.edu/125780574/Poems_by_Alberto_Caeiro_heteronym_of_Fernando_Pessoa_Translated_by_M_M_Lisboa_Quando_vier_a_Primavera

In extracts from a conversation with John McEwen, two years before he died and already almost completely incapacitated, Willing stated that painting was 'a means of having a sort of conversation with [himself...] Like an open door one hesitates to go through' (McEwen, 2019b, pp. 120–23). As a young artist, he had worked a lot on portraiture, including self-portraiture, and that particular 'conversation' continued throughout his life (Fig. 4.8).

Fig. 4.8 Victor Willing, *Self-Portrait* (1957), oil on canvas, 56 × 56 cm. ©The Estate of Victor Willing, https://www.creativeboom.com/inspiration/visions-a-major-retrospective-of-the-mid-century-british-painter-victor-willing/
http://hdl.handle.net/20.500.12434/0365929c

Lynne Cooke sees Willing's *Self-Portrait* of 1957 (Fig. 4.8) as singular in that 'although he portrays himself as a painter at work, there is no sense of occasion, nothing portentous or rhetorical about the stance and presentation'. His surroundings, appearance and clothing are neutralized or obscured, attention being directed to the figure, not the face. 'He seems to regard himself as no more significant, [than any other figure he might have chosen to portray]. The image is divested of narrative and anecdotal time, the sense of presence can be sharpened and distilled' (Cooke, 2000, p. 12).

Placidity may not have been always attainable in these circumstances, and might not have come naturally anyway to a man steeped in Jungian psychoanalysis and who named Nietzsche's *The Birth of Tragedy* as one of his favourite books.

Even so, images such as *Place*, *Mud* and *Rien* suggest an on-going process of, if not Stoical (in the original Zeno sense of the word), at least philosophical (in the common-parlance usage of the term) acceptance of a different type: namely an attempt at envisaging the Epicurean utopia (more of which later).

> You have to accept the lot to be religious. I don't. But... I have found myself aware also of those images that have been insistent [...], archetype because they are more than coincidental. The sense of the numinous takes us further then humanist ethics. When we enter caverns measureless to man, we are already treading a path also to do religious experience. Too timid, in the event, to do more than peep at what might be there. (Willing, quoted in McEwen, 2019a, p. 47).

All the Unhealthy People: Where Does It Hurt?

May you stay forever young.

Bob Dylan, 'Forever Young'

In Willing, the human figure gradually gave way to empty spaces, although it never entirely disappeared, a palimpsest remaining even if only *in absentia*, in images that suggest its erstwhile presence (empty chairs; discarded clothing).

In 'Uncanny Motions: Facing Death, Morphing Life', Anu Koivunen discusses an exhibition of the Finnish artist Helene Schjerfbeck's paintings and drawings, which included a frame that, in lieu of a painting, featured a video loop: an animated rendition of Schjerfbeck's self-portraits that merged thirteen works into an apparently seamless unfolding of the artist's different ages, her face transforming from that of an eighteen-year-old to that of an eighty-three-year-old.

> Whereas the artist's paintings and drawings hanging on the walls of this art gallery, engaged in the commemoration of her work and the times that had passed, the video—titled *Metamorphosis* and running as a fifty-second loop—seemed to bring the dead artist alive, over and over again [...] The curatorial decision to include it has been based on the particular sense of liveness that it engenders. [...] One is faced with a morph that allows one to perceive aging as movement. [...] It imposes the trajectory of life and the approaching death on the viewer, [...] viewers are faced with death—looking the transforming, aging subject of the portraits into the eyes—but also, as an effect of the loop, with rebirth. (Koivunen, 2013, pp. 248–52)

Lynne Cooke discusses the difference between likeness and lifelikeness (what Sartre called existential posture, Cooke, 1986, p. 127) in portraiture, the former relating to naturalistic representation and the latter being concerned with 'being witness to the living being' (Cooke, 1986, p. 125). With regard to Willing's *Heads*, she argues that like Picasso, who 'never seems to have quailed before the revelations of his mind, however appalling they might prove' (Cooke, 1986, p. 125), 'the series [was] marked by a heightened sense of anguish [...and] a shift to a smaller scale [...] necessitated by the worsening of his multiple sclerosis' (Cooke, 1986, pp. 125–26).

Koivunen draws on Deleuze's view that 'the close-up of the face is detached from the frames of social roles, individuation, and communication, turning the face into a phantom (Koivunen, 2013, p. 258) with the result that a close-up is not about individuation but instead it is about suspending it, the dread expressed by the face confronting with its impending nothingness. Not unlike the video, in which the viewer's attention is directed at the transformation of facial features that come to resemble a skull, Willing's trajectory, too, morphed from self-portraits to images devoid of animate life (even plants seem to acquire sci-fi, uncanny, triffid-like qualities and appear to chart a similar path: from ontological beginning to unavoidable end (from burgeoning greenery to dead leaves).

Place of Exile (Fig. 4.9), a preparatory drawing for *Place* (fig. 10), differs from it because it features a shadowy human figure that has disappeared in *Place* (top right-hand side). Writing about Willing, Hellmut Wohl stated that 'the paintings are pregnant with the implied presence of a protagonist' (Wohl quoted in McEwen, 2000, p. 39).

Fig. 4.9 Victor Willing, *Place of Exile* (1976), charcoal and pastel on paper, 31.4 × 50 cm. ©The Estate of Victor Willing, courtesy Marlborough Fine Art, https://artscouncilcollection.org.uk/artwork/place-exile

http://hdl.handle.net/20.500.12434/2f38f9ef

Fig. 4.10 Victor Willing, *Place Triptych* (1976–78), oil on canvas, 66 × 116 cm (left panel, 190 × 216 cm (centre panel), 166 × 116 cm (right panel). ©The Derek Williams Trust, https://derekwilliamstrust.org/news/victor-willing-takes-his-place-in-the-collection/#

http://hdl.handle.net/20.500.12434/b2f5f4bb

Paula Rego, who as Willing's wife and an artist herself had a ring-side seat to his thought processes, saw him not as a conceptual artist but as 'a physical picture maker. He thought that emotion could be felt physically and expressed formally' (Rego, 2000a, p. 101). Writing about *Place*, Rego saw each panel of the triptych as intending to represent 'an alchemical symbol with intense personal meaning to the artist: the flesh, the self, and the possibilities for traveling in the mind'.[12]

---

12 Quoted in https://derekwilliamstrust.org/news/victor-willing-takes-his-place-in-the-collection/#

> *Place* [Fig. 4.10] is without doubt the best thing Vic ever did. [...] It is not uncheerful—he likes it there. He isolates himself deliberately. The chair is Vic. [...] the central panel is balanced between the ways of the flesh—the big fleshy plant on the right, pure sex Vic's way—and the ways of the mind—and the drawings on the left. (Rego, 2000b, p. 71)

Cruelly, she detailed what she thought he needed to make pictures, and this included almost everything (bar the first one) that his illness had destroyed:

> The intellect and hope and travel and sex. [...] The huge size of it was important to Vic. [...] For him it had something to do with his relationship to his own body. (Rego, 2000b, p. 71)

This view is replicated in her own artwork of the mid- to late-1980s, in which she chronicles his path through increasing disability to death, in particular the *Girl and Dog* series created two years before he died (Chapter 5, Figs, 5.17, 5.18, 5.19), which she insisted were all 'about Vic' (Tusa, 2001, p. 10) and *The Family* (Fig. 4.11, whose provisional title had been *The Raising of Lazarus*), done the year he died. As mentioned before, she had a privileged view of that particular tragedy.

Fig. 4.11 Paula Rego, *The Family* (1988), acrylic on paper on canvas, 213.4 × 213.4. ©Victoria Miro, https://www.victoria-miro.com/artworks/29907/

http://hdl.handle.net/20.500.12434/42c4d32f

Place may also represent Willing's ideal of the 'aedicula' or 'shelter', a place of refuge or retreat. A retreat (in the sense of withdrawal from a battle lost), it would appear, if compared with the earlier drawing (*Place of Exile*), seeing as in the painting, as opposed to the precursor drawing, even the last encumbrance of human life (the self) has been elided. In ancient Greece, an *aedicula* (diminutive of *aede*) was a small building or construction designed to frame, shelter and honour a sacred object. It could also be used as a shrine or a niche for a statue. Aediculae are typically made up of two or four columns that support a flat or domed shape and had featured in his drawings and paintings. This particular painting uses a symbolic vocabulary of geometric shapes and disparate objects, framed within an architecture of blank walls and deserted spaces. Aediculae could be open on all sides or set into a wall.

Rego suggested that the objects in *Place* capture the lonely abode of the artist. In the centre panel, as in an abandoned stage set, the triptych features Willing's empty chair and bag within a covered shelter. The atmosphere of disquiet, and the dislocation caused by the split of images between three panels which do not entirely flow into each other, has a very particular source (the quasi-hallucinations Willing experienced, as mentioned earlier). Hettie Judah (2020) looks back at his works of the last phase and remarks that 'a symbolic vocabulary soon emerged: a chair; feathers; sprouting plants, clothes suspended from a line; a little sailing boat; two and three-dimensional geometric forms. As with his early figurative paintings, all are tightly framed, mysterious objects contained by architecture, like history paintings denuded of heroes'. In *Place*, content and form are perfectly symbiotic. The content of the left-hand and right-hand side panels feed off from the central panel and into it but with breaks in continuity, and they are still separate, though the effect of enclosure is maintained. Scale is also disrupted by non-sensical proportions: the chair on the platform under the awning is either tiny in comparison with the handbag, or the bag is gigantic. One leaf from the potted plant on the right-hand panel breaks into the background of the central panel, but again, the implied proportions, if applied to the right-hand panel, would suggest that the plant is as large as a tree, which however, would not thrive in a pot. Some elements are reliable (the shadow of the small cuboid object, the plant, the awning and the platform appear correct), but there is much that is imponderable (the unidentifiable objects scattered on the ground) or disconcerting. Moreover, are they walls (is this an indoors setting) or is the blue backdrop in all three panels the sky? That ambiguity is presumably resolved in *Mud* (Fig. 4.12).

Fig. 4.12 Victor Willing, *Mud* (1979–80), oil on canvas, 183.2 × 426.1 cm. ©The Estate of Victor Willing. Arts Council Collection, Southbank Centre, London, https://artuk.org/discover/artworks/mud-64323

http://hdl.handle.net/20.500.12434/5a7666a4

In this triptych, created one year after *Place*, the backdrop of mud, like the flooring in *Place*, feeds from the central panel into the lateral ones, only even more clearly, in what seems to be a depiction of a corner of a room. But how do the straight edges of floor and walls fit into the setting of what appears to be a muddy swamp, in which, moreover, a plastic sunflower that makes no pretence at being anything but artificial, seemingly grows. What is animate or inanimate here? Are those butcher cuts of meat hanging in the background in the centre panel real (and decaying) or ornamental? Either way, when did a signifier of rotting flesh become an *objet d'art*? To what does the half-buried wheel in the left-hand panel belong? Was there once a vehicle attached to it? Was there someone in it? Where are they now? Is he or she in the tent (*aedicula*), waiting for help? For autopsy? Buried in the mud where dead bodies fossilize? Compost for a flower that isn't real? Dead bodies in swamps emit methane which combusts to produce will-o'-the-wisp light effects in the dark. Like the art of those about to die? Who have already died.

In the last stages of MS, one's ability to move can be entirely destroyed and one can be confined either to a chair or to a bed. The old self vacates the space it had previously claimed as its own. In its place, it leaves nothing: a pile of discarded clothing with nobody inside. With *no body* inside (Figs. 4.2, 4.13 and 4.14).

Fig. 4.13 Victor Willing, *Stepladder* (1976), oil on canvas, 183 × 152 cm. ©The Estate of Victor Willing. Pallant House Gallery, Chichester, https://artuk.org/discover/artworks/painting-with-stepladder-70480

http://hdl.handle.net/20.500.12434/5a1558fa

Fig. 4.14 Victor Willing, *Swing* (1978), oil on canvas, 152 × 83 cm. ©The Estate of Victor Willing, https://artuk.org/discover/artworks/swing-70536

http://hdl.handle.net/20.500.12434/edfe3989

John McEwen (2019b, p. 121) was told by the artist of a childhood memory of his unstable mother hanging him by his braces inside a wardrobe and leaving him there when he was naughty: something recalled in a seemingly matter-of-fact way by Willing, but that leads to the possibility that he might have been an abused child. *Swing* (Fig. 4.14) may be based on that memory. Elsewhere, again in conversation with McEwen, however, he gives another version of the inspiration for the image:

> Swing for instance recalls when I was a small boy and took great delight in going backwards and forwards on a swing, upside down. What was marvellous about that was the disorientation. You had the impression that the world was swinging, not you. Later I discovered that the' 'hanged man' card in the tarot pack is an upside down figure, representing chaos. So there seemed a connection. It is chaotic if the whole world is moving. (McEwen, 2019b, p. 121)

Well, it was *his* party and he could change his story if he liked. In *Rien, Stepladder* and *Swing* (Figs. 4.2, 4.13 and 4.14), clothing with no body, not even a mannequin's, may signify someone that once wore them but is no longer there: clothes without an emperor to wear them, which has to be more poignant than even a naked monarch. But even more so is a setting where the clothes themselves have disappeared, and all that remains is something we cannot fathom (indoors or outdoors? Blue sky or blue walls?). What happens if something/someone slips under that small—is it small?—arch in *Place with a Red Thing* (Fig. 4.15)? Is that a door or a window? What happens after we pass that gate? What if what awaits us there is a Jonah-like whale (Willing's favourite story in the Bible: in conversation he suggested that the 'red thing' was the whale's tail waiting to swallow us). Is the whale itself buried in the mud? Is it also dead? Preserved into the faux immortality (or memento mori) of a fossil? Whatever the case may be, in all instances the aftermath is a world which life has already vacated:

Fig. 4.15 Victor Willing, *Place with a Red Thing* (1980), oil on canvas, 200 × 250.2 cm. ©The Estate of Victor Willing, https://www.tate.org.uk/art/artworks/willing-place-with-a-red-thing-t03186
http://hdl.handle.net/20.500.12434/71a0fc41

Scott McCracken argues as follows:

> Although [Willing] avoids any direct representation of the human figure, his paintings do embody an unassailable human presence. [...] We can surmise that there must be an inhabitant of the scenes pictured, forever absent [...]. '*Scenarios in which something has happened or is about to happen.*' [...]. All that remains before us are the props. They occupy the unpopulated sets, replacing the actors who have exited stage left. (McCracken, 2019, p. 1)

Regardless: No Country for Old Men

> That is no country for old men.
> [...]
> Whatever is begotten, born, and dies.
> Caught in that sensual music all neglect
> Monuments of unageing intellect.
>
> William Butler Yeats, 'Sailing to Byzantium' (1990, p. 57)

The line 'no country for old men' may describe a world that is so for some, more than for others. Which makes it just as well that MS—though it may only shave a few years off one's life expectancy if one is lucky—at worst (in the cases of Victor Willing and Jacqueline du Pré) ensures the impossibility of the patient making old bones. What could be more fitting for a Baby Boomer (like Willing), raving it up in the sixties and telling his elders that he wouldn't trust anyone over thirty? The Beatles, with an eye on Vera, Chuck and Dave, may have envisioned getting past the age of sixty-four (although half of them did not), but not everyone was that lucky. Certainly not Vic, born not in Byzantium but in Alexandria (exotic, either way), and dead before he 'got old' (or at least only twice-thirty).

The symbology of empty spaces (Fig. 4.16) becomes unavoidable as one prepares to disappear oneself.

Fig. 4.16 Victor Willing, *Breathe* (1982), pastel and charcoal on paper, 42.2 × 30 cm. ©The Estate of Victor Willing, https://www.artsy.net/artwork/victor-willing-untitled-breathe

http://hdl.handle.net/20.500.12434/6e6e4155

> They are not long, the weeping and the laughter,
> Love and desire and hate:
> I think they have no portion in us after
> We pass the gate. (Dowson, 'Vitae summa brevis')[13]

In the aftermath, after passing the gate, there is a world which one has already left behind, creating empty spaces where an unoccupied chair reminds us of prior occupancy (Figs. 4.9 and 4.10), as does a funeral bier

---

13   See https://www.theotherpages.org/poems/dowson01.html

stuck in the sand, with a bird of prey flying overhead Fig. 17).

 Fig. 4.17 Victor Willing, *Cart* (1978), oil on canvas, 188 × 208 cm. ©The Estate of Victor Willing. Bridgeman Images, https://www.bridgemanimages.com/en/willing/the-cart-1978-oil-on-canvas/oil-on-canvas/asset/1079709
http://hdl.handle.net/20.500.12434/9755ad39

In conversation with McEwen (2000, p. 24) Willing said that *Cart* related to a childhood memory of vultures in the desert outside Alexandria scavenging a dead donkey. In this image, the carrion birds shadow the shaded tumbrel. Even as a child, the terror of bodily decay (in this case not leading to a multiply-sclerotic, multiply-scarred death but after it) seems to have loomed large in his imagination.

 Fig. 4.18 Victor Willing, *Effigy* (1978), crayon and pastel on paper, 25 × 32.5 cm. ©The Estate of Victor Willing. Timothy Taylor, https://www.timothytaylor.com/artworks/16711-victor-willing-effigy-1978/
http://hdl.handle.net/20.500.12434/2544a2bc

I used to believe that story
that said a real man doesn't cry.
I thought of myself as a man.
As a boy
my favourite action films
made me anything but a coward
with that childish arrogance of the invincible hero.
Now I tremble.
And now I cry.
Like a man trembles.
Like a man cries! (José Craveirinha, (1974)

When She whom no one loves arrives
(Be she harsh or tender)
I may be afraid.
I may smile, or say:
'Hello there, Unavoidable One!
My day went well, let night come.
(Night, with all its sorceries).
She will find the field ploughed, the house clean,
The table laid,
Everything in its place. (Manuel Bandeira, 'End of Day', 1974, p. 307)

This Used to Be Me (or: *exeunt* pursued by a bear)

You must go on. I can't go on. I'll go on.

Samuel Beckett, 'The Unnamable'

In his essay, 'Images of the Self', McEwen quotes from one of Willing's favorite books, Friedrich Nietzsche's *The Birth of Tragedy*, given to him when he was fresh out of the Slade by Francis Bacon (who, during Willing's lean years, often bought him breakfast: a Bacon sarnie?): 'With sublime gestures he reveals to us how the whole world of torment is necessary so that the individual can create the redeeming vision, and then, immersed in contemplation of it, sit peacefully in his tossing boat amid the waves' (John McEwen, 2000, p. 3). McEwen notes that the quote from Nietzsche 'is uncannily apposite to [Vic's] own experience [...].The necessary "torment" created, for him and many others, what was indeed a "redeeming vision." Thus, to an extraordinary degree he fulfilled what seems like his destiny'(McEwen, 2000, p. 23).

McEwen also remembers the following occasion:

> One afternoon, musing on the terrace of the *quinta*[Quinta Ribeira da Baleia] after a simple but delicious Portuguese lunch [...] Willing thought: 'This is it! for God's sake! People work all their lives to be in my situation, and here I am, young and healthy, getting it now—yet I know there's something wrong with my life'. (McEwen, 2000, pp. 31–32)[14]

Not long after that, he collapsed with a heart attack, and not long after *that* he was diagnosed with MS.

The Epicurean path to happiness involved the avoidance or minimization of pain, anxiety and suffering, rather than the search for pleasure as such. The cultivation of the pleasures of the flesh were not deemed sufficient and ought to balance with those of the mind. The latter involved mental processes that cultivated feelings of joy, lack of fear and pleasant memories. Freedom from hardship was to be achieved by the formation of a community of friends outside the traditional political state. Was that what Willing—'pursued by a bear', exiting life, his body ravaged by an illness that, like the gods, likes to attack the young—was trying to find in those *aediculae*?

---

14 On the Quinta, see https://www.ericeiramag.pt/en/financial-times-dedicates-article-to-paula-regos-house-in-ericeira/ and https://www.ericeiramag.pt/en/arte-channel-highlights-the-life-of-paula-rego-in-ericeira/

One of the remarkable qualities in his later work is the combination of flatness and lack of workable perspective. McEwen (2019b, p. 124) discusses the influence of Erwin Panofsky in his thinking.

> Panofsky had pointed out that in the Renaissance artists introduced perspective (measurable space) into pictures because Time had become measurable (meaning that the notion of future and past time was made believable [...] which in turn had produced [...] socio-economic results [...]: inherited wealth became possible [...] Vertical mobility [...] replaced the brutish battles for kingship. In a 20th century traumatized by the brutality of war and a pandemic that largely killed the young, however, 'the lack of a credible future explains the flatness of modern painting, because we've been forced into thinking principally of the present.' In the same conversation Willing stated that he believed in the continuity of life, enough 'at least to allow myself a shallow space—but there's an emphatic back wall in my paintings—*no distant horizons*. [...] A sense of the numinous takes us further than humanist ethics. When we enter caverns measureless to man we are already treading a path also known to religious experience. I have been too timid, in the event, to do more than peep at what might be there. I would like another go'. (McEwen, 2019b, p. 124)

✱✱✱

Conclusion

In Nick Willing's film about his mother, he reads a letter Vic wrote to Paula to be read to her after he died, kept in a file titled 'Adieu':

> Paula, I'm uncomfortable now all the time. Most of me is gone already. It only remains for me to dispose of the other little bits while I still can. I don't want to know what the bitter end is.[15]

Turning feminist wisdom (and other kinds: some things have always already been said) back to front, in some respects the political is personal. Personally—as opposed to politically—speaking (as it were) the last remnants of Willing's presence populate our hauntology.[16] There is no Degree Zero of seeing. If one looks, one is implicated:

---

15 The documentary can be viewed at: https://archive.org/details/paula-rego-secrets-and-stories-2017-bbc
16 On hauntology, see Derrida, 2006, p. 10.

> But to learn to live, to learn it *from oneself and by oneself*, all alone, to teach *oneself* to live ('I would like to learn to live finally'), is that not impossible for a living being? Is it not what logic itself forbids? To live, by definition, is not something one learns. Not from oneself, it is not learned from life, taught by life. Only from the other and by death. In any case from the other *at the edge of life*. At the internal border or the external border, it is a heterodidactics between life and death. (Derrida, 2006, p. xvii, second italics added)

Heterodidactics: let's learn together while we still can, but be prepared to sing for your supper just before you say goodbye. As 'Sam', he of that long-past awkward lunch once wrote, 'no trace anywhere of life, you say, pah, no difficulty there, imagination not dead yet, yes, dead, good, imagination dead imagine' (Beckett, 1965). The last word, however, belongs to Willing's and Rego's long-time friend, the poet Alberto Lacerda, a Portuguese citizen born in Mozambique but permanently settled in London, whose planned autobiography, never actually written, went by the intended title of *Sunny Intervals* (the reference, for the African-born Lacerda, being the terminology of British weather forecasts). Both men knew all about existential diasporas as well as the slings and arrows of outrageous fortune:

> A visionary painter? Not really [...]. Even the most disturbed works have a curious tranquillity. [...] He gives form not to the invisible but to absence. (Lacerda, quoted in McEwen, 2000, p. 38).
>
>> I believe in angels that roam the world,
>> I believe in the goddess with sparkling eyes,
>> I believe in moonlit love with a piano soundtrack,
>> I believe in legends, in fairies, in the natives of Atlantis.
>>
>> I believe in a missing device capable of
>> Instilling harmony into discord,
>> I believe that everything becomes eternal in a second.
>> I believe in a future heaven that used to be.
>> I believe in the gods of a more perfect galaxy,
>> In the humble flower that grows against the wall,
>> I believe in flesh that enchants what lies beyond,
>>
>> I believe in the unbelievable, in astonishing things.
>> In a world invaded by roses,
>> I believe love has golden wings.
>> Amen. (Natália Correia, 'Credo')[17]

---

17 Original text available here: https://textosdepoesia.wordpress.com/2013/03/07/

Works Cited

Bersani, Leo, 1976, *A Future for Astyanax: Character and Desire in Literature* (London: Little, Brown).

Bachelard, Gaston, 1992, *The Poetics of Reverie: Childhood, Language, and the Cosmos* (Boston, MA: Beacon Press).

Baker, Peter, 2006, 'Au contraire', *Slugger O'Toole* (20 March), https://sluggerotoole.com/2006/03/20/au_contraire/

Bandeira, Manuel, 1974, *Poesia completa e prosa* (Rio de Janeiro: Aguilar).

Beckett Samuel, 1965, 'Imagination Dead Imagine', https://www.johnderbyshire.com/Readings/imaginationdeadimagine.html

Black, Daisy, 2019, 'Commanding Un-empty Space: Silence, Stillness and Scopic Authority in the York "Christ before Herod"', in *Gender in Medieval Places, Spaces and Thresholds*, ed. Victoria Blud, Diane Heath and Einat Klafte (London: University of London Press), pp. 237–50.

Bradley, Fiona (ed.), 2000, *Victor Willing* (London: August).

Caeiro, Alberto, 1993, 'Poemas Inconjuntos', in *Poemas de Alberto Caeiro*, 10th ed. (Lisbon: Ática), p. 87, http://arquivopessoa.net/textos/991

Camões, Luis Vaz de, 1980, *Os Lusíadas*, Canto VIII, 2 (Porto: Porto Editora).

Cooke, Lynne, 1986, 'Thought Made in the Mouth', in *Victor Willing, A Retrospective Exhibition 1952–85. Whitechapel, 6 June–20 July 1986. Catalogue* (London: The Trustees of the Whitechapel Art Gallery), pp. 9–18.

Cooke, Lynne, 2000, 'Imaginary Portraits', in *Victor Willing*, ed. Fiona Bradley (London: August), pp. 123–32.

Craveirinha, José, 1974, 'Real Men Don't Cry', https://www.escritas.org/pt/t/13382/um-homem-nao-chora

Deleuze, Gilles, 1986, *Cinema 1: The Movement-Image*, trans. Hugh Tomlinson and Barbara Habberjam (Minneapolis: University of Minnesota Press).

Derrida, Jacques, 2006, *Specters of Marx: The State of the Debt, the Work of Mourning and the New International* (New York and London: Routledge).

Derrida, Jacques, 2017, *The Truth in Painting*, trans. Geoffrey Bennington and Ian McLeod (Chicago: University of Chicago Press, 2017).

Gilmore, Elizabeth, and Victoria Howarth, 2020, *Introduction to Victor Willing: Visions* (Hastings: Hastings Contemporary), pp. 10–13.

Gleadell, Colin, 2022, 'Victor Willing: Could Paula Rego's Husband Hit the Big Time?', *The Telegraph* (2 August), https://www.timothytaylor.com/press/11-victor-willing-could-paula-rego-s-husband-hit-the/

creio-natalia-correia/

Harvey, Marcus, 2019, *Victor Willing: Turps Spotlight II* (London: Turps Banana).

Hastings Independent, 2019, 'Victor Willin: "Visions"', *Hastings Independent* (1 November), https://www.hastingsindependentpress.co.uk/articles/culture/arts/victor-willing-visions/

Judah, Hettie, 'Victor Willing: An Observer of Everyday Life', *Art UK* (15 January), https://artuk.org/discover/stories/victor-willing-an-observer-of-everyday-life

Koivunen, Anu, 2013, 'Uncanny Motions: Facing Death, Morphing Life', *Discourse*, 35.2, 248–62.

Kosoi, Natalie, 2005, 'Nothingness Made Visible: The Case of Rothko's Paintings', *Art Journal*, 64.2, 20–31.

Lacerda, Alberto, 2000, Unpublished essay quoted in McEwen, 'Images of the Self', in *Victor Willing*, ed. Fiona Bradley (London: August, 2000), pp. 23–45 (p. 38).

Lefebvre, Henri, 1984, *The Production of Space*, trans. Donald Nicholson-Smith (Oxford: Blackwell).

Lewison, Jeremy, 1983, *Victor Willing: Paintings since 1978. Catalogue of an Exhibition Held at Kettle's Yard Gallery, 20 January to 20 February 1983. Exhibition Organised by Jeremy Lewison* (Cambridge: Kettle's Yard Gallery and the Authors).

McCracken, Scott, 2019, 'Notes Towards an Essay on Victor Willing', *Turps Banana*, 21, https://static1.squarespace.com/static/59060cbe15d5db2857dfea1d/t/5d4c7b87d5115f0001d09918/1565293476260/Victor+Willing+Turps+%2321+2.pdf

McEwen, John, 1983, 'Time as a Shallow Stage', in Victor Willing, *Paintings since 1978. Catalogue of an Exhibition Held at Kettle's Yard Gallery 20 January to 20 February 1983. Exhibition Organised by Jeremy Lewison* (Cambridge: Kettle's Yard Gallery and the Authors), pp. 4–11.

McEwen, John, 1986, 'Victor Willing in Conversation with John McEwen', in *Victor Willing, A Retrospective Exhibition 1952–85. Whitechapel, 6 June–20 July 1986. Catalogue* (London: The Trustees of the Whitechapel Art Gallery), pp. 19-31.

McEwen, John, 2000, 'Images of the Self', in *Victor Willing*, ed. Fiona Bradley (London: August, 2000), pp. 23–45.

McEwen, John, 2019a, 'When Was Now?', in *Victor Willing: Visions*, ed. John McEwen, Elizabeth Gilmore and Victoria Howarth (Hastings: Hastings Contemporary), pp. 13–47.

McEwen, John, 2019b, 'Extracts of a Conversation', in *Victor Willing: Visions*, ed. John McEwen, Elizabeth Gilmore and Victoria Howarth (Hastings: Hastings Contemporary), pp. 120–25.

Mills, John, 2000, 'Early Days: A Memoir', in *Victor Willing*, ed. Fiona Bradley (London: August), pp. 133–39.

Pessoa, Fernando, 1942 [1995], 'Autopsicografia', in *Poesias* (Lisboa: Ática), http://arquivopessoa.net/textos/4234

Plath, Sylvia, 1974, *Ariel* (London: Faber and Faber).

Racine, Jean, *Andromache*, (E-book). http://uploads.worldlibrary.net/uploads/pdf/20121103000318andromachepdf_pdf.pdf (Accessed 30 November 2025).

Rego, Paula, 2000a, 'Callot: Harridan' in *Victor Willing* edited by Fiona Bradley (London: August, 2000), pp. 101-22.

Rego, Paula, 2000b, 'Place' in *Victor Willing* edited by Fiona Bradley (London: August, 2000), pp. 71–89.

Rego, Paula, 2000c, 'Salome' in *Victor Willing* edited by Fiona Bradley (London: August, 2000), pp. 90–100.

Rego, Paula, 2000d, 'Standing Figure and Nude', in *Victor Willing* edited by Fiona Bradley (London: August, 2000), pp. 58-70.

Rego, Paula, 2000e, *Victor Willing* edited by Fiona Bradley (London: August, 2000, pp. 58-122.

Sandler, Irving (April, 1983), *Mark Rothko: Paintings 1948-69*, exhibition catalogue (New York: Pace Gallery, pp. 11).

Serota, Nicholas, 2000, 'Trapping Reality', in *Victor Willing*, ed. Fiona Bradley (London: August), pp. 17–22.

Serota, Nichola, 2020, 'Foreword' to *Victor Willing: Visions* (Hastings: Hastings Contemporary), pp. 8–10.

Serota, Nicholas, 1986 (c), in *Victor Willing, A Retrospective Exhibition 1952–85. Whitechapel, 6 June–20 July 1986. Catalogue* (London: The Trustees of the Whitechapel Art Gallery).

Serota, Nick, and Rachel Kirby, 1986, *Victor Willing, A Retrospective Exhibition 1952–85. Whitechapel, 6 June–20 July 1986. Catalogue* (London: The Trustees of the Whitechapel Art Gallery).

Sylvester, David, 'Writings by Victor Willing ("Travel by Bus"; 'Thoughts After a Car Crash"; "Now"; "Blood")', in Nicholas Serota, *Victor Willing, A Retrospective Exhibition 1952–85. Whitechapel, 6 June–20 July 1986. Catalogue* (London: The Trustees of the Whitechapel Art Gallery), pp. 57–65.

Tusa, John, 2001, 'Interview with Paula Rego', *The Independent on Sunday* (3 June), 10 [Also broadcast in full on BBC Radio 3, Sunday Feature, 3 June 2001].

Walsh, Timothy, 1992, 'The Cognitive and Mimetic Function of Absence in Art, Music and Literature', *Mosaic: An Interdisciplinary Critical Journal*, 25.2, 69–90.

Willing, Victor, 1983a, 'Now', in *Victor Willing: Paintings since 1978. Catalogue of an Exhibition Held at Kettle's Yard Gallery, 20 January to 20 February 1983*.

Exhibition Organised by Jeremy Lewison (Cambridge: Kettle's Yard Gallery and the Authors), pp. 13-28.

Willing, Victor, 1983b, *Victor Willing: Paintings since 1978. Catalogue of an Exhibition Held at Kettle's Yard Gallery, 20 January to 20 February 1983. Exhibition Organised by Jeremy Lewison* (Cambridge: Kettle's Yard Gallery and the Authors).

Willing, Victor, 1993, 'A Conversation with John McEwen', in *Victor Willing: Selected Writings and Two Conversations with John McEwen*, ed. Karsten Schubert (London: Karsten Schubert Ltd), p. 46.

Willing, Victor, 2000a, 'Masks', in *Victor Willing*, ed. Fiona Bradley (London: August), pp. 46–57.

Willing, Victor, 2000b, 'Thoughts After a Car Crash', in *Victor Willing*, ed. Fiona Bradley (London: August), pp. 140–43.

Willing, Victor, 2000c, 'Travel by Bus', in *Victor Willing*, ed. Fiona Bradley (London: August), p. 151.

Yeats, W. B., 1990, *Collected Poems* (London: Picador).

5. Paula Rego: A Brick through a Window Never Comes with a Love Note[1]

Tell all the truth but tell it slant —
Success in Circuit lies
Too bright for our infirm Delight.

Emily Dickinson, 'Tell all the truth but tell it slant'

'I call it purring, not growling', said Alice.
'Call it what you like', said the [Cheshire] Cat.

Lewis Carroll, *Alice's Adventures in Wonderland*

Introduction

In Paula Rego's work produced over almost sixty years, a lot gets broken: bodies, minds, institutions and structures of power within the spheres of the personal and the public/political. She takes a battering ram mostly to what used to be strong until it isn't (after she's had her way with it). Less uplifting are her attacks on what was already a little broken and which she sets about finishing off briskly. Never hit someone when they are already down? That may be no more than a platitude. And one platitude deserves another: in the case of some acts of revenge, if a job's worth doing, it is worth doing well.

---

1 Variation on 'A rock through a window/ Never comes with a kiss', the opening lines to 'Madness to the Method' (Blue Öyster Cult, 1985).

Handmaids with a Difference: Who Broke This?

> We were the people who were not in the papers.
> We lived in the blank white spaces at the edge of print.
> It gave us more freedom.
>
> Margaret Atwood, *The Handmaid's Tale*

Paula Rego, perhaps unsurprisingly considering her nationality and her upbringing by a very religious mother who undoubtedly told her stories from the Bible and the Catechism, repeatedly drew upon religious or religion-adjacent themes throughout her life (*Crivelli's Garden*, Fig. 5.1; *The Crime of Father Amaro*; the *Abortion* series; the *Virgin Mary* cycle; the images on genital mutilation). In all of them, as one would expect, we witness a reversal of traditional readings that almost invariably up-end conventional distributions of strength and weakness, dominance and subjection.

Judith's Sword

> This is a low flying panic attack
> Sing a song on the jukebox that goes
> Burn the witch
> Burn the witch
> We know where you live
>
> Radiohead, 'Burn the Witch'

The story of Judith and Holofernes was first told in the earliest extant version of the *Book of Judith* (Ioudith) in the Septuagint: a Greek version of the Hebrew Bible (or Old Testament, including the *Apocrypha*), created for Greek-speaking Jews in Egypt in the third and second centuries BCE and adopted by the early Christian Churches. Judith was a beautiful and virtuous widow from the Israelite town of Bethulia. In the course of the Assyrian siege of her city, she entered the enemy's camp, and over three days and nights succeeded in striking up relations with Holofernes, the Assyrian general, by holding out the prospect of sex. On the third night, Holofernes was induced into excessive drinking and lost consciousness. Judith beheaded him with his own sword and carried his head back home, ending the siege and bringing peace to Israel.

> The Jews of Bethulia, following Judith's advice, subsequently take the offensive, attacking the Assyrian army and defeating them. Judith, praised by all, sings a victory song and then goes back to her quiet life at home. She lives until the age of 105 and is mourned by all of Israel when she dies. [...] Judith resembles other biblical characters as well, such as David in his encounter with Goliath (1 Sm 17) and Ehud, who assassinates King Eglon of Moab (Jgs 3:12–30). Above all, Judith is reminiscent of a series of biblical women, including, of course, Jael, who slays the general Sisera in her tent (*Judges* 4:17–22; 5:24–27), and Esther, who charms a foreign king with her beauty. (Levine Gera, 2010, p. 25)

The *Book of Judith* was not included in the Hebrew Bible, and, before the tenth century, Jewish literature does not refer to her. It was preserved by Christian tradition, and played a formative influence on the creation of models of Christian female piety, Judith becoming an unlikely model for Christian female spirituality. Bizarrely, she was specifically twinned with Mary as the model of chaste womanhood. Elena Ciletti mentions Judith's lineage as being the longest of any woman in the Old Testament, reinforcing Mary's descent from the royal house of David, and quotes Tortoletti who depicted her as a prefiguration of Mary, as the *Regina degli Angeli* (Queen of Angels) (Ciletti, 2010, pp. 355–56).

Kevin R. Brine, referring to Otto Rank as well as to ancient Greek traditions regarding the practice of decapitation, discusses the fact that in Roman times, beheading was considered a privileged mode of execution, reserved for Roman citizens, whilst crucifixion was inflicted on those who were to be publicly shamed: make of that what you will. Be that as it may, Brine argues as follows:

> The author of the *Book of Judith* makes it amply clear that the beheading of Holofernes was an act of war and uses the celebratory scene of the presentation of the head to Judith as a military heroine. Judith brings the head back from the Assyrian camp to the battlements of Bethulia to inspire the Jews to rout the Assyrian aggressors. The head of Holofernes is exhibited as a war trophy. Judith is honoured with the captured booty of Holofernes' armour. The same ancient military convention of exhibiting a tyrant's head to establish that the enemy has been vanquished appears elsewhere in the Old Testament. (2 *Maccabees*: Brine, 2010, p. 8)

Ciletti labours the argument that Judith did not actually seduce Holofernes (i.e. she maintained her sexual purity) as befitted God's warrior (*Guerriera di Dio*). Caryn Tamber-Rosenau, however, does see Judith's bathing activities in the Roman camp as foreplay to sexual seduction:

> The *Book of Judith* cuts out the middle step between male gaze and male punishment: here, gazed-upon does not suffer. Instead, the reader skips right to the retribution visited upon the gazer: Holofernes looks with predatory intent and then dies. Furthermore, the retribution comes straight from the gazed-upon woman and is loaded with images of sexual conquest. Judith manages, in essence, to reverse the direction of the gaze. The reader's gaze is focused, finally, not on Judith in her state of undress but on Holofernes at the highly sexualized moment of his demise. (Tamber-Rosenau, 2017, p. 70)
>
> Reading Judith this way, one admires the way the story uses the trope of the bathing beauty, taking a motif centered on a lovely but helpless woman. [...] The story of Judith (contrary to those of Bathsheba peeped upon by David or Susanna by the lecherous elders), with its decidedly, deliberately, and devastatingly sexual heroine, shows us what it actually looks like when a biblical bathing woman wants to be looked at. (Ibid., pp. 71–72)

Fig. 5.1 Paula Rego, *Crivelli's Garden* (1990–91), acrylic on canvas, 189.9 × 945.3 cm. ©National Gallery, London, https://artlyst.com/whats-on-archive/paula-rego-crivellis-garden/
http://hdl.handle.net/20.500.12434/38aed26e

In Paula Rego's *Crivelli's Garden*, Judith holding out Holofernes' head inside a tote bag for inspection (Fig. 5.1, upper panel) resembles nothing so much as an affectionate mother showing her daughter a treat she brought her. 'Look what I've got for you, darling'. The use of homely images for depicting the outrageous was of course not new. Artemisia Gentileschi's own Judith looks not unlike a good wife prepping vegetables for supper, and Jan Massys' Judith and other wives appear at first glance to be demonstrating affection for their husbands (were it not for the titles) (Figs. 5.2 and 5.3). As is often the case in Paula Rego, when does love and care morph into abuse (Figs. 5.17, 5.18 and 5.19)? 'The sense of rage is real. It is the honestly confessed frustration of a woman who finds herself the helper of a paralysed husband' (Jones, 2022).

Fig. 5.2 Artemisia Gentileschi, *Judith Beheading Holofernes* (1614–20), oil on canvas, 199 cm x 162.5 cm, Uffizi Gallery, Florence. Wikimedia Commons, public domain, https://commons.wikimedia.org/wiki/File:Judit_decapitando_a_Holofernes,_por_Artemisia_Gentileschi.jpg

Fig. 5.3 Jan Massys, *The Ill-matched Pair* (1566), oil on panel, 97 × 134 cm, National Museum, Sweden. Wikimedia Commons, public domain, https://commons.wikimedia.org/wiki/File:The_Ill-matched_Pair_(Jan_Massys)_-_Nationalmuseum_-_17511.tif

Judith's reformulation in scripture as a saintly patriot, albeit one who, for a housewife, was unexpectedly handy with a sword, may have been historically contrasted with her more helpless Biblical sisters (Vashti,

Bathsheba, Susanna). In *Crivelli's Garden*, Rego does two things: she introduces us to a matter-of fact Judith sharing the sight of Holofernes' head with a youthful companion (a future member of the monstrous regiment?); and, in the adjacent panel she associates her with another Old Testament woman, but now an entirely irredeemable one: Delilah.

Delilah's Scissors

> She tied you to a kitchen chair
> She broke your throne, and she cut your hair
> And from your lips she drew the Hallelujah.
>
> Leonard Cohen, 'Hallelujah'

Delilah, whose name is a wordplay on the Hebrew *layla*, 'night' (Samson, *Shimshon*, being related to 'sun:' *shemesh*), is mentioned in the sixteenth chapter of *Judges* in the Old Testament. She is loved by Samson, a Nazirite, famous for his superhuman strength, previously verified by feats such as slaying a lion with his bare hands and massacring a Philistine army using a donkey's jawbone as his sole weapon. Delilah is bribed by the Philistines to discover the source of his strength. After three failed attempts at doing so (that number again), she finally lures Samson into telling her that his strength is derived from his long hair. She calls upon a woman servant (another accomplice in yet another monstrous regiment) to help her shear his hair while he sleeps, thereby depriving him of his strength and enabling his delivery to the enemy. The Philistines gouge out his eyes and condemn him to do hard labour in Gaza City but while there, his hair begins to grow again. When the Philistines take him to their temple he prays to God and recovers his strength, enabling him to bring down the temple's columns thus collapsing the building, killing both himself and his enemies.

James D. G. Dunn and John William Rogerson note (with disapproval) that Delilah is not 'identified by a male relationship—the wife, daughter or sister of anyone' but simply as someone in her own right' (Dunn and Rogerson, 2003, pp. 200–01), and in his blockbuster biblical epic (*Samson and Delilah*, 1949), the sometimes-sanctimonious Cecil B. DeMille comforts his viewers with the spectacle of Delilah dying in the temple with Samson and her fellow countrymen. The Bible, however, interestingly, does not discuss her fate.

For Kahr, 'of all the destructive women in the Bible and legends, perhaps no other was so familiar to the Christian world and so sure to strike terror into the hearts of men as Delilah' (Kahr, 1973, p. 240). But even in *Judges*, however, there may be some extenuating circumstances for her: she may have plotted Samson's destruction in the course of three nights, but he himself had deceived her three times before that:

> And she said unto him, How canst thou say, I love thee, when thine heart *is* not with me? Thou hast mocked me these three times, and hast not told me wherein thy great strength *lieth*. (*Judges* 16:15)

Samson, it should be noted, even in *Judges*, comes across as both arrogant (he did, after all, catch Delilah trying to trap him twice before she finally succeeded at the third attempt) and slow to learn from experience: before Delilah he had been involved with two foreign women, a harlot from Gaza and a woman from Timnah (i.e. a Philistine like Delilah). This propensity for love entanglements with Gentile women (daughters of the enemies of his people) is thought by some to have been the beginning of a moral decline which ended in his death (Kahr, 1973, pp. 245–49). Beware on whose lap you rest your uncut locks, even if, as in Rego, after brandishing the tensorial instrument, she dutifully sweeps up the shorn hair like a good housewife (Fig. 5.1, centre left).

Fig. 5.4 Artemisia Gentileschi, *Samson and Delilah* (1930–38), oil on canvas, 90.5 cm x 109.5 cm, Palazzo Zevallos Stigliano, Naples. Wikimedia Commons, public domain, https://commons.wikimedia.org/wiki/File:Samson_und_delilah.jpg

A Girl's Best Friend

> All is not lost, the unconquerable will,
> and study of revenge, immortal hate,
> and the courage never to submit or yield,
> And what is else not to be overcome.
>
> John Milton, *Paradise Lost*, Book 1

In Greek myth, literature and philosophy, the dog acted as a polymorphous symbol: either faithful companion and co-worker (to ward off cattle-robbers and scavengers, big cats and wild dogs: Lonsdale, 1979, pp. 149–50), or, contradictorily, exemplifying a generalized form of spiritual force or a dangerous/hellish animal.

In *The Republic*, Plato recognized the intelligence of dogs as well as their wisdom in distinguishing between an unknown person, an acquaintance or an enemy. The dog was also seen as a magical creature with therapeutic functions, which included licking the sick and wounded back to health. At the opposite end of the spectrum, dogs were expressions of monstrosity. Kerberos was the dog guarding Hades, and more akin to a wolf than a dog (Lonsdale, 1979, p. 151). Closer to our time and paradigms, Joseph Manca (2013) discusses the unclean nature of dogs, and we can note that in many Western languages 'dog' is either an insult ('dirty dog'; 'bitch') or an expression of despair ('a dog's life'; 'being treated like a dog'; or, in Rego's mother tongue, 'abaixo de cão', 'lower than a dog'). In the art canon, dogs, good or bad, abound: from the dogs of Hecate and Artemis, through Roman terracotta and marble hounds, medieval *Livres de Chasse*, medieval funeral statuary and high art, from Renaissance hounds (Anthony Van Dyck, John Wootton), to Jean-Honoré Fragonard and Joshua Reynolds (in the eighteenth century) to Charles Landseer and John Singer Sargent (in the nineteenth). In the twentieth and twenty-first centuries, we find dogs in Amadeo de Souza Cardoso, Pablo Picasso, Francis Bacon, Lucian Freud, Jeff Koons and David Hockney. And of course, Paula Rego, drawing inspiration and a title for a recent triptych (Fig. 5.12) from William Hogarth's six-part *Marriage à la Mode* (Fig. 5.13). In the mid-1980s, two years or so before her husband, Victor Willing— by then severely incapacitated—died of multiple sclerosis, Paula Rego did a series of images collectively titled *Girl and Dog*, depicting a young girl interacting with a seemingly weakened dog and subjecting it to a combination of love/eroticism and violence. She went on record as saying that she did them as 'one does harm to those one loves' (McEwen, 1997, p. 138) and specifically that the *Girl and Dog* images (Figs. 5.17, 5.18 and 5.19) were all 'about Vic' (Tusa, 2001, p. 10).

Theirs was a famously turbulent marriage, as attested by interviews given by Rego herself, friends, and two documentaries made by their son, Nick Willing.[2] In a volume on Willing released in 2000, Rego recollects the following remarks made during their married life by her then-more famous husband:

> A lot of people don't know what they're doing until they do it, trusting that it will come out in the end. That's more how I painted—the monkey with the typewriter, [Vic] called me. The monkey who will write Shakespeare if he keeps at it long enough. (Rego in Bradley, 2000, p. 58)

Which monkey did she have in mind, though? Did she resent his comments? Is it always true that sticks and stones may break your bones but words will never hurt you? And if they do hurt, need one take it lying down? Not necessarily.

Fig. 5.5 Paula Rego, *Red Monkey Beats His Wife* (1981), acrylic on paper. 65 × 105 cm. ©The Estate of Paula Rego. Victoria Miro, https://www.victoria-miro.com/artworks/29917/

http://hdl.handle.net/20.500.12434/4afa4ec1

The *Red Monkey* series (see also *Wife Cuts off Red Monkey's Tail*, Fig. 5.16), alluding to scenes of domestic violence, includes some of the most brutal images in her portfolio, but they were by no means an exception. Paintings of women and dogs are so numerous in the art canon as to constitute a subgenre of its own, and one in which the lines between domesticity (love for one's pet), perversion (bestiality) and cruelty are sometimes blurred, the boot/stiletto being definitely on Cinderella's foot. The use of dogs in her work is a constant in Paula Rego, and as any appreciator of her work will know, her female dogs (Figs. 5.6 and 5.7), unlike her hapless male ones (Figs. 5.8, 5.17, 5.18 and 5.19), are definitely bitches.

---

2   See *Paula Rego, Secrets & Stories*, 2017, BBC2, https://archive.org/details/paula-rego-secrets-and-stories-2017-bbc and Turps, 'Gallery Talk: Nick Willing & Scott McCracken on Victor Willing', *YouTube* (2 December 2019), https://www.youtube.com/watch?v=dyU01sG2yVs

Fig. 5.6 Paula Rego, *Dog Woman* (1952), pencil on paper, 15.5 × 21.5 cm. ©The Estate of Paula Rego, https://shop.tate.org.uk/paula-rego-dog-woman/paureg2122.html

http://hdl.handle.net/20.500.12434/b961052d

Fig. 5.7 Paula Rego, *Dog Woman* (1994), pastel on canvas, 120 × 160 cm. ©The Estate of Paula Rego. Victoria Miro, https://www.victoria-miro.com/artworks/29910/

http://hdl.handle.net/20.500.12434/c87f0f3b

Presently the use of images of dogs to depict broken masculinity will be discussed. For now, and bearing in mind that MS often causes impotence in men, much need not be added to the picture of *Girl Lifting up Her Skirt to a Dog* (Fig. 5.8), completed two years before her husband died, and *The Family* (Fig. 4.11, see Chapter 4), done the very year he died.

Fig. 5.8 Paula Rego, *Girl Lifting Up Her Skirt to a Dog* (1986), acrylic on paper mounted on canvas, 76 × 55.5 cm. ©The Estate Paula Rego. Bridgeman Images, https://www.bridgemanimages.com/en/rego/girl-lifting-up-her-skirt-to-a-dog-1986-acrylic-paint-on-paper-mounted-on-canvas/acrylic-paint-on-paper-mounted-on-canvas/asset/8369496?offline=1

http://hdl.handle.net/20.500.12434/49137433

Girls Are Not Boys

Moody females steal your power.
It's dangerous for a man.
A man must remain focused.

Andrew Tate[3]

Surprisingly, the depiction of girls/women and dogs involved in suspicious activities did not have to wait for Rego's iconoclastic tendencies. We find them at least as far back as supposedly chocolate-boxy artists such as Fragonard and Antoine Watteau (Figs. 5.9, 5.10 and 5.11) and endlessly reproduced in old-fashioned kitsch. Did you ever

---

3   Andrew Tate is the perfect spokesman for the toxic masculinity against which Paula Rego has fought all her life.

look closely at those plastic place mats your granny put on the table to protect the wooden surface when you went for tea? Did *she*? Was there a glint in her eye when she did it? Never underestimate a granny.

Fig. 5.9 Antoine Watteau, *The Toilette* (first half of the eighteenth century), oil on canvas, 45.2 × 37.8 cm, the Wallace Collection, London. Wikimedia Commons, public domain, https://commons.wikimedia.org/wiki/File:Antoine_Watteau_-_The_Toilette_-_WGA25473.jpg

Fig. 5.10 Jean-Honoré Fragonard, *Two Girls on a Bed Playing with their Dogs* (date unknown), oil on canvas, 74.3 × 59.3 cm, Resnick Art Collection, Los Angeles. Photo by Sotheby's (2022), Wikimedia Commons, public domain, https://commons.wikimedia.org/wiki/File:Jean-Honor%C3%A9_Fragonard_-_Two_girls_on_a_bed_playing_with_their_dogs_-_collection_Resnick.jpg

In 'Rococo Representations of Interspecies Sensuality and the Pursuit of "Volupté"', Jennifer Milam discusses the figure of the dog in Fragonard as a means of pushing the boundaries of human sexuality in the pursuit of pleasure (Milam, 2015, p. 129 and Fig. 5.11):

Fig. 5.11 Jean-Honoré Fragonard, *Young Girl and her Dog* (1770–75), oil on canvas, 89 × 70 cm, Alte Pinakothek, Munich. Photo by Jebulon (2014), Wikimedia Commons, public domain, https://commons.wikimedia.org/wiki/File:Jeune_fille_et_son_chien,_Jean-Honor%C3%A9_Fragonard,_HUW_35,_Alte_Pinakothek_Munich.jpg

Referring to Claude Yvon's entry 'Âme des bêtes' in *L'encyclopédie* (1751), Charles Bonnet's *Essai de psychologie* (1755) and Louis-Sébastien Mercier's *Tableau de Paris* (1782–88), Milam agrees that animal emotions may be gendered depending on whether they are evoked by a man or a woman. Animal emotions associated with male masters were linked to loyalty and protection, whereas at least in literary representations dogs (specifically lapdogs) were associated with the woman's body and her bed, with 'thinly veiled intimations that the dog has usurped the place that properly belongs to a male lover' (Milam, 2015, p. 129). Fragonard's paintings 'portray the dog as an erotic stimulus [... in which] physical parts of the animals are painted to draw attention to female sexual organs, whether bare bottom or bare breast. [...] Louis de Jaucourt defined [...] practices that create a feeling of voluptuousness have in common the notion of excess leading to character, debauchery, and licentiousness' (Milam, 2015, p. 193). Fragonard was by no means alone.

Ultimately, however, it is in Hogarth, much admired by Paula Rego, who paid homage to him in her own rendition of *Marriage à la Mode* (Fig.

5.12), that we find the clearest expressions of human-dog bestiality as an expression of social/moral collapse (Fig. 5.13).

Fig. 5.12 Paula Rego, *The Betrothal: Lessons: The Shipwreck, after 'Marriage à la Mode' by Hogarth* (1999), pastel on paper mounted on aluminium, 165 × 500 cm, Tate, London. ©Paula Rego. Tate, https://www.tate.org.uk/art/artworks/rego-the-betrothal-lessons-the-shipwreck-after-marriage-a-la-mode-by-hogarth-t07919

http://hdl.handle.net/20.500.12434/8cf06e1f

Kaitlyn Farrell (2013, p. 35) sees the dogs in Hogarth as 'serving as symbols of warped fidelity in the overarching satire of [...] their masters. [...] They became the physical embodiment of the influence and whims of their owners and thus served as ideal subjects for the critique of the society which bred them' (ibid., p. 35), 'based on their black markings, which eerily echo the foreboding syphilitic spot' (ibid., p. 35) on several of the human figures. In Hogarth's *The Tête à Tête* (Fig. 13), the inclusion of a domestic lap dog in this first depiction of the newlyweds in their own quarters ought to connote harmony but instead draws direct attention to the discord and lack of honesty in the portrayed marriage. The dog's interest in the lacy cap left by the newly-wed husband's mistress contrasts with the bride's indifference to it (ibid., p. 36).

Fig. 5.13 William Hogarth, *Marriage A-la-Mode: The Tête à Tête* (c. 1743), oil on canvas, 69.9 × 90.8 cm, the National Gallery, London. Wikimedia Commons, public domain, https://commons.wikimedia.org/wiki/File:William_Hogarth_-_Marriage_A-la-Mode_2_The_T%C3%AAte_%C3%A0_T%C3%AAte.jpg

132   Broken

Fig. 5.14 William Hogarth, *A Harlot's Progress*, Plate 1 (1732), etching and engraving on paper, 31.6 × 38.8 cm, British Museum. Wikimedia Commons, public domain, https://commons.wikimedia.org/wiki/File:A_Harlot%27s_Progress,_Plate_1_(BM_1858,0417.544).jpg

Fig. 5.15 William Hogarth, *Hudibras and the Skimmington* (1725–26), engraving (second plate of three), 26.9 × 50.8 cm, New York Metropolitan Museum of Art. Wikimedia Commons, CC0, https://commons.wikimedia.org/wiki/File:Hudibras_and_the_Skimmington_(Twelve_Large_Illustrations_for_Samuel_Butler%27s_Hudibras,_Plate_7)_MET_DP826937.jpg

 Fig. 5.16 Paula Rego, *Wife Cuts off Red Monkey's Tail* (1981), acrylic on paper, 68 × 101 cm. ©The Estate of Paula Rego. Marlborough Fine Art, https://www.researchgate.net/figure/Paula-Rego-Wife-Cuts-off-Red-Monkeys-Tail-1981-Acrylic-on-paper-68-x-101-cm_fig3_335537543

http://hdl.handle.net/20.500.12434/cfbc9f66

And Aaron Santesso develops a rather circuitous argument for Moll's scissors (barely visible but still there hanging from her waist, associating her profession, as seamstress) with her descent from innocence to harlotry in Hogarth's *A Harlot's Progress* (Fig. 5.14). He returns to the same point in *Hudibras and the Skimmington* (Fig. 5.15). Bearing in mind Rego's inclination *not* to portray women as victims, it is more likely that those scissors hanging from the harlot's waste in *A Harlot's Progress* and the ones depicted in the sign hanging over in the shop's doorway in *Hudibras* belonged in the same sewing box as those of the wife cutting off/castrating her husband's tail/penis in Rego's *Wife Cuts off Red Monkey's Tail* (Fig. 5.16).

Mother, Mother, Why Have You Forsaken Me?

> No one knows where she comes from
> Maybe she's a devil in disguise
> I can tell by looking in her eyes
> Little miss strange.
>
> Jimi Hendrix, 'Little Miss Strange'

In 1988, Victor Willing, died of multiple sclerosis after many years of worsening disability (see Chapter 4). Rego's *Girl and Dog* series (Figs. 5.17, 5.18 and 5.19) was inspired by his profound deterioration in the last phase of his life (Lisboa, 2019, pp. 310–11). As she said in conversation and in the documentary *Paula Rego, Secrets & Stories*, her reaction to his growing incapacity was partly one of anger: 'this wasn't what I signed up for'.

Fig. 5.17 Paula Rego, *Girl and Dog* (1986), acrylic on paper, 112 × 76 cm. ©The Estate of Paula Rego. Marlborough Fine Art, https://www.researchgate.net/figure/Paula-Rego-Girl-and-Dog-Untitled-b-1986-Acrylic-on-paper-112-x-76-cm-Photograph_fig11_335537284

http://hdl.handle.net/20.500.12434/23018b9c

Fig. 5.18 Paula Rego, *Snare* (1987), acrylic on paper on canvas, 150 × 150 cm. ©The Estate of Paula Rego / Bridgeman Images. British Council Collection, https://artuk.org/discover/artworks/snare-176993

http://hdl.handle.net/20.500.12434/92a80acc

Interestingly, at least one of these images (*Two Girls and a Dog*, Fig. 5.19) was intended to represent both the dying Vic and a Christian descent from the cross. If, as the song would have it, 'they ain't making Jews like Jesus anymore',[4] the same might be said of strong Biblical males in general, even if in the art canon, and even more so in Rego, Jesus himself is mostly portrayed as having been on the scrawny and feeble side (Fig. 5.20). Particularly so when he had just been crucified, although in that respect, what else might one expect? Especially if that crucifixion was unwarranted: 'We Jews believe it was Santa Claus that killed Jesus Christ'.[5]

 Fig. 5.19 Paula Rego, *Two Girls and a Dog* (1987), acrylic paint on paper on canvas, 150 × 150 cm, Calouste Gulbenkian Foundation, Lisbon. ©The Estate of Paula Rego, https://gulbenkian.pt/cam/en/publications/paula-rego-4/
http://hdl.handle.net/20.500.12434/5ba183bc

 Fig. 5.20 Paula Rego, *Descent from the Cross* (2002), pastel on paper on aluminium, 75 × 72 cm. ©The Estate of Paula Rego. Bosc d'Anjou (2021), https://www.flickr.com/photos/boscdanjou/52136949210
http://hdl.handle.net/20.500.12434/f42710d3

And sometimes, for instance in Rego's work, Jesus doesn't feature at all in his own crucifixion. It might have been his party but in her fantasies he wasn't necessarily invited (Figs. 5.21 and 5.22).

 Fig. 5.21 Paula Rego, *Lamentation* (2002), watercolour and ink on paper, 21 × 29 cm, property of the Portuguese State (Portuguese State Contemporary Art Collection). ©The Estate of Paula Rego. Victoria Miro, https://www.artsy.net/artwork/paula-rego-lamentation-at-the-foot-of-the-cross
http://hdl.handle.net/20.500.12434/3f736db8

 Fig. 5.22 Paula Rego, *Deposition* (1998), pastel and graphite on paper mounted on aluminium, 160 × 120 cm, private collection, https://www.christies.com/en/lot/lot-5335320
http://hdl.handle.net/20.500.12434/485ba8fd

---

4   'They Ain't Making Jews Like Jesus Anymore' (Kinky Friedman and the Texas Jewboys, 1992).
5   Ibid.

Do you know what the Kabbala teaches? That the sum total of the evil and miseries of humankind arose when a lazy or incompetent scribe misheard, took down erroneously, a single letter, one single solitary letter, in Holy Writ. Every horror since has come on us through and because of that one erratum. You didn't know that, did you? (George Steiner, quoted in Soeiro, 2007, p. 219)

In other words, don't believe everything they tell you. Once again, the things that you're liable to read in the Bible, it ain't necessarily so... (see Chapter 3).

The Savage Breast

> Music has charms to soothe a savage breast.
>
> William Congreve, *The Mourning Bride*

> You know the meaning
> When she smiles at you.
>
> The Stranglers, 'The Savage Breast'

'In the beginning Disney created the heavens and the earth. He saw all that he had made, and it was very good'. Or deeds to that effect. As a matter of fact mostly it *was* very good, with some exceptions, such as the death of Bambi's mother, something that traumatized countless generations of children until the revised version in the 1990s made the shooting of the doe cryptic to the point of unintelligibility (which was just as well: at least our children did not leave the cinema weeping and sobbing as their parents' generation had done). Before Disney, of course, children who read the original texts by the likes of Charles Perrault, Hans Christian Andersen and the nominatively-determined Brothers Grimm, either grew a thick skin or never quite forgot the horrors of childhood tales. And horrible they were indeed.

> [...A]t last the magic draught was ready [...]. 'There it is for you', said the witch. Then she cut off the mermaid's tongue, so that she became dumb, and would never again speak or sing. [...] She fell into a swoon, and lay like one dead. When the sun arose and shone over the sea, she recovered, and felt a sharp pain. [...] She [...] became aware that her fish's tail was gone, and that she had as pretty a pair of white legs and tiny feet as any little maiden could have. [...] The prince asked her who she was, and where she came from, and she looked at him mildly and sorrowfully with her

deep blue eyes; but she could not speak. Every step she took […] she felt as if treading upon the points of needles or sharp knives. (Andersen, 1836)

Fig. 5.23 Paula Rego, *The Little Mermaid* (2003), pastel on paper mounted on aluminium, 140 × 110 cm, Kunsthal Charlottenborg, Copenhagen, https://www.christies.com/en/lot/lot-5608702

http://hdl.handle.net/20.500.12434/844b595a

If you are inclined to feel sorry for a woman/fish silly enough to give up her voice and her habitual means of locomotion for the love of a man who in the end ditches her in favour of someone more unquestionably of his own species (Fig. 5.23), you might empathize with Virginia Woolf's approach to such a submissive female (the angel in the house): 'I turned upon her and caught her by the throat [Fig. 5.24]. I did my best to kill her. My excuse, if I were to be had up in a court of law, would be that I acted in self-defence. Had I not killed her she would have killed me' (Woolf, 1995, p. 59). As indeed they did, those terrible role models, begging to be knocked off their pedestals, and shown for what they probably were in reality: in Rego, thunder-thighed females (the metamorphosis from fish tail to legs didn't necessarily go according to plan, see Fig. 5.23). Be that as it may, neither the sisters or mothers or stepmothers of those ineffectual angels (the Little Mermaid, Cinderella, Snow White, Little Red Riding Hood, Peter Pan's witless Wendy, Blue Beard's dim bride) nor Rego herself were themselves in general well-disposed towards trad wives.

Fig. 5.24 Paula Rego, *Mermaid Drowning Wendy* (1992), coloured etching and aquatint, 27.7 × 20 cm, Cristea Roberts Gallery, London, https://cristearoberts.com/artists/206-paula-rego/works/90242/

http://hdl.handle.net/20.500.12434/6f7cdffa

Mothers, Mothers, Everywhere (and Lots of Blood to Drink)

If I was bound for hell, let it be hell. No more false heavens. No more damned magic. You hate me and I hate you. We'll see who hates best. But first, first I will destroy your hatred. Now. My hate is colder, stronger, and you'll have no hate to warm yourself. You will have nothing.

Jean Rhys, *Wide Sargasso Sea*

As I discovered almost thirty years ago, at the dawn of the internet (for humanity) and of motherhood (for me), frequenting children's bookshops disclosed a new reality: the story of Bluebeard, the serial wife killer, had by then been removed from the marketplace. The reason for the ban is unclear. Once upon a time, Bluebeard had been a staple of Perrault tales and one might argue that now, in these days of love (or sex) by App, Andrew Tate, Wayne Couzens and incel violence, it is more than ever a vital cautionary tale (Bates, 2021, 2025). Blue Beard is thought to have been inspired by Gilles de Rais, a fifteenth-century nobleman from Britanny and convicted serial killer (who, however, fought for Joan of Arc: even psychopathic misogynists have their soft spots).

In the standard version of the story, Bluebeard is a rich nobleman who has been married six times to beautiful women (in that respect, at least, he was not an incel). Each wife inexplicably disappears. After the last one vanishes, he visits his neighbour in the castle down the road and asks to marry one of his daughters. One of the girls is pressured by her father to accept the match in order replenish the family's coffers. Bluebeard takes her to his palace and not long afterwards tells her that he must go on a trip. He gives her the palace keys, telling her that she may open any room with them, except for an underground chamber that he forbids her from entering. She is, of course, overcome curiosity and does.

> Arrived at the door of the closet, she paused for a moment, bethinking herself of her husband's prohibition, and that some misfortune might befall her for her disobedience; but the temptation was so strong that she could not conquer it. She therefore took the little key and opened, tremblingly, the door of the closet. At first she could discern nothing, the windows being closed; after a short time she began to perceive that the floor was all covered with clotted blood, in which were reflected the dead bodies of several females suspended against the walls [Fig. 5.25]. These were all the wives of Blue Beard, who had cut their throats one after the other. (Perrault, 1895)

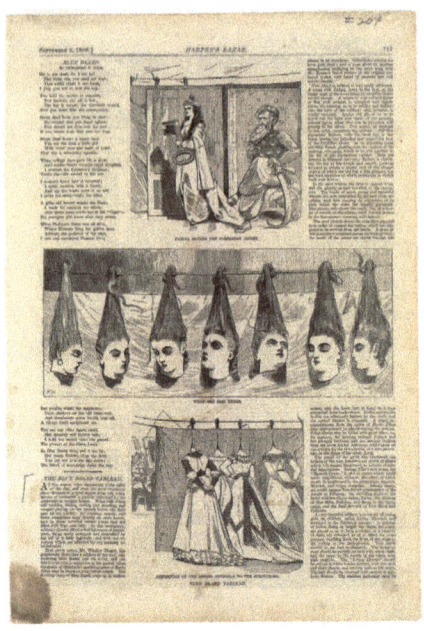

Fig. 5.25 Winslow Homer, *The Blue Beard Tableau: Fatima Enters the Forbidden Closet* (1868), wood engraving, 11.4 × 11.7 cm, Boston Public Library, Print Department. Wikimedia Commons, public domain, https://commons.wikimedia.org/wiki/File:Blue_beard_tableau_(Boston_Public_Library).jpg

Squeamish bookshops may censor children's literature, but as adults we can hand over the narrative to Angela Carter, who re-wrote the original and can match any childhood horror story shriek for shriek. In Perrault, the problem is solved by Anne, the sword-brandishing sister of the slightly dim heroine (aren't they always?). In Carter, it is not the sister but the mother who saves the day (and the girl):

> You never saw such a wild thing as my mother [...] one hand on the reins of the rearing horse while the other clasped my father's service revolver [...]. As if she had been Medusa, the sword still raised over his head as in those clockwork tableaux of Bluebeard that you see in glass cases at fairs. [...] On her eighteenth birthday, my mother had disposed of a man-eating tiger that had ravaged the villages in the hills north of Hanoi. Now, without a moment's hesitation, she raised my father's gun, took aim and put a single, irreproachable bullet through my husband's head. (Carter, 1995, pp. 39–40)

Which of course is what a mother is good for. Swords, knives, axes, guns.

Scissors (Figs. 5.14, 5.15 and 5.16). The instrument is a matter of choice, as long as it is capable of cutting a foe down to size (aka emasculating him, Fig. 5.26). Curiously, or perhaps fittingly, *Dressing Him up as Bluebeard* (i.e. dressed-up-*as, not* the real thing: and a simulacrum, of course, can't hurt you) was part of Rego's *Jane Eyre* series. What could she be thinking? The idea that Mr. Rochester—the man with whom every right-thinking girl (or woman, or matron) falls in love—might be akin to the notorious wife killer is grotesque. And yet... Bertha, his first wife, the original madwoman in the attic, might have seen some merit in the comparison. And even Jane, after all, only agreed to marry him after he'd lost a hand (castration by any other name works just as well), his eyesight and all his property. As a matter of fact in this case, in comparison to Brontë, Rego uncharacteristically lowers the stakes: trauma for trauma, being dressed in silly clothes (Fig. 5.26) pales in comparison to what befell the original heart throb.

Fig. 5.26 Paula Rego, *Dressing Him Up as Bluebeard* (2002), lithograph, 73 × 54 cm, part of a limited set, Museum of Modern Art, Tate, The Metropolitan Museum of Art, Art Institute of Chicago, https://www.artsy.net/artwork/paula-rego-dressing-him-up-as-bluebeard-from-the-jane-eyre-series

http://hdl.handle.net/20.500.12434/b4657e7c

'Little Red Riding Hood' by the Brothers Grimm also merited Rego's attention (Figs. 5.27 and 5.28). In the original tale, as is well known, the wolf does eat both her and her grandmother but they are rescued by a passing woodcutter who disembowels him, releases them, fills his belly with stones and throws him in the river where he drowns:

> The huntsman heard him as he was passing by the house, and thought, 'How the old woman snores- I had better see if there is anything the matter with her.' Then he went into the room, and walked up to the bed, and saw the wolf lying there. 'At last I find you, you old sinner!' said he; 'I have been looking for you a long time.' And he made up his mind that the wolf had swallowed the grandmother whole, and that she might yet be saved. So he did not fire, but took a pair of shears and began to slit up the wolfs body. When he made a few snips Little Red Riding Hood appeared, and after a few more snips she jumped out and cried, 'Oh dear, how frightened I have been! It is so dark inside the wolf'. (Grimm and Grimm, 1812)

If, however, you are a woman re-writing or visualizing the story, this is what you might get:

> 'What big teeth you have!' [...]
> 'All the better to eat you with'. The girl burst out laughing; she knew she was nobody's meat. She laughed at him full in the face, she ripped off his shirt for him and flung it into the fire, in the fiery wake of her own discarded clothing. [...] She will lay his fearful head on her lap [...] See! sweet and sound she sleeps in granny's bed, between the paws of the tender wolf. (Carter, 1995, p. 118)

Or else:

> At childhood's end, the houses petered out
> [...] till you came at last to the edge of the woods.
> It was there that I first clapped eyes on the wolf.
> He stood in a clearing, reading his verse out loud
> in his wolfy drawl, a paperback in his hairy paw,
> red wine staining his bearded jaw. What big ears
> he had! What big eyes he had! What teeth!
> In the interval, I made quite sure he spotted me,
> sweet sixteen, never been, babe, waif, and bought me a drink,
> [...] I took an axe
> to a willow to see how it wept. I took an axe to a salmon
> to see how it leapt. I took an axe to the wolf
> as he slept, one chop, scrotum to throat, and saw
> the glistening, virgin white of my grandmother's bones.
> I filled his old belly with stones. I stitched him up.
> Out of the forest I come with my flowers, singing, all alone. (Carol
>   Ann Duffy, 'Little Red-Cap')[6]

Or even:

Fig. 5.27 Paula Rego, *Mother Takes Revenge* (2003), pastel on paper, 104 × 79 cm. © The State of Paula Rego. Bridgeman Images, https://www.bridgemanimages.com/en/rego/mother-takes-revenge-red-riding-hood-series-2003-pastel-on-paper/pastel-on-paper/asset/8835840?offline=1
http://hdl.handle.net/20.500.12434/f05bf1d2

---

6   Duffy, 1999.

 Fig. 5.28 Paula Rego, *Mother Wears Wolf's Pelt* (2003), pastel on paper, 84 × 67 cm. © The Estate of Paula Rego. Bridgeman Images, https://www.bridgemanimages.com/en/rego/mother-wears-the-wolf-s-pelt-red-riding-hood-series-2003-pastel-on-paper/pastel-on-paper/asset/8835842?offline=1
http://hdl.handle.net/20.500.12434/788ac529

The Wrath of (M)others

God could not be everywhere, and therefore he made mothers.

Rudyard Kipling

Even Rudyard Kipling, like a stopped clock, gets it right every so often. The final part of this chapter will consider two images (*Night Bride* and *Escape*) based on the issue of female genital mutilation (FGM) which combines all the horrors of sexual, familial, ideological and biological violence. The genital mutilation images of 2009 are more straightforward than the abortion ones of 1998 in the bloodiest possible sense of the word. They address personal cataclysm where choice was never even a possibility. Most white women in the West will never suffer FGM. At least not if the term is used only literally. But what if it isn't? Violence comes in many shapes and forms, including violence by proxy.

What goes into the making of a good wife? Bearing in mind Rego's title for one of the images of female genital mutilation (*Night Bride*, Fig. 29) what does the small print in the marriage contract stipulate, not only for this particular bride but for others all over the world? Is the figure standing upright the double of the reclining one, holding out her own mutilated flesh in a makeshift hold-all (Fig. 5.29)? Who is the passive spectator? Is she complicitous through inaction (this is none of my business)?

 Fig. 5.29 Paula Rego, *Night Bride* (2009), etching and aquatint, 36.5 × 50 cm, Royal Academy Collection, https://www.royalacademy.org.uk/art-artists/work-of-art/night-bride
http://hdl.handle.net/20.500.12434/4da66494

Female genital mutilation, euphemistically misnamed as female circumcision, is an old tradition in some parts of the world. By 'tradition', of course, we/they mean rituals that historically have included the stoning to death of lepers, the burning at the stake of Jews, the ducking of would-be witches and the hanging, drawing and quartering of traitors. They all share common ground: pain, violence and death in the name of someone else's greater good. The motivation for performing genital mutilation upon girls may be to guarantee pre-marital virginity or to enhance male sexual pleasure (a tight vagina), or both. Or to cater to the pure or garden-variety delights of misogyny *regarding* (in both senses of the word: concerning and contemplating)[7] the spectacle of the pain of (female) others. Bros before hoes every time. The practice of cutting girls is frequently based on a traditional belief in the need to control a girl's sexuality and ensure her virginity until marriage, or to prepare her for marriage. A girl who remains intact will often be considered unsuitable as a wife. There are also often misconceptions that an uncut girl will be promiscuous, unclean, bad luck or less fertile. And in some communities, there is also the belief that it is a religious obligation to mutilate girls.

Even international organizations working towards eradicating this crime can be curiously mealy-mouthed about it. They avoid a lexicon of criminality against girls and shelter behind concepts of customs and cultural differences so as to justify the mutilation of the bodies of pre-pubescent female children. The endgame is their demarcation as the property of men and the maximization of male sexual pleasure: the latter predicated upon female pain during penetration: 'if you really love me you will be happy to suffer for me'.

The World Health Organization informs us that FGM involves the partial or total removal of external female genitalia or other injury to the female sex organs for non-medical reasons. It can cause bleeding and problems urinating, cysts, infections, complications in childbirth, an increased risk of stillbirths and death. It is recognized internationally as a violation of the human rights of girls. Asked about the women's issues that she tackled in her work (domestic violence, sex trafficking, illegal abortion, and female genital mutilation, among others), Rego stated that 'emotions don't have to come into it. I feel what I feel but that's it. I'm

---

7   Sontag (2004).

trying to get the picture to be as near the truth as possible. [...] I don't use the ideas directly but I try and get justice for women [...] at least in the pictures. *Revenge too*' (quoted in Gosling, 2022, italics added).

Women, of course, don't always stand together. Traditionally girls are taken by their mothers or grandmothers to the mutilation ritual that 'culturally' is part of 'becoming a woman'.

In what can only be called paternalistic complicity ('this is none of my business'; 'that's the kind of thing they do in faraway countries of which we know little'), genital mutilation is excused by those wary of being deemed racist. In the end, however, respect for so-called cultural diversity (aka violence) notwithstanding, Paula Rego, at least, went her own way. In *Escape* of 2009 (Fig. 5.30), a mother snatches her little girl from the hacking knife. One can only hope that that knife/those scissors might also have been repurposed in other ways (Fig. 5.16): much like that 'irreproachable bullet' that took care of Bluebeard (Carter, 1995, p. 40). Occasionally, though not nearly often enough, her cup runnethed/boiled over.

✻✻✻

Conclusion

It may have been Confucius (in general not a good friend of women, but everyone is entitled to a few moments of wisdom) who said that 'you travel to get away from yourself, but when you arrive at your destination, there you still are'. This rather fatalistic axiom may encapsulate the thousand-mile journey that women in the work of Rego undertake in lives lived under a broad spectrum of hardship and oppression. At the optimistic (or vindictive) end of this spectrum sits (and sniggers) Paula Rego, who, over a period of almost seventy years, showed us a vista, both dark and sunlit, of other possibilities.

> Thou art thy mother's glass, and she in thee
> Calls back the lovely April of her prime. (Shakespeare, 'Sonnet 3')[8]

Or something like that.

---

8   Text available at: https://www.poetryfoundation.org/poems/50644/sonnet-3-look-in-thy-glass-and-tell-the-face-thou-viewest

Fig. 5.30 Paula Rego, *Escape* (2009), etching and aquatint, 49 × 36.5 cm. ©Ostrich Arts Ltd/Amgueddfa Cymru - Museum Wales, https://museum.wales/collections/online/object/2e7a7812-96c6-357f-98d1-681ff3ae4012/Escape/?field0=string&value0=roman&field1=with_images&value1=1&page=196
http://hdl.handle.net/20.500.12434/d8ddbe49

Works Cited

Andersen, Hans Christian, 1836, *The Little Mermaid*, http://hca.gilead.org.il/li_merma.html

Bates, Laura, 2021, *Men Who Hate Women: From Incels to Pickup Artists, the Truth about Extreme Misogyny and How it Affects us All* (London: Simon and Schuster).

Bates, Laura, 2025, *The New Age of Sexism: How the AI Revolution is Reinventing Misogyny* (London: Simon and Schuster).

Bradley, Fiona (ed.), 2000, *Victor Willing* (London: August).

Brine, Kevin R., 2010, 'The Judith Project', in *The Sword of Judith Book: Judith Studies Across the Disciplines*, ed. Kevin R. Brine, Elena Ciletti and Henrike Lähnemann (Cambridge: Open Book Publishers), pp. 3–21, https://doi.org/10.11647/obp.0009.01

Carter, Angela, 1995, *The Bloody Chamber* (London: Vintage).

Ciletti, Elena, 2010, 'Judith Imagery as Catholic Orthodoxy in Counter-Reformation Italy', in *The Sword of Judith Book: Judith Studies Across the Disciplines*, ed. Kevin R. Brine, Elena Ciletti and Henrike Lähnemann (Cambridge: Open Book Publishers, 2010), pp. 345–68, https://doi.org/10.11647/OBP.0009.19

Cohen, Simona, 2014, 'Animal Imagery in Renaissance Art', *Renaissance Quarterly*, 67.1, 164–80, https://doi.org/10.1086/676155

Duffy, Carol Ann, 1999, 'Little Red-Cap', in *The World's Wife* (London: Picador), https://www.poetryfoundation.org/poems/1527555/little-red-cap

Dunn, James D. G., 2003, *Eerdmans Commentary on the Bible*, ed. James D. G. Dunn and John William Rogerson (Grand Rapids, MI: William B. Eerdmans Publishing Company, 2003).

Grimm, Jacob, and Wilhelm Grimm, 1812, *Kinder und Hausmärchen*, trans. D. L. Ashliman, 1st ed. (Berlin: Realschulbuchhandlung, 1812), English translation at https://pinkmonkey.com/dl/library1/story089.pdf

Gosling, Emily, 2022, '"I'm All Too Human": Artist Paula Rego on Depicting People', *Another Mag* (8 June), https://www.anothermag.com/art-photography/10634/im-all-too-human-artist-paula-rego-on-depicting-people

Farrell, Kaitlyn, 2013, 'A Dog's World: The Significance of Canine Companions in Hogarth's "Marriage A-la-Mode"', *The British Art Journal*, 14.2, 35–38.

Jones, Jonathan, 2022, '"She is Dancing among the Greats": The Dangerously Honest, Richly Ambiguous Paula Rego', *The Guardian* (8 June), https://www.theguardian.com/artanddesign/2022/jun/08/paula-rego-jonathan-jones-tribute

Kahr, Madlyn, 1973, 'Rembrandt and Delilah', *The Art Bulletin*, 55.2, 240–59.

Levine Gera, Deborah, 2010, 'The Jewish Textual Traditions', in *The Sword of Judith Book: Judith Studies Across the Disciplines*, ed. Kevin R. Brine, Elena Ciletti and Henrike Lähnemann (Cambridge: Open Book Publishers, 2010), pp. 23–39, https://doi.org/10.11647/OBP.0009.02

Lisboa, Maria Manuel, *Essays on Paula Rego: Smile When You Think About Hell* (Cambridge: Open Book, 2019), https://doi.org/10.11647/OBP.0178

Lonsdale, Steven H., 1979, 'Attitudes towards Animals in Ancient Greece', *Greece & Rome*, 26.2, 146–59.

Lucas, Peter J., 1992, '"Judith" and the Woman Hero', *The Yearbook of English Studies*, 22, 17–27.

Manca, Joseph, 2013, 'Dogs of Infamy in Lorenzo De' Medici's Birth Tray', *Notes in the History of Art*, 32.4, 1–6, https://doi.org/10.1086/sou.32.4.41955678

McEwen, John, 1997, *Paula Rego*, 2nd ed. (London: Phaidon).

Milam, Jennifer, 2015, 'Rococo Representations of Interspecies Sensuality and the Pursuit of "Volupté"', *The Art Bulletin*, 97.2, 192–209, https://doi.org/10.1080/00043079.2015.979104

Perrault, Charles, 1895, *The Story of Blue Beard* (London: Lawrence and Bullen), https://www.gutenberg.org/cache/epub/44288/pg44288-images.html

Rego, Paula, and Bessa-Luís, Agustina, 2001, *As Meninas: Pinturas Paula Rego*, Texto Agustina Bessa-Luis, 2nd ed. (Lisbon: Três Sinais Editores).

Santesso, Aaron, 1999, 'William Hogarth and the Tradition of Sexual Scissors', *Studies in English Literature*, 39.3, 499–521, https://doi.org/10.1353/sel.1999.0030

Schipper, Jeremy, 2011, 'What Was Samson Thinking in Judges 16: 17 and 16: 20?', *Biblica*, 92.1, 60–69.

Soeiro, Ricardo Gil, 2007, 'Dreams in the Mirror: George Steiner by George Steiner', in *Stories and Portraits of the Self*, ed. Helena Carvalhão Buescu and João Ferreira Duarte (Leiden: Brill), p. 220, https://doi.org/10.1163/9789401205290_018

Sontag, Susan, 2004, *Regarding the Pain of Others* (London: Penguin).

Tamber-Rosenau, Caryn, 2017, 'Biblical Bathing Beauties and the Manipulation of the Male Gaze: What Judith Can Tell Us about Bathsheba and Susanna', *Journal of Feminist Studies in Religion*, 33.2, 55–72, https://doi.org/10.2979/jfemistudreli.33.2.05

Tusa, John, 2001, 'Interview with Paula Rego', *The Independent on Sunday* (3 June), 10 [Also broadcast in full on BBC Radio 3, Sunday Feature, 3 June 2001].

Woolf, Virginia, 1995, *Killing the Angel in the House: Seven Essays* (London: Penguin Books Ltd UK).

6. Menstrous/Monstrous: Bleeding, Amenorrhea and Feminine Hygiene in the Art of Ana Palma and Paula Rego[1]

> I don't trust any creature that bleeds for one week every month and doesn't die.
>
> Neil LaBute (dir.), *In the Company of Men* (1997)

> Mignonne, allons voir si la rose
> Qui ce matin avait déclose
> Sa robe de pourpre au soleil,
> A point perdu cette vesprée,
> Les plis de sa robe pourprée,
> Et son teint au vôtre pareil.
>
> Pierre de Ronsard, 'Mignonne, allons voir si la rose'[2]

Introduction

Ana Palma is one of a young generation of Portuguese artists who, half a century after the country emerged from a long period of extreme political

---

1 A version of this text in Portuguese appears in *Faces de Eva*, 52 (Lisboa, 2024), and is translated here with permission.
2 'Sweetheart, let us go see if the rose
   Which this morning had unfurled
   Its purple gown to the sun,
   Has lost this evening,
   The folds of its scarlet robe,
   And its complexion akin to yours'.

and religious oppression, is now able engage with topics relating to the female body (in this instance, menstruation) that conventionally respectable people, let alone nice ladies, did not mention without a heavy protective carapace of euphemism. In doing so, she engages also with centuries-long tradition of using propriety as a vehicle for the practice of misogyny.

***

Visible/Speakable

Men are afraid that women will laugh at them. Women are afraid that men will kill them.

Margaret Atwood

In war scenarios, as in the Garden of Eden after the Fall, everyone suffers, but typically women, after Eve, suffer differently from men and the problem is often related to gynaecological matters: rape; childbirth in pain; lack of pain relief. Lack of sanitary products? The latter might seem a trivial problem, and possibly it is, but as regards making life miserable, it all adds up.[3] More on this later. Motherhood is one of the key themes of the visual arts in the West, beginning with centuries of Marian motherhood, but not only: see, for example, the *Acts of Creation: On Art and Motherhood* exhibition launched in March 2024. The press release tells us that 'the exhibition addresses diverse experiences of motherhood across three themes: Creation, which looks at conception, pregnancy, birth and nursing; Maintenance, which explores motherhood and caregiving in the day-to-day; and Loss, which touches on miscarriage and involuntary childlessness, as well as reproductive rights. The heart of the exhibition is a series of revelatory self-portraits—a celebration of the artist as mother'.[4] But one aspect is missing.

Menstrual art (or *Menstrala*—a term coined by the artist Vanessa Tiegs in a series of eighty-eight images of birds and flowers created

---

3 See Mousa, 2024.
4 See https://arnolfini.org.uk/whatson/actsofcreation/ and https://arnolfini.org.uk/press-releases/actsofcreation/

between 2000 and 2003[5] that use her menstrual blood as the medium) had made itself known as far back as the early 1970s, when radical feminist artist Judy Chicago produced works such as *Red Flag* and *Menstruation Bathroom*. The former is a photolithograph of the artist removing a bloodied tampon from her vagina: the latter presents women's blood as taboo and, by implication, puberty as the moment of shame when signs of womanhood appear in the form of bloodied sanitary pads spilling out of an overfull bin. By now an established sub-genre (as well as a commercial gimmick: look on Etsy for earrings in the shape of used tampons), *Menstrala* has inspired well-known artists, such as Lani Beloso who uses her menstrual output as the medium in her artworks. Her 2010 project, *The Period Piece*, is a series of thirteen canvas paintings representing a year's worth of menstrual cycles, all done using her own blood and referring to the acute suffering she experienced in every menstrual cycle. Carolee Schneemann poignantly addressed the vulnerability of her own body in matters that included menstrual bleeding.[6] And in Chile we have Cecilia Vicuña's striking *Quipu Menstrual* (2006/2021).[7] Vicuna's work brings what in the mainstream (male) vision is at best ignored and at worst pulled into the foreground, in what might be described as floods of suffering. Menstrual record-keeping is a part of the female lived experience: When will I start menstruating? When will be my last period? How much will I suffer in the lead up to it (perimenopause) and after (menopause: will I go gently into that good night)? And how much pain, inconvenience, fear, embarrassment will I suffer during my years as school girl, young woman, mature woman? Will I underperform in exams, job interviews, professional activities? As an academic, I am always aware that in any given exam hall, one in four female students will be in some degree of pain.

In 'If Men Could Menstruate', a notorious article first published in the women's magazine *Ms* in 1978, Gloria Steinem satirizes a hypothetical boastful culture surrounding menstruation, were it the lot of men rather than women. Regardless of what Steinem might have said or done, however, even fifty years later, few women do not still dread the public

---

5   See https://www.vanessatiegs.com/menstrala/
6   See https://www.barbican.org.uk/sites/default/files/documents/2022-03/FINAL_Carolee%20Schneemann_Press%20Release_March22_0.pdf
7   See Santos, 2021; Park Hong, Lozano and De La Torre, 2022; and also Sinclair, 2015.

embarrassment of a menstrual accident in a public setting. More about this later. But what of women who err in the opposite direction? The ones who are of an age to menstruate but for a variety of reasons do not? Are they akin to the preoccupying spinsters that feature as the old hags of society and culture? Women whose childbearing (validating/ conforming) years come to nothing?

It is the case of unexplained absent menstruation that will be discussed regarding the work of Ana Palma, a London-based Portuguese artist whose work, often carrying a strong autobiographical component, falls perfectly within the scope of Derrida's loose understanding of a self-portrait ('everything that happens to me, that I can affect, or that affects me', Derrida, 1993, p. 65). Like Paula Rego (for example, in her 1998 abortion images), Palma, Rego's fellow countrywoman and like Rego London-based, addresses the body (her own body) in its most visceral and vulnerable plights. Women artists often look at themselves and at each other. Do they look *after* each other? Every woman needs a sister. But before we go looking for her, let us look at the rule that Palma's exception may prove (and illuminate).

Felix Culpa: The Rule That the Exception Proved

> When a woman has her regular flow of blood, the impurity of her monthly period will last seven days, and anyone who touches her will be unclean till evening. (*Leviticus* 15:19)

Leviticus is nothing if not thorough. The list of contaminations (who and what she touches) goes on from verses 10–25. Since regardless of all these interdictions, a menstruating woman is still supposed to go to church (let alone cook and look after her family), some contradictions remain unsolved, although presumably that is what *midrash* is for.

Similarly, the finer points regarding the Virgin Mary's bodily functions were debated by the Patristic Fathers over many centuries. This prolonged rumination in due course led to the following conclusions regarding the Mother of God: first, that she did not menstruate; second, that she did not undergo a ruptured hymen either prior to impregnation or during childbirth; third, that she did not give birth in pain[8]—unlike

---

8   The Catechism of the Council of Trent, which states Mary gave birth 'without

Eve and all her daughters, or, more recently, Rego's Mary in *Nativity* (Fig. 6.1), or Monica Sjöö's daringly gender transgressive *God Giving Birth*; and, fourth, that her body did not corrupt in the grave.[9] Other physical aspects of her maternity (visible pregnancy: *Maria Gravida*; breastfeeding: the nursing Virgin) also fell out of favour in artistic representations, although they did not entirely disappear.

 Fig. 6.1 Paula Rego, *Nativity* (2002), property of the Portuguese State (Portuguese State Contemporary Art Collection), https://www.researchgate.net/figure/Paula-Rego-Nativity-2002-Pastel-on-paper-mounted-on-aluminium-54-x-52-cm-Belem_fig1_335537454

http://hdl.handle.net/20.500.12434/16a1d4d5

Mary's only uncontroversial secretion was tears because she wept at the foot of the cross, and although in the most ghoulish representations she weeps tears of blood, only the most irreverent would suggest that that was a euphemism for menstruation.

In many respects, therefore Mary might have been the exception that fortuitously atoned for the sins of Eve (*Felix Culpa*)[10] but she also contributed to the impossible double bind that all women face: the requirement that they emulate her while stipulating that they will inevitably fail do so: the only acceptable role for women may be motherhood although to that effect, with the single exception of the Holy Mother, women cannot bear children whilst remaining virgins, because like Eve they are tainted by/guilty of original sin.

Beauty Bare

Euclid alone has looked on Beauty bare.
Let all who prate of Beauty hold their peace,
And lay them prone upon the earth and cease
To ponder on themselves, the while they stare

---

experiencing ... any sense of pain' (see https://www.catholicapologetics.info/thechurch/catechism/ApostlesCreed03.shtml) and, the Church's Liturgy, which states, 'She who had given him birth without the pains of childbirth . . .' (BVM Collection of Masses, p. 117).

9 See https://en.wikipedia.org/wiki/Tomb_of_the_Virgin_Mary
10 See https://en.wikipedia.org/wiki/Exsultet

> At nothing, intricately drawn nowhere
> In shapes of shifting lineage.
>
> Edna Millay, 'Euclid Alone Has Looked on Beauty Bare'

Women, of course, are known to be tricky beasts and need to be controlled. The Gospel according to *Mark* 5: 25–34 stands out from related prescriptions because it allows an exceptional deviation from Jewish purity rules that banned menstruating women from partaking in religious and social activities during their 'infectious' time (*Leviticus* 15: 19–33 listed numerous prohibitions that accrued to gynaecological conditions associated with menstruation). During their monthly bleeding, women were termed ἀκάθαρτος ('unclean') and had to be secluded for at least seven days. If the cycle was irregular or lengthy or otherwise anomalous, the woman was deemed 'polluted' until she was 'cured' (*Leviticus* 15:19–33). If a menstruating woman touched or was touched by anyone, that person was also banished until evening (Selvidge, 1984, p. 619). And the Pentateuch didn't even get there first: 'Restricting woman because of her menstrual flow is not uncommon among primitive religions. According to B. J. Bamberger, "Ancient man reacted to the phenomenon of menstruation with a horror that seems to us grotesque and hysterical..."' (Selvidge, 1984, p. 621). Anthropologists, psychologists, sociologists, and theologians are still attempting to explain this phobia. Suggested hypotheses for this exclusionary practice range from male 'castration anxiety' to a 'protective device' used by women against their husbands (Selvidge, 1984, p. 621): all the more effective because it may be a yuckier and therefore more-effective version of 'not tonight, dear, I have a headache'. Be that as it may, and Selvidge also points it out, Christ's followers, as was so often the case, were less generous than their master: in *Mark* 5: 25–34, he (who in another tradition was known as Jesus, son of Mary: Īsā ibn Maryam, *Qur'an* 3: 45)[11] welcomed the menstruating woman in the crowd, allowed her to touch him and then go about her business, rather than confining her to her home during her bleeding. But those he taught did not follow suit, a subsequent Jesus movement reinstating the taboo (Selvidge, 1984, p. 623).

---

11 See https://quran.com/3/45?translations=48,84,17,39,101,20,46,85,18,95,38,19,22,33,27

Menstruating women are considered ritually unclean in Judaism, Christianity, Hinduism, and Buddhism. Interestingly, Islam does not view a menstruating woman as carrying any sort of 'contagious pollution'. She is neither 'cursed' nor 'untouchable'. (Abdullah, 2022)

Barren Women: Another Kind of Curse

There are three things that are never satisfied,
Four that never say, 'Enough!':
The grave, the barren womb,
Land, which is never satisfied with water,
And fire, which never says, 'Enough!'

Proverbs 30:16

At the other end of the spectrum, the failure to menstruate may be indicative of general infertility, in which case the absence of 'the curse' becomes itself a scourge condemning women not to fulfil their prescribed role as mothers. For Herbert Spencer, for example, at the endpoint of his transition from advocate of female suffrage to Andrew Tate *avant la lettre* (it is a man's privilege to change his mind), an excess of education made women barren (Francis, 2007, pp. 51–68). The barren woman has always been suspicious: unnatural, a witch, a hag, a rebel, an old crone, a voluntary abortee, a spinster (by choice? A lesbian; a man-hater; a slut; a whore). An empty womb by another name would stink as badly as the blood-soiled products of menstruation. The menarche, like the lack of it, is a negative blade that cuts only one way. But is that really so? Blood has a rusty metallic odour, not something any self-respecting blacksmith would wish to touch: but who is wielding the forging hammer in the furnaces of this particular hell? The lack of a period may also indicate that the body is in fight-or-flight mode: under threat and just about able to sustain itself alone, but not another creature within itself.

Natural Woman or Forever a Loser?

You came from someone who menstruates. It's a sacrament, it should be a sacrament in our society.

Mary Lou Ballweg

The bloodshed of menstruation is both bad (abject[12] in most cultures) and necessary in order to prove that you are a dutiful ('natural'/breeding) woman. But motherhood comes with a caveat: is the mother Mary (God's chosen one) or Eve (the postlapsarian mother)? Immaculate or tainted? Forever perfect or irredeemably flawed? Nature, via the turmoil of love, always exacts a price from those who fall short of the ideal. Heads you win, tails I lose. Being a natural woman, as we know, is usually a problem. As well as all the blood, mess and pain, it can kill you, sometimes even before you even cross the line into womanhood. In 1935, Chad Varah, a young Anglican priest, officiated at the funeral of a fourteen-year-old girl in England: she had killed herself when her menstruation started. She had never been told the facts about puberty and when she began to bleed in pain she thought she was dying. This prompted Varah to found the suicide helpline, the Samaritans. But even in less extreme circumstances, menstruation remains a social (as opposed to a somatic) problem. In the fountain of knowledge that is the internet, we find many pearls of wisdom. Mostly, however, they reveal female embarrassment and male disgust.[13] Would you ask your Dad to go and buy you Tampax or even let him know you are menstruating? Certainly not women in most countries, or women over a certain age anywhere.

And, it would appear, one is damned if one does (menstruate) and damned if one doesn't. In '"A Strange Infirmity": Lady Macbeth's Amenorrhea', Jenijoy La Belle (1980) debates how Lady Macbeth's many flaws are linked (possibly causally) to her desire not to menstruate as a means of preserving her abject, murderous (true) self. Perhaps that notorious damned spot not only came from her victim's blood but also gestured, *in absentia*, to the Lady's refusal to spill her own in any form, be it from wound or womb. Sometimes the process of compensation tries to reclaim menstruation as not only natural but even positive (Fedele, 2014). Mostly, however, the taboo surrounding it and its abjectification comes second only to incest in its horror and universality. In 'The Mother-Shaped Hole', Julia V. Hendrickson (2019) discusses how messy maternity and its associated bloods created a representational difficulty for Modernist art. And in 'Menarche and the (Hetero)sexualization of

---

12 Kristeva, 1982.
13 See Armitage, 2017.

the Female Body', Janet Lee explores the cultural complications of the onset of menstruation and argues that 'the menarche—or a woman's first menstrual period—is a central aspect of body politics':

> Through explorations of oral and written narratives, I suggest that girls' subjective sense of themselves as maturing women at menarche develops simultaneously with a process of sexualization whereby young women experience themselves as sexualized, and their bodies are produced as sexual objects. While women internalize negative scripts associated with the bleeding female body, they also respond with consciousness and resistance. (Lee, 1994, p. 43)

Meanwhile, out in the market place where women do their shopping, Roseann Mandziuk (2010) discusses the early twentieth-century advertising campaign by Kotex in the marketing of 'feminine hygiene' products (they are still called that one hundred years later) as a means of keeping 'clean'. And more recently, Peggy McCracken discusses the double standard highlighted in Ridley Scott's *G.I. Jane*, whereby the matter of women shedding blood cannot include menstrual blood, a problem fortunately circumvented by the fact that women who participate in strenuous physical activity (for example athletes or, in this case, women in the military) often cease to menstruate as a result of losing body fat (or of being in fight-or-flight mode, as suggested above).

> The different values associated with women's blood and men's blood reinforce the notion of a 'natural' gendered social order in which men fight and women do not. And one way in which women's blood is devalued in relation to men's blood is through the association of women's blood with women's reproductive biology. [...] *G.I. Jane* makes a point of representing menstruation, but only in order to show its absence. Any blood Lieutenant O'Neil sheds must have come from the cuts and abrasions she continues to accumulate in training exercises. [...] The film reveals a profound anxiety of its own about a woman who performs as a man, a woman who bleeds profusely from her wounds but not from her genitals, a woman who escapes what the film constructs as the 'natural' categories of sex and heterosexuality. This is a sign of the movie's profound ambivalence about [...] women's ability to perform in combat [...]. *G.I. Jane* exposes a perceived incompatibility between women's blood and heroic bloodshed, which is usually defined as masculine. (McCracken, 2003, pp. 626–27)

It Never Rains But It Pours: Rivers of Blood

Leaders bleed, period.

Silvia Young

In the ancient Irish epic tale *Táin bó Cúallnge* (*The Cattle-Raid of Cooley*), Medb is prevented from pursuing her unwomanly activities as a warrior by an excessive shedding of menstrual blood, which forces her to enlist the help of a man. Women's blood—the blood of menstruation, like the blood of parturition—is shown to be incompatible with the noble pursuit of war and Medb's role in battle is replaced by Fergus, who came to her rescue and 'covered the retreat of the men of Ireland' (McCracken, 2003, p. 629). But even so, Medb's menstrual flood might in the end win the day. In the first version of the narrative she is able to draw on her supposed female shortcomings, and produces a menstrual flow of such power that 'it made three great trenches in each of which a household can fit,' (McCracken, 2003, p. 629) thus covering the men's retreat.

> Medb voided her water, so that it made three large dikes, so that a mill could find room in each dike. Hence the place is known as Fual Medbha ('Medb's Water'). (McCracken, 2003, p. 629)[14]

In a later version, menstrual blood is replaced by urine. But is that really less repulsive? Apparently so. Whatever the case might have been regarding Medb, in general, women's biological specificity is a rare topic whether in Hollywood or Late Antiquity. The cases of Medb (in the first version of the narrative) and G.I. Jane are the exceptions that, until recently, proved the rule.

Even in the not uncommon cases of women who cross-dress to pass themselves as men and go to war, their female biology—the reality of what they are—is often the trigger for reinstating gender-role orthodoxy (women in the home, men in the battlefield). When this problem is circumvented, it is because a woman ceases to be a 'proper woman'. Quicherat (1841–49), for example, notes that Joan of Arc's successful military career went hand in hand with contemporary

---

14 The text of the *Táin* is available to read for free at https://www.gutenberg.org/files/16464/16464-h/16464-h.htm; the episode in question appears at https://www.gutenberg.org/files/16464/16464-h/16464-h.htm#Page_51

reports (including from her valet) that she did not menstruate. And Marina Warner, discussing a nineteenth-century account, suggests that 'the maiden [was] "womanly in modesty, but exempt, by a particular design, from the weaknesses of her sex, she was also not subjected to those periodic and inconvenient dues, which, even more than law and custom, prevent women in general fulfilling the functions that men have taken over"' (Warner, 1981, p. 19). In Shakespeare's *Henry VI*, on the other hand, Joan's blood (which, from the point of view of the English, it is desirable to shed) is female blood, either inherited from her mother or an unspecified witch's blood; in either case, it becomes key to her demonization (McCracken, 2003, p. 639). A woman's blood, particularly—but not exclusively—menstrual blood, has no place on the battlefield. The pre-condition for a woman to become a warrior is that at the very least she should not menstruate. If she does, as was the case with Medb, a man's helping hand must be called upon, and in general any blood she may shed will be besmirched by its association with her sex. A woman's ability to fight is only acceptable if it is deployed in the defence of her home and family, i.e., driven by her maternal instinct and therefore safely within the parameters of acceptable female agency.

The Female of the Species

> She who faces Death by torture for each life beneath her breast
> May not deal in doubt or pity, must not swerve for fact or jest.
> These be purely male diversions, not in these her honour dwells.
>
> Rudyard Kipling, 'The Female of the Species'

> Kipling's feelings about women were complex and often contradictory but he believed that female suffrage would weaken the Empire, and [...] that women would ruin their reproductive system by standing on their feet for hours and working.
>
> Andrew Lycett, *Rudyard Kipling*

Although he opposed women's suffrage, Kipling surprisingly recognized childbirth as a bloody battlefield in its own right, and indeed, as historical data shows, before the advent of antibiotics, more than one in every ten combatants in this particular struggle died: they were literally decimated. One startling statistic tells us that in one specific year, in the

French province of Lombardy, no women survived childbirth (Gordon, 2018). And the World Health Organization tells us that even with the advantages of modern surgery and advances in infection control, a maternal death occurred every two minutes in 2020.[15]

The battle for jurisdiction over the bodies of women is old hat (numbers in childbirth deaths, for example, increased significantly when, in the eighteenth century, male doctors already infected in surgical wards took over from midwives the care of women in labour).[16] But it is also part of both middle-brow poetry and the high art canon. One doesn't hesitate to admire and memorialize the female body ravaged in war as depicted by Old Masters (Tiepolo's *The Rape of Europa*, c. 1743; Rubens' *The Rape of the Daughters of Leucippus*, 1617–18; Poussin's *The Abduction of the Sabine Women*, c. 1633–34, to name but a few), but only if it is shed by passive female victims, usually in the context of rape (in which case there is no doubt as regards the gender/ power stakes). It is always a good idea to think about a museum from the point of view of a child: 'Mummy, what are those men doing to that lady?' Etc., etc., etc.

Aristophanes' *Lysistrata* introduced a rare instance of women intervening in conflict between men by withholding sex—rather than falling prey to sexual violence as a weapon of war. In general, however, women are claimed as war trophies. And there is another instance in which the trope of violence has been recruited in battle grounds mapped out over the woman's body. In 'Bodies of Evidence: Feminist Performance Art', Erin Striff (1997) debates the abundant deployment of emotional imagery used by anti-abortion campaigns that present the foetus as the victim of its murderous not-to-be mother, as well as the difficulty in finding images of similar power enlisted on the pro-choice side. There are examples, of course, that address the sorrows of the abortee, including the famous 'coat-hanger' image that depicts the instrument used by women upon themselves in backstreet abortions (Fig. 6.2); or the ambivalent Frida Kahlo's images that might or might not depict abortion (*A Few Small Nips*, 1935);[17] or, notably, the abortion

---

15 See https://www.who.int/news-room/fact-sheets/detail/maternal-mortality
16 Chamberlain, 2006.
17 See   https://useum.org/artwork/A-Few-Small-Nips-Unos-cuantos-piquetitos-Frida-Kahlo-1935

images of 1998 by Ana Palma's fellow countrywoman, Paula Rego (Figs. 6.3 and 6.4).

Fig. 6.2 'We Won't Go Back', coat hanger sign from demonstration in front of SCOTUS, 3 May 2022. Photo by Janni Rye (2022), Wikimedia Commons, CC0, https://commons.wikimedia.org/wiki/File:We_wont_go_back_-_coat_hanger_-_sign_-_Demonstration_in_front_of_SCOTUS_May_3_2022_754.jpg

Fig. 6.3 Paula Rego, *Untitled Triptych; Abortion* (left-hand panel) (1998–99). Pastel on paper mounted on aluminium, 110 × 100 cm. ©The Estate of Paula Rego and Victoria Miro, https://womensartblog.wordpress.com/2018/05/21/the-abortion-pastels-paula-rego/

http://hdl.handle.net/20.500.12434/f03859a7

Fig. 6.4 Paula Rego, *Untitled* (Abortion) (1988), pastel on paper mounted on aluminium, 110 × 100 cm. ©The Estate of Paula Rego and Victoria Miro, https://www.nationalgalleries.org/sites/default/files/features/EFENJJWW4AADxdy_1.jpg

http://hdl.handle.net/20.500.12434/8ce01b69

But what if abortion and other obstetric events (amenorrhea) are the means by which motherhood is rejected by women? It ought to be emphasized that what follows is pure speculation by the author of this chapter, rather than anything that transpired from conversations with Ana Palma.

Ana Palma: All by Herself

> I tell you
> someone will remember us
> in the future.
>
> Sappho

In an interview conducted in August 2023, Ana Palma shared the following reflections about her body and her work:[18]

> My work has become more intimate and autobiographical over the years. The 'Femina' series started as a way to voice and process what I was going through since I could not express it in any other language. [...] It took me literally years to start talking openly about my amenorrhea, and I think sometimes I still avoid it for fear of judgement.
> [...]
> Before the amenorrhea journey started, I was working on the idea of the death-life-rebirth cycle that women experience in their bodies and minds [...]. Back then, I had no idea I was just about to embark on the most profound physical, emotional, and spiritual metamorphosis. It's almost like I was anticipating and preparing for it.
> [...]
> This temporary condition brought me so many questions around identity, gender, sexuality, and inevitably social conditioning and inequalities. [...] Although there were negative aspects of this journey, which included burnout and depression, I always saw the transformation I have experienced over the past 5 years as a blessing. [...] This undiagnosed condition threw me into what astrophysicists call a wormhole [...]. I'm closer to myself than I have ever been; I have been able to make life-changing decisions that I never had the confidence or courage to do. [...] I'm no longer apologetic.[...] As a woman, my body was always a source of shame, guilt, and fear. [...] A woman's body is a scary place to live in, and it will continue to be if society does not address the root cause of these issues. (Ana Palma in interview with M. M. Lisboa)

The result is a body of work that is autobiographical but also reaches out to collective concerns, both contemporary and Antique.

---

18   Full interview available below, see 'Interview with Ana Palma'.

The End of the World

> Of Adam's first wife, Lilith, it is told
> (The witch he loved before the gift of Eve,)
> That, ere the snake's, her sweet tongue could deceive,
> And her enchanted hair was the first gold.
> And still she sits, young while the earth is old,
> And, subtly of herself contemplative,
> Draws men to watch the bright web she can weave,
> Till heart and body and life are in its hold.
>
> Dante Gabriel Rossetti, 'Body's Beauty'

Here's a real-life story of very recent occurrence. In my teaching room there is a comfortable white armchair, courtesy of my College's furniture stocks. I noticed that students seldom chose to sit on it. Some of them. Just recently, one of the more outspoken of the female sisterhood (or nursery: like Prime Ministers, students get younger every year) commented that neither would I if I still menstruated. Just in case of an accident. *Touchée* (as it were). The chair seat is now covered in a throw made of fabric in patterned shades of pink and red. Why should the boys enjoy all the comfortable furniture? The negativity that surrounds the specific female concern that is the menarche crosses boundaries of time and place. It would be easier to find countries, cultures and periods where menstruation is *not* at the very least an embarrassment, and at worst a taboo. Given that, however, how does society, even now, engage with a woman who not only does not endure one of the aspects of Eve's 'curse' but who also happens not to be the Virgin Mary? Even now, depending on location, how does one approach the oddity of a woman who does not suffer that which behoves her sex as a consequence of Eve's special role in the Fall (menstruation, motherhood, childbirth in pain)? Is she blessed? Almost certainly not. Is she cunningly evading what ought to be the defining parameters of postlapsarian consequentiality (menses pain, agonizing parturition) that ensure no less than the continuation of the species? Is she the herald of a forthcoming apocalypse? Many famous sci-fi narratives imagining the end of the world (Margaret Atwood's *The Handmaid's Tale*, John Wyndham's 'Consider Her Ways', P. D. James' *The Children of Men,* to name but a few), start from the premise of a doomed status quo in which women no longer reproduce. Fertility is the *sine qua non* of species' survival, and the 'curse' is the price to be paid (by women) for that future, lest she become the embodiment of the dark Eve, Lilith: Adam's first wife, who refused to accept the duty of obedience to her husband, was expelled from the Garden of Eden, and banished to the margins of the Dead Sea, where she proceeded to consort with demons and bear them babies which she would then kill and eat. And, if that became the norm, then presumably there would be no future for humanity. A flawed second wife (Eve) who was over-friendly with serpents, ate forbidden fruits and caused her husband and all his descendants to be excluded from Paradise, was even so better than the first one, since after the Fall there were admittedly still ordeals to endure (especially for her: pain from menstruation and childbirth), but, if you suffered enough and atoned accordingly, salvation might still be possible (Fig. 6.5).

Fig. 6.5 Paula Rego, *Agony in the Garden* (2002), pastel on paper on aluminium, 79.5 × 76.5 × 4.5 cm, Virgin Mary Series. ©Paula Rego. All rights reserved 2025/Bridgeman Images, https://www.bridgemanimages.com/en/rego/agony-in-the-garden-2002-pastel-on-paper-on-aluminium/pastel-on-paper-on-aluminium/asset/8617906

http://hdl.handle.net/20.500.12434/d41732e1

But the first verdict seemed the worst verdict
When Adam and Eve were expelled from Eden;
Yet when the bitter gates clanged to
The sky beyond was just as blue.
[...]
And when from Eden we take our way
The morning after is the first day. (Louis MacNeice, 'Apple Blossom')

Which is some consolation, although not, surely, for those barren, amenorrhoeic, resisting, defiant, never-to-be mothers who surely signal the end of the world.

Ana Palma's *Entrails II* and *The Cycle* (Figs. 6.6 and 6.7) may be read in conjunction. The uplifting celestial blue background and pastel pink hues of the former may give the lie to the title which itself draws attention to what we are actually viewing: namely a would-be anatomical drawing of a woman's body (the shape of a pink dress with a frilly hem suggests it is a woman's body)[19] which, however, anatomizes the harsh sharpie lines of the viscera, leading down to what would appear to be an effluent vagina. It is not however clear whether there is any blood flowing out. And if there isn't, why not? If there is, given the autobiographical information made available to us by Palma, is the bleeding a sign of wishful thinking? An attempt at self-normalization? Or rather regret regarding a prior individuality (amenorrhea) that, if no longer a problem, propels this particular individual back to the norm: that of a menstruating woman, with all the benefits and problems that reabsorption into ordinariness entails. The advantages of being recouped back into the herd speak for themselves: becoming 'normal', being a 'natural woman', being fertile, being like most other members of one's sex. But also being subjected to the problems that afflict the majority: pre-menstrual tension; menstruation pain and inconvenience; possible embarrassment; the possibility of potentially unwanted pregnancy, with the undeniable negative aspects that Mary alone escaped because she was excused from them (childbirth in pain; death in childbirth); the perimenopause and menopause.

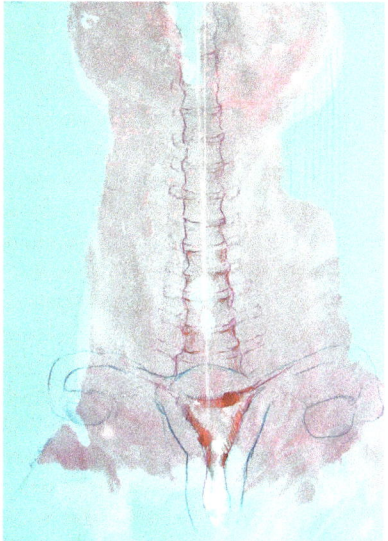

Fig. 6.6 Ana Palma, *Entrails II* (2021), acrylic and watercolour pencil on paper, 35 × 50 cm, CC BY-NC-SA 4.0.

---

19 Palma describes this image as a self-portrait, a print of her own body.

The Cycle, which pre-dates *Entrails*, is even less compromising. In this instance, the palette uses colours that are either sombre (a clenched fist in grey/brown) or a cryptic semi-humanoid figure in red/brown, evocative of clotting blood. Is the clenched fist a sign of pain or defiance or both? If the figure is gesturing towards a human shape, is it attacking or running away? Is the arm-shape warding off blows or threatening them? Is that a skull, and if so, whose? Someone certainly died here, but did someone escape too?[20]

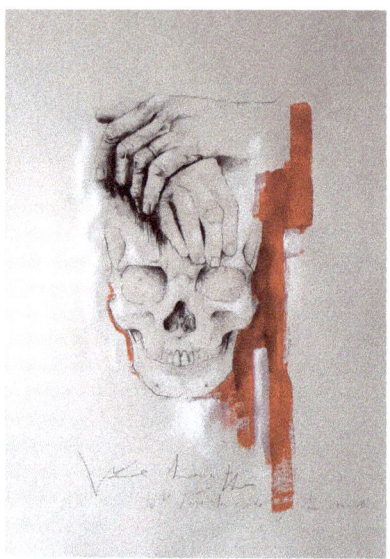

Fig. 6.7 Ana Palma, *The Cycle* (2016–19), graphite pencil and acrylic on paper, 59.4 × 84.1 cm, CC BY-NC-SA 4.0.

The next figures to be discussed, *Morreste-me* (*You Died on Me*) and *Rebirth* (Figs. 6.8 and 10) respectively of 2013 and 2017, unlike the previous two, bespeak chronological progress. *Morreste-me* uses an unusual verb structure in Portuguese. *Morrer* ('to die') is an intransitive verb which here, however, becomes transitive. As such, it imbues the expression 'you died' with a dimension of personal involvement on the part of the speaker: 'you died on me' suggests that that death (someone else's) was something that

---

20 Let us hear Palma herself: '*The Cycle* was about the countless life/death/rebirth cycles we go through in human life (and nature) on a physical and psychological level. It talks about accepting and welcoming these cycles with resilience and curiosity'. Quoted in interview with Ana Palma in this volume.

was done *to* the purveyor of the voice, the latter thus claiming centre stage in the theatre of loss and grief. The image leaves unclear what is implied by the cradling arms of the female figure: possibly breast-feeding/failing to breast feed; a miscarried baby; an aborted foetus; a stillbirth; a death in infancy; infanticide. Whatever the case may be, what is evoked is the possibility of maternity come to nothing for causes unknown. Again, the pastel pink backdrop in *You died on me*, like the sex of the figure, claims this as a stereotypical female concern: pink is for girls. Was this a female baby or merely the affirmation/rejection of blood continuity? Euripides' Medea, never fully convinced of the benefits of maternity ('Men say of us that we live a life free from danger at home while they fight wars. How wrong they are! I would rather stand three times in the battle line than bear one child', Euripides, *Medea*, Act l, pp. 24–25, lines 247–50), committed infanticide to punish Jason for his infidelity, and, in this play, at least, got away with it, escaping to find a welcome in, of all places, Athens, the seat of law and order as it was then articulated. Paraphrasing the Brazilian poet Mário de Andrade, to love and to hate may be intransitive verbs, but in both cases the death toll might be unfathomably distributed. 'Let the little children run from her'.[21]

Fig. 6.8 Ana Palma, *You Died on Me* (2013), graphite and watercolour on paper, 47 × 42.5 cm, CC BY-NC-SA 4.0.

---

21 'Jeseus said, "Let the little children come to me, and do not hinder them, for the kingdom of heaven belongs to such as these"'. *Matthew* 19:14.

Palma's titles, as we shall see presently, often carry resonances of mysticism, and religious allusions, whether Christian or Ancient Greek/Roman. Bearing that in mind, what possibility of organic return, redemptory or ominous, is envisaged in the *Rebirth* (Fig. 6.10)? Is that a round pregnant belly? Is the eye drawn down to what might be a quickened womb filled again with the possibility of new life – a second coming? But if so, what do we make of the impassive expression of the female figure and the crab/insect-like shape on the wall beside her and in *Orange* (Fig. 6.9)? In Antiquity, insects and blood were plagues (swarms of locusts: *Exodus* 19:4–6; rivers of blood: *Exodus* 7:17–22).

Insects and other beasties (locusts, beetles) foretold death: both Biblical plagues and cancer (similar because of the disease's finger-like metastases). The Roman physician, Aulus Cornelius Celsus translated the Latin word for 'crab' as 'cancer', and in *Leviticus*, the crab is one of the unclean animals. Is whatever is being cradled in that womb a lethal growth rather than the promise of future life and personal perpetuity (Fig. 6.9)?

Fig. 6.9 Ana Palma, *Orange* (2017), watercolour on paper, 29.7 × 42 cm, CC BY-NC-SA 4.0.

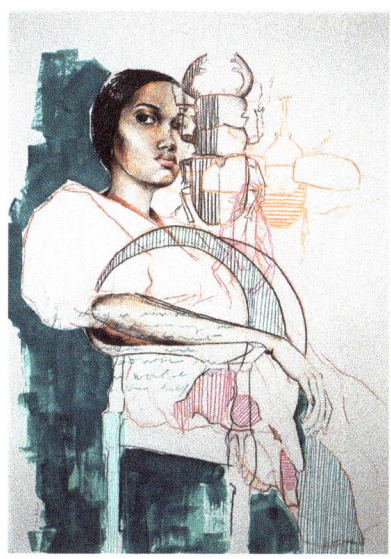

Fig. 6.10 Ana Palma *Rebirth* (2017), coloured pencil and acrylic on paper, 42 × 59.4 cm, CC BY-NC-SA 4.0.

And as for blood, the Ancient Greeks and the Bible considered blood (*haema*) to be the same as the soul/psyche (ψυχή), the non-material source of life being called spirit (πνεύμα/*pneuma*). In the Bible, blood signifies either sacrificial atonement or a curse (the latter, if it was wantonly shed, unless it is duly expiated: *Genesis* 9:4; *Leviticus* 7:26 and 17:11–13). Do menstruating women wantonly shed their blood and their souls every month? Are they *desalmadas*? Is that why they are feared? Is that why they may bleed to death in childbirth (the extreme punishment for Eve's original sin: 'Unto the woman [the Lord] said, "I will greatly multiply thy sorrow and thy conception. In sorrow thou shalt bring forth children"', *Genesis* 3:16)? Is that why until not that long ago, pain relief in childbirth was deemed not acceptable because it impeded female atonement for the sin of Eve?

And nothing, of course, prevents different adversaries (cancer/blood/plagues of insects) from joining forces: my enemy's enemy is my friend. The human placenta and cancer share striking similarities in their invasive behaviour and molecular characteristics, such as shared genetic modifications and epigenetic patterns. Both are characterized by invasive cells that evade the maternal or local immune system, share molecular pathways for hyperproliferation, and exhibit widespread DNA hypomethylation.

When cells go forth and multiply, the result may be not perpetuity (eternal life) but (cancerous) self-destruction, the body turning on itself. Which is a deadly sin. How selfish is a selfish gene? Deadly selfish? Does it have inbuilt into itself its own de(con)struction? In *Literature and Evil*, Georges Bataille argues that for the woman, maternity represents the loss of the self in its uniqueness:

> *Sexuality* implies death, not only in the sense in which the new prolongs and replaces that which has disappeared, but also in that the life of the being who reproduces himself is at stake. To reproduce oneself is to disappear [...]. He who was, by reproducing himself, ceases to be what he was—because he doubles himself. [...] Sexual reproduction itself is only one aspect—the most complicated—of the immortality of life which is at stake in asexualised reproduction. It is an aspect of immortality, but at the same time of individual death. [...] The basis of sexual effusion is the negation of the isolation of the ego which only experiences ecstasy by exceeding itself, by surpassing itself in the embrace in which the being loses its solitude. [...] The death of the being, becomes apparent. (Bataille, 2012, p. 7)

Whose re-birth is envisaged in Palma's *Rebirth* (fig. 6.10)? The woman who reclaims her non-breeding self in its uniqueness? What is the truth? Endurance through one's flesh and blood? Or is that a possibility that applies exclusively to men (Bataille's curiously tone-deaf 'he'?), whose male progeny guarantee the continuity of bloodline, name and property (the load-bearing joists that uphold the infrastructure of patriarchy). But what if the joists will no longer cooperate? What if the necessary womb withdraws consent? Even at the price of its own (bloody) destruction? What a terrible price. What a terrible possibility. What a terrible truth. And in *Truth* (Fig. 6.11, from Palma's *Femina* exhibition (2019)), that truth is looking you in the eye, uncompromisingly, the confrontation being instigated by a black woman against the backdrop of one of Palma's frequent images of an insect (*Found It!*, Fig. 6.12, from the *Human Nature* exhibition, 2017). Is the beetle alive or impaled, and if the latter, is it a zoologist's exhibit from Portugal's past imperial adventures? Is the insect the woman? Is the woman the insect? Kafka, where are you when we need you?

Fig. 6.11 Ana Palma, *Truth* (2019), graphite pencil and acrylic on paper, 29.7 × 42 cm, CC BY-NC-SA 4.0.

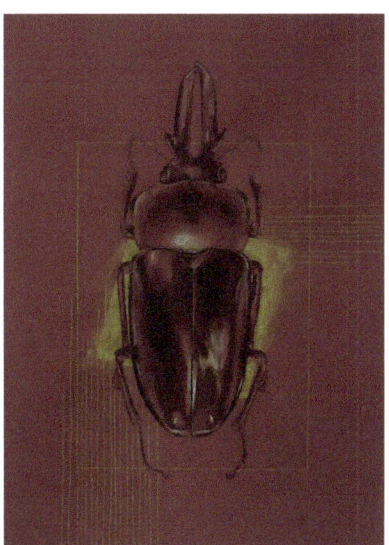

Fig. 6.12 Ana Palma, *Found It!* (2017), watercolour pencils on paper, 70 × 50 cm, CC BY-NC-SA 4.0.

Paraphrasing Alice Walker in *The Colour Purple*, 'you pore, you ugly, you bleed, you a woman. Goddam it, he say, you nothing at all' (Walker,

1986). But what of the female refusenik at the end? In the constrained Barbie-pink reality that was all that was traditionally available to women, the only option might have been that of negativity: the withdrawal of biological possibility (the withholding of the fertile womb). The option of not bleeding.

Fig. 6.13 Ana Palma, *Inner Spring* (2019) , graphite, watercolour pencils and acrylic on paper, 29.2 × 42 cm, CC BY-NC-SA 4.0.

In the past fifty years, an abundance of studies have pondered the link between femaleness, anorexia and amenorrhea as phenomena constituted under patriarchal discourses concerning girls'/women's social disempowerment (Orbach, 1978, 1986; Malson and Ussher, 1996; Redland, 2018; Mahowald, 1992, to name but a few of the many scholars working in the fields of human biology, psychology, psychoanalysis and sociology). But what if, in time-honoured Derridean/Bataillean logic, that restrictive assignation of roles according to sex has inbuilt into it the deconstruction of its own cantilevers and the crumbling of its foundation walls? After all, menstruation is the result of an unfertilized egg being discarded from the womb, and as regards reproduction, a menstruating woman whose body ejects an egg every month even at the price of a small injury to the lining of her own womb (hence menstrual bleeding and pain), is after all not unlike one who does not menstruate at all/ an abortee/one who uses contraception/does not become pregnant (possibly because she will not). *Will not*? Over her surviving body? Over her non-bleeding body? Is that a tragedy? Yes, for many women it is. But for others it might also be the opening of bright new blue heavens where, under reviewed possibilities, (inner/personal) hope springs in different, uncharted forms (Fig. 6.13) and, in an unorthodox paradise, 'the sky beyond is just as blue'.

Let us look finally at two images of a mother and daughter, Demeter and Persephone: Greek Antiquity's famous mother's-daughter's *folie-à-deux*, whose mutual love and resentment against autocratic male gods achieved at least a partial victory against the masculine urge for fruitfulness, by plunging the world into barrenness for one half of every year.

> [Woman is either] positioned in a patrilinear structure, giving a son to her father and husband, or she functions in a matrilinear chain, offering a daughter to her mother. [...] Women who have children in male-authored fiction are a small enough group, commonly becoming pregnant—frequently as the result of a super-potent wedding night—in order that they can suffer obstetrical trauma. Women who give birth to daughters are an even smaller sub-group and a startlingly high number of them are adulteresses. [...] There is something in women who are perceived as desiring which, it seems, deserves the punishment of reproducing themselves; they have disqualified themselves from the uniquely gratifying form of motherhood that Freud identifies in the birth of a son. (Segal, 1995, pp. 136–37)

Segal identifies a further possibility: namely that of a powerful pact between mother and daughter, such that, beyond or outside the perceived act of narcissism and self-reproduction that according to a male perspective damns the mothers of daughters, we glimpse another world—clandestine and menacing—'a potential other-world in which women speak of love' (Segal, 1995, pp. 136–37). Let us look at Antiquity's and Palma's Demeter and Persephone in this light.

Persephone and Demeter: Seasonal Deaths/Re-Births Foretold

> Theseus, the hero,
> And like all heroic Greeks, a cunt,
> Laughed in the Minotaur's respectable snout…
>
> Jorge de Sena, 'In Crete with the Minotaur'

In ancient Greek mythology, Demeter is the Olympian goddess of the harvest and agriculture, presiding over crops, grains and the fertility of the earth. Through sexual congress with her brother Zeus, she became the mother of Persephone, also a fertility goddess. The *Homeric Hymn to Demeter* (c. seventh to eighth century BCE) tells the story of Persephone's abduction and Demeter's search for her. When Hades, King of the Underworld, wished to make Persephone his wife, he kidnapped her with Zeus' permission. Demeter searched everywhere for her missing daughter to no avail, until she was informed that Hades had taken her to the Underworld. In her grief and anger, Demeter neglected her duties as goddess of agriculture, plunging the earth into famine. To avert disaster, Zeus ordered Hades to return Persephone to her mother but, because Persephone, possibly tricked by her abductor/uncle/lover had eaten food from the Underworld (pomegranates), she could not stay with Demeter forever, being forced thenceforward to divide the year between her mother on Earth and Hades in the underworld. This explains the seasonal cycles, as Demeter permits flowers and crops to grow bountiful in Spring and Summer while Persephone is with her, but not when she returns to the Underworld (in Autumn and Winter).

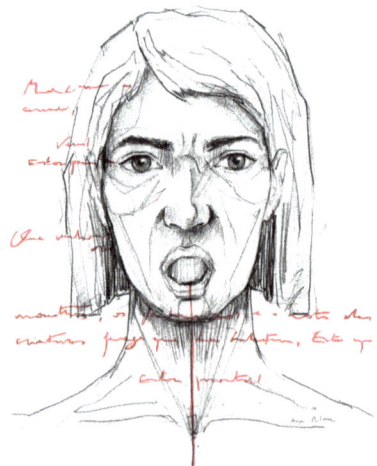

Fig. 6.14 Ana Palma, *Demeter* (2021), graphite and watercolour on paper, 29.7 × 42 cm, CC BY-NC-SA 4.0.

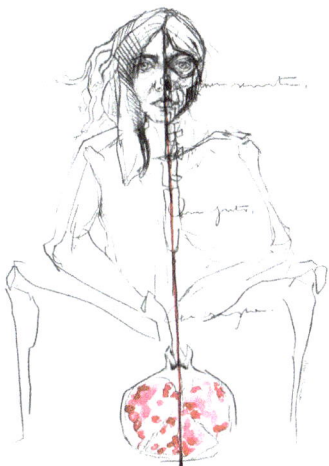

Fig. 6.15 Ana Palma, *Persephone* (2021), graphite and watercolour on paper, 29.7 × 42 cm, CC BY-NC-SA 4.0.

Palma's *Demeter* and *Persephone* (Figs. 6.14 and 6.15) were both created in 2021, a time when the world had come to a standstill under the modern plague that was Covid. Both involve textual inscriptions that are almost illegible, but whose content was kindly provided by the artist (although in conversation we agreed that this article would preserve the difficulties in deciphering the handwriting: the artist's original intention being to convey an emotional charge to the viewer, even if the meaning of the words remains unavailable).[22] This Sybiline artist will retain her cryptic privilege, at least here. Not unlike the taunt presented by Linear A (as opposed to Linear B) in Greek Antiquity. Linear A was a writing system used by the Minoans of Crete from 1800 to 1450 BC. It was succeeded by Linear B, which was an early form of Greek. The latter was deciphered by the archaeologist Michael Ventris in the 1950s. No texts in Linear A have yet been deciphered. Is Palma playing on the boundaries between her personal Linear A and Linear B in her classics-themed works (*Demeter* and *Persephone*)? Is that why sometimes we can decipher what is

---

22   In conversation, Palma kindly disclosed the content of the writing in *Demeter* and *Persephone*. After debating the matter, we agreed that the difficulties of unlocking the script would be left to each individual viewer. Linear A rather than Linear B. This Sybiline artist will retain her cryptic privilege, at least here.

written and sometimes we cannot? What is truth (see Fig 6.11)?

Each of Palma's images speaks of rage and internalized anger on the part of both mother and daughter, but more so the mother. In *Demeter* (Fig. 6.14), as indeed is the case in the original myths, it is the bereaved mother's rage against her daughter's abductor that speaks loudest. Hell, and particularly Hades' Underworld, has no rage like that of a mother grieving for her child. Palma's *Persephone* (Fig. 6.15), in turn, spectral in visage, is birthing or haemorrhaging between her legs a pomegranate, the consumption of which, as was the case with Eve's forbidden fruit, led to banishment from Earth/Paradise and condemned them each to life in a less desirable place (Hell/Earth respectively). The result, it would appear, both for humanity's first mother and Demeter's lost daughter, was complicated childbirth: sons born in travail for Eve, or blood-red issue that may be a fruit but also looks like the deformed product of a miscarriage for Persephone.

Ubiquitous in most parts of the planet, pomegranates come to life in the Southern Hemisphere from March to May (Autumn), and in the Northern Hemisphere from September to February (Autumn and Winter). In Ancient Greek mythology, the pomegranate was known as the 'fruit of the dead', and was believed to have sprung from the blood of Adonis, the Greek ideal of male beauty who was the lover of both Aphrodite and Persephone. Aphrodite had found Adonis abandoned as a newborn and taken him to the Underworld to be fostered by Persephone. She returned for him once he was grown to manhood and fell in love with him. Persephone, however, also desired him, and Zeus settled the dispute by decreeing that Adonis would spend one third of the year with Aphrodite, one third with Persephone, and one third with whomsoever he chose. Adonis ('like all heroic Greeks, a cunt')[23] chose the higher rather than the lesser goddess, his life being thence inequitably divided (two thirds/one third) between the two rivals: one who loved him above the earth, the other beneath it. Persephone had no children with Adonis but had earlier had two with Hades, including one daughter, Melinoë who became the goddess of nightmares and madness: not the happiest of progenies. Is that what provoked Demeter's scream in Palma's image? Would barrenness, whether due to amenorrhea or not, have been a

---

23 Jorge de Sena, 'In Crete with the Minotaur'; see https://ruadaspretas.blogspot.com/2008/11/jorge-de-sena-em-creta-com-o-minotauro.html for the original text.

preferable option? Are nightmares and madness worse than even a scorched earth that miscarries the fruit of the dead (Fig. 6.15)? Or is this just another version of Hobson's choice, the non-option offered by that famous Cambridge provider of rental horses for transporting voyagers from the Fens to London, or, like an earlier colleague (Charon, the Ferryman), from the world of mortals across the Styx to the Underworld (and in the case of Persephone, seasonally back again)?

Conclusion

> And then, there's the Sybil: with my own eyes I saw her, at Cumae, hanging up in a jar; and whenever the boys would say to her 'Sybil, Sybil, what would you?' she would answer, 'I would die'.
>
> Gaius Petronius, *Satyricon*[24]

The nine Sybiline books were notoriously lost, then found by an unnamed woman who used extortion against King Tarquin (Lucius Tarquinius Superbus, the last Roman king prior to the implementation of the Republic), before agreeing to return them. At first he refused, so she burnt them three by three until only three were left and she was paid the price she'd originally demanded for all nine. Copies of the lost ones were sought from all corners of the empire, and those deemed legitimate were later stored in the Temple of Apollo on the Palatine Hill on the orders of Emperor Augustus. Augustus, if some historians (Tacitus; Cassius Dio) are to be believed, was murdered by his wife, Livia, who miscarried the only child she conceived by him (the other two by her first husband she also disposed of in due course: Drusus allegedly by murdering him and Tiberius again allegedly by making him temporarily emperor, whilst convenient, and then conniving in his murder).[25] The Sybil, who foretold it all, may have claimed to want to die, but do we believe her? Perhaps her death was just an early instance of performance art in the course of which men's lineages come to nothing as a consequence of women's sabotage. Tragedy, comedy or satyr play? Almost certainly the first. Bleeding/breeding or rather the refusal to do either is rebellion by any other name, and all can be reclaimed by

---

24 Full text available at https://www.gutenberg.org/files/5225/5225-h/5225-h.htm
25 As imagined in Graves's *I, Claudius* (2006).

women. Is it surprising that Persephone, later known to the Romans as Proserpina, was the Mistress of the Erinyes/Furies? The Golden Bough, sacred to her, was the Underworld destination of dead heroes, bleeding and slain in battle, and directed to it and to her by her accomplice the Sybil, who herself never died. Instead, her bloodless body withered in a jar, but her voice was heard through eternity. Some art endures whilst there is anyone left to enjoy it. As the tablet of the Siena Sybil (Fig. 6.16) states—commandeering a man's words for her own purposes—'[S]he will put an end to the fate of death [...]. Then having returned from the dead, [s]he will come into the light]'.[26]

Fig. 6.16 Siena, *Sibilla Cumea*, Sienna Cathedral, mosaic floor detail. Photo by Sailko (2011), Wikimedia Commons, CC BY-SA 3.0, https://commons.wikimedia.org/wiki/File:Siena,_sibilla_cumea_01.JPG

Works Cited

Abdullah, Sharifah Zahhura Syed, 2022, 'Menstrual Food Restrictions and Taboos: A Qualitative Study on Rural, Resettlement and Urban Indigenous Temiar of Malaysia', *PLoS One*, 17.12, https://doi.org/10.1371/journal.pone.0279629

---

26 The inscription on the pavement Sybil is from St Augustine, *City of God*, one of the Sibylline prophecies about the coming of Christ.

Armitage, Susie, 2017, 'This Is What Period-Shaming Looks Like Around the World', *BuzzFeed* (22 June), https://www.buzzfeed.com/susiearmitage/this-is-what-period-shaming-looks-like-around-the-world

Atwood, Margaret, 1987, *The Handmaid's Tale* (London: Virago).

Bataille, Georges, 2012, *Literature and Evil*, trans. Alistair Hamilton (London: Penguin Modern Classics).

Campos, Álvaro, 1944, *Poesias de Álvaro de Campos* (Lisbon: Ática).

Chamberlain, Geoffrey, 2006, 'British Maternal Mortality in the 19th and Early 20th Centuries', *J R Soc Med*, 99.11, 559–63, https://www.ncbi.nlm.nih.gov/pmc/articles/PMC1633559/

Derrida, Jacques, 1993, *Memoirs of the Blind: The Self-portrait and Other Ruins* (Chicago, Il: University of Chicago Press).

Euripides, 2004, *Medea*, trans. with an introduction by Philip Vellacott (London: Penguin Classics).

Fedele, Anna, 2014, 'Reversing Eve's Curse: Mary Magdalene, Mother Earth and the Creative Ritualization of Menstruation', *Journal of Ritual Studies*, Special Issue: *Ritual Creativity, Emotions and the Body*, 28.2, 23–36.

Francis, M., 2007, 'The Problem with Women', in *Herbert Spencer and the Invention of Modern Life* (London: Acumen Publishing), pp. 51–68.

Gordon, Jane Anna, 2018, 'Of Woman Born: Mary's Monster', *The Bicentennial of Mary Shelley's Frankenstein Issue* (26 October), https://commonreader.wustl.edu/c/of-woman-born/

Graves, Robert, 2006, *I, Claudius* (London: Penguin).

Green-Cole, R., 2020, 'Painting Blood: Visualizing Menstrual Blood in Art', in *The Palgrave Handbook of Critical Menstruation Studies*, ed. C. Bobel, I. T. Winkler, B. Fahs et al. (London: Macmillan), pp. 787–801, https://doi.org/10.1007/978-981-15-0614-7_57

Hendrickson, Julia V., 2019, 'The Mother-Shaped Hole: Lise Haller Baggesen's Mothernism', in *Inappropriate Bodies Book: Art, Design, and Maternity*, ed. Rachel Epp Buller and Reeve Charles (East Gwillimbury, Ontario: Demeter Press, 2019), pp. 31–59, https://doi.org/10.2307/j.ctvpg860f.4

Hessel, Katy, 2024, 'Can a Painting of Childbirth Be Blasphemous and Obscene? The Police Seemed to Think So', *The Guardian* (4 March), https://www.theguardian.com/artanddesign/2024/mar/04/childbirth-blasphemous-obscene-police-god-birth

Hughes, Bee, 2018, 'Menstrual Art: Why Everyone Should Go and See It', *The Conversation* (12 November), https://theconversation.com/menstrual-art-why-everyone-should-go-and-see-it-105778

James, P. D., 2018, *The Children of Men* (London: Faber and Faber).

La Belle, Jenijoy, 1980, '"A Strange Infirmity": Lady Macbeth's Amenorrhea', *Shakespeare Quarterly*, 31.3, 381–86.

Lee, Janet, 1994, 'Menarche and the (Hetero) Sexualization of the Female Body', *Gender and Society*, 8.3, 343–62.

Lisboa, Maria Manuela, 'Monstruosa/Menstruosa: Sangue, menstruação e higiene íntima na arte de Ana Palma e Paula Rego', *Faces de Eva*, 52 (2024).

Kristeva, Julia, 1982, *Powers of Horror: An Essay on Abjection* (New York and Oxford: Columbia University Press).

Mahowald, Mary Briody, 1992, 'To Be or Not Be a Woman: Anorexia Nervosa, Normative Gender Roles, and Feminism', *The Journal of Medicine and Philosophy: A Forum for Bioethics and Philosophy of Medicine*, 17.2, 233–51.

Malson, Helen, and Jane M. Ussher, 1996, 'Bloody Women: A Discourse Analysis of Amenorrhea as a Symptom of Anorexia Nervosa', *Feminism and Psychology*, 6.4, 505–21.

Mandziuk, Roseann M., 2010, 'Ending Women's Greatest Hygienic Mistake: Modernity and the Mortification of Menstruation in Kotex Advertising, 1921—1926', *Women's Studies Quarterly*, 38.3/4, 42–62.

McCracken, Peggy, 2003, 'The Amenorrhea of War', *Signs*, 28.2, 625–43.

Mousa, Aseel, 2024, '"My Period Has Become a Nightmare": Life in Gaza without Sanitary Products', *The Guardian* (5 March), https://www.theguardian.com/global-development/2024/mar/05/my-period-has-become-nightmare-life-in-gaza-without-sanitary-products

Orbach, Susie, 1978, *Fat Is a Feminist Issue: The Anti-diet Guide to Permanent Weight Loss* (New York: Paddington Press).

Orbach, Susie, 1986, *Hunger Strike: The Anorectic's Struggle as a Metaphor for Our Age* (New York: Norton).

Quicherat, Jules, 1841–49, *Procès de condamnation et de réhabilitation de Jeanne d'Arc*, 5 vols. (Paris: Renouard).

Park Hong, Cathy, Brenda Lozano and Mónica de la Torre, 'The Sound and Feel of Cecilia Vicuña's Art', *Frieze* (31 August), https://www.frieze.com/article/sound-feel-cecilia-vicuna-art

Redland, Danielle Fortunee, 2018, *A Far Cry From A No Thing: Psychoanalytic Perspectives on Women and Secondary Amenorrhea* (Doctoral thesis, Goldsmiths, University of London), https://research.gold.ac.uk/id/eprint/23049/

Santos, Juan José, 2021, 'Word-Weapons: *Cecilia Vicuña: Seehearing the Enlightened Failure* Reviewed', *Bomb Magazine* (3 May), https://bombmagazine.org/articles/2021/05/03/word-weapons-cecilia-vicu%C3%B1a-seehearing-the-enlightened-failure-reviewed/

Segal, Naomi, 1980, 'Patrilinear and Matrilinear', in *The Body and the Text: Hélène Cixous, Reading and Teaching*, ed. Helen Wilcox et al.(New York and London: Harvester Wheatsheaf), pp. 131–46.

Selvidge, Marla J., 1984, '*Mark* 5:25-34 and *Leviticus* 15:19-20: A Reaction to Restrictive Purity Regulations', *Journal of Biblical Literature*, 103.4, 619–23.

Sinclair, Leah, 2015, 'The History of Bodily Fluids in Feminist Art', *Vice* (6 October), https://www.vice.com/en/article/the-history-of-bodily-fluids-in-feminist-art/

Steinem, Gloria, 1978, 'If Men Could Menstruate', in *Ms.* Magazine (October), https://www.ncbi.nlm.nih.gov/books/NBK565636/

Striff, Erin, 1997, 'Bodies of Evidence: Feminist Performance Art', *Critical Survey*, 9.1, 1–18.

The Ta´in from the Irish Epic Ta´in Bo´Cuailnge, 1969, trans. Thomas Kinsella (Oxford: Oxford University Press).

Vicuña, Cecilia, 2006/2021, *Quipu Menstrual*, installation view, 13th Shanghai Biennale, Power Station of Art, Shanghai, 2021.

Walker, Alice, 1986, *The Colour Purple* (London: The Women's Press).

Warner, Marina, 1981, *Joan of Arc: The Image of Female Heroism* (New York: Knopf).

Wyndham, John, 2014, 'Consider Her Ways', in *Consider Her Ways and Others* (London: Penguin).

INTERVIEWS AND RECOLLECTIONS

Interview with Lila Nunes

Lila Nunes was Paula Rego's main female model for almost forty years. Many women artists, including some mentioned in the chapters in this book, have spoken about the nature and importance of their female models. We are extremely lucky that Lila agreed to answer several questions about her years with Paula.

***

Maria Manuel Lisboa: *How and when did your association with Paula begin?*

Lila Nunes: I arrived in London in December 1985 as an au pair to help Vic, who was suffering with multiple sclerosis and study English. Julieta, an old friend of Paula and mother-in-law to one of my aunts, introduced us. After Vic died, I left to study nursing but we always kept in touch.

Lisboa: *Did you speak to each other in Portuguese, English or a mixture of the two?*

Nunes: A mixture of the two but mostly Portuguese.

Lisboa: *Paula sometimes spoke of you as her artistic partner. How would you characterize that partnership? Did you, for example, ever suggest specific poses to her?*

Nunes: Our collaboration developed over many years. In the beginning she did drawings of me at home that she would take to the studio to include in the work. I was not going to the studio at this time, so I did not know what she was doing. Later, in 1994, I started going to the studio to pose for her, so I was able to see what she was doing and learned more about her work and what was important for her. Usually, she had an idea of the pose she wanted me to do but it was in trying the pose that we really found what she was looking for. Discovering the way the body twists in different physical and emotional situations... Expressions of what we feel/do can be found in all parts of our body... The way we dress, the way we stand, walk, crouch... are all expressive of how we feel. We did a lot of sessions just drawing, so that she could find what she was looking for. For example, a lot of drawings were done in preparation for 'Dog Women'; some of them became paintings others did not.

Lisboa: *Is it physically demanding maintaining a pose? What's the secret of managing it?*

Nunes: It's quite demanding, and tiring, and it can be painful because we have to keep still. Your body does not like it. Even though I did not realize it in the beginning, I believe the way I did it was by going into a kind of 'zen' state. My mind would wonder inwards in such a way that by the time we stopped, I couldn't remember what I had been thinking about.

Lisboa: *Paula often said that you had an instinct for knowing what she wanted from you. Were you very much on the same wave length?*

Nunes: Quite often we discussed the subject and situation she wanted to portray so; we would be on the same wave length. And of course, there was trust, we were free to express ourselves, laugh at ourselves, imagining ourselves in those situations and talk about other people that we imagined had been in those situations.

Lisboa: *Did Paula let you see the pictures before they were finished?*

Nunes: Of course. Every time we had a break, I would see what was going on in the painting.

Lisboa: *Did you discuss the literary works which served as the inspiration for the pictures?*

Nunes: Yes, we discussed many of them, especially the Portuguese ones which I was more familiar with. We spend hours talking about *Father Amaro* by Eca De Queiros. We also discussed a lot of films and when she did the work for the Unbound exhibition, we went to see a lot of films together.

Lisboa: *What about the polemical topics (fascism, abortion, etc.).*

Nunes: We often talked about fascism and abortion, its consequences and impact, as these were very important topics for her and me.

Lisboa: *In interviews, Paula said that her model got to choose the music played. Can you name some of the music? Or is a secret?*

Nunes: The routine was listening to an opera in the morning (Aida, Traviata, La Forza Del Destino, Carmen... and Rigoletto, which was her favorite for many years). Early afternoon, we listened to all kinds of music from Frank Sinatra to Amy Winehouse, Rod Stewart, Bob Dylan, Portuguese folklore... Late afternoon we listened to Fado: Alfredo Marceneiro, Camane, Mariza, Maria Teresa De Noronha... and her favourite Amália Rodrigues. I very rarely chose music unless I wanted to introduce her to something new. Other models like Tom, Tony and Pedro brought in their favourite music to listen to while they were posing.

Lisboa: *Did you laugh together? Weep together? Did you eat Portuguese snacks together?*

Nunes: We spend many hours talking about all kinds of things: sad things, happy things, our lives... I only saw Paula well up once and shed a few tears another time. And we laugh a lot together, mainly about ourselves and sometimes other people. We both had sandwiches for lunch, sometimes I made Portuguese soup like 'caldo verde' and sometimes she would bring in cakes. At the end of the day, we had champagne to help us unwind.

Lisboa: *From the many images for which you modelled, do any hold a special place in your heart, and if so which ones and why?*

Nunes: There are many paintings that I love. It is very difficult to choose one because as soon as I do that, another one pops into my head that I also like... As a group I love the *Ostriches*, I always called them 'as peruas' [female turkeys], but I also love *Dog Women*, *Possession*, *Abortion*... As a painting I love *Target*, *Angel*... there are so many... I find it very difficult to choose one.

Lisboa: *Was it important that you were both Portuguese living in another country?*

Nunes: I think that was very important. When we discussed what went on over there, we were physically removed which allowed us a wider view of the 'stage' if we can call it that. We were aware that the reason we understood some things was because we were not living there anymore.

Lisboa: *You have become immortal through Paula's immortal works. Do you like the way she depicted you? Do you recognize yourself in her pictures?*

Nunes: I do not see myself in the pictures, as they are not portraits. But I understand and identify with them as a woman.

Reference

Nunes, Lila, 2022, "Paula Rego Remembered by Lila Nunes', *The Guardian* (11 December), https://www.theguardian.com/artanddesign/2022/dec/11/obituaries-2022-paula-rego-remembered-by-lila-nunes

Interview with Ana Palma

Ana Palma is a Portuguese figurative artist currently living in London. Brought up in the countryside, surrounded by nature, she was a strong-willed child who loved to learn, explore and create: traits that haven't faded with adulthood and are an intrinsic part of her practice. She studied Fine Art in Porto and Madrid, and she holds a Master's degree in Art Education. Ana's work has a strong autobiographical component. Through it, she explores themes related to identity, gender, sexuality and inevitably social conditioning and inequalities while voicing and processing her own experiences. Ana Palma has exhibited as a solo artist and in collective shows in the UK and abroad.

***

Maria Manuel Lisboa: *This interview is taking place in the context of the inclusion of an essay on your art works, in a monograph by me. Like Paula, you are a Portuguese woman artist living in London. Paula famously was encouraged by her father to leave Portugal in the early 1950s because 'it was no country for a woman'. What led you to leave Portugal?*

Ana Palma: Paula Rego and the following generation were the reason I was fortunate enough to be born in a less oppressed Portugal. However, growing up in a small village, I still faced many challenges directly and indirectly, by witnessing the lives of the women around me. I moved to London in my late twenties. At the time, I was feeling stagnant at personal and professional levels. I wanted to give myself the opportunity to grow that my mum and grandmothers did not have. I have always been a very curious person, so learning, discovering and being exposed to new ways of seeing the world is a core part of my identity. I find it profoundly inspiring, and this constant research and discovery informs my practice. London brought me all of this and the stimulus I needed to propel my artistic career forward. The quality of the cultural offer here is outstanding and, generally speaking, people here value art and artists more. I still feel embarrassed to say that when I left Portugal, the Department for Culture had been suppressed by the government. As an artist this felt like an invitation to leave the country. I believe that Portugal has changed positively since then, but there is still a long way to go.

Lisboa: *Although she drew upon many themes that were in no sense Portuguese (nursery rhymes, Charlotte Brontë, Jean Genet, etc.), Paula Rego often said that her work was always about Portugal. What about your work?*

Palma: I believe that, on a surface level, my work is not at all about Portugal. Nevertheless, I was born and raised there, and since my work is autobiographical and I'm a product of my upbringing, if we start digging into it, we'll inevitably find traces of Portuguese culture.

Lisboa: *Paula sometimes avoided putting labels on herself (religious, feminist, etc.), even though her work did point us in certain directions. What about you? Are you a feminist? Does religion have a presence in your work? Does your work have any other socio-political dimensions?*

Palma: Even if we don't put labels on ourselves, society will end up doing it for us, right?! As an artist, I think labels can be limiting and influence how others will perceive our work because some are tied to negative connotations, often based on wrong assumptions, lack of knowledge and stereotypes. Nonetheless, they are useful to provide the framework needed to start the discussion and acknowledge the 'elephant in the room'... and someone needs to do it. I'm not fond of labels but I don't avoid them anymore.

I have values and beliefs that led me to stand up against injustice and inequality all my life. In this sense, I have put on a few labels, and feminist is one of them, and I actually think that this should be everyone's cause regardless of gender. Feminism is about freedom of choice, equal opportunities and fairness for everyone. Every human being can benefit from this, because what frees women, also frees underrepresented groups and inevitably will free men.

As a person aware of the world around me, it's impossible to not express my concerns through my work. So, of course, my practice has social-political dimensions, it must have! I believe that having a voice comes with responsibilities. One can choose to create neutral work or considerate pieces with content that, at the very least, will try to contribute positively to social change. Perhaps all of my causes will unavoidably emerge in my work, from my inability to accept or understand inequalities and oppression, to any form of violence inflicted upon human beings and the Earth. I dream of living in a society that embraces change based on integrity. I want to be part of a more compassionate civilization that acknowledges everything is interconnected and holds us accountable for our actions because even the smallest thing has an impact on other human beings and the environment.

Regarding your question about the presence of religion in my work, although I was raised Catholic, I don't consider myself religious. I discarded that label long ago, for I was struggling to justify the contradictions and inconsistencies of their teachings and actions. So, even though I stepped away from it, a lot of the Catholic principles are deeply rooted in the Portuguese culture, hence have conditioned me in ways that I'm still discovering, some positive and some very detrimental. So if we take this into consideration, we can say that religion is present in my work since it has influenced how I see myself as a woman as well as my relationship with my own body in all its dimensions.

Lisboa: *Do you think some of the historical problems she addressed in her work (state violence, religious autocracy, gender antagonism, whether physical or emotional) are still a reality now, in the 2020s?*

Palma: Unfortunately, I think so. In the past decade, we have been witnessing across the globe the deterioration of democracy and a serious backlash against the rights of underrepresented groups in the most direct and subtle ways. Sometimes I feel like we are moving backwards and I ask myself what we are doing to honour the ones who came before us and fought for the rights and privileges that we now take for granted. We keep harming ourselves, one another, and the Earth.

Although nowadays we have access to so much information, I wonder to what extent it is being used to raise awareness, to ensure that our rights, e.g. our freedom of choice and speech, are not taken away from us. Misleading information or information overload can lead to brainwashing or numbness, and if we really think about it, the most corrosive forms of oppression are the ones that we struggle to see.

Despite all of this, I haven't lost hope and every day I see more and more people taking action and trying to make the world a better place. I have never heard so many men advocating for women's rights and even calling themselves feminists; museums and galleries showcasing work by underrepresented communities; artists becoming more vocal and contributing to social change; EDI (equality, diversity and inclusion) becoming a core part of some organizations, etc. I still can't see the impact that I would like to see right now (we are running out of time when it comes to climate change), but I do believe in the butterfly effect and the power of the collective. Power with(in), as opposed to power over.

Lisboa: *It is clear from Paula's titles as interpretative handles to her work, as well as from her many interviews and the documentary directed by her son, Nick Willing, that her work has a strong autobiographical component. You have said the same about your own work. You have spoken openly, for example, about your amenorrhea. Would you say some more about how that has inflected your work?*

Palma: That's a long story! The body of work I developed in the past five years couldn't reflect it more authentically. My work has become more intimate and autobiographical over the years. The 'Femina' series started as a way to voice and process what I was going through since I could not express it in any other language.

There's so much stigma around health issues related to sexuality and the reproductive system. We struggle to talk about infertility, menstrual cycles, prostate problems, miscarriages, abortions, sexual dysfunctions, etc., and if we do, suddenly the level of embarrassment rises, and some people will try to change subjects or even remove themselves from the conversation. This is so isolating and damaging for everyone! It took me literally years to start talking openly about my amenorrhea, and I think sometimes I still avoid it for fear of judgement.

Before the amenorrhea journey started, I was working on the idea of the death-life-rebirth cycle that women experience in their bodies and minds, which I believe is deeply connected to the ones we observe in the natural world—it's interesting how we mirror Nature in so many ways. Back then, I had no idea I was just about to embark on the most profound physical, emotional and spiritual metamorphosis. It's almost like I was anticipating and preparing for it.

This temporary condition brought me so many questions around identity, gender, sexuality and inevitably social conditioning and inequalities. I had to start looking for answers. I realized how fascinated I am by human beings, and, as a consequence, I delved into subjects such as psychology, biology, neuroscience, philosophy and even spirituality. We are such fascinating, complex creatures!

Although there were negative aspects of this journey, which included burnout and depression, I always saw the transformation I have experienced over the past five years as a blessing. I believe life's challenges are opportunities to learn, grow, and become better human beings, and this undiagnosed condition threw me into what astrophysicists call a wormhole. It has been an incredible discovery journey about myself as an individual who is part of a society, a planet and the universe. I'm closer to myself than I have ever been; I have been able to make life-changing decisions that I never had the confidence or courage to do; I became more compassionate and more committed than ever to act from a place of integrity, and if that causes discomfort in others, I'm no longer apologetic.

As I recover, I continue to find ways to restore trust between myself and my body (interestingly, I still separate the two!). It's unbelievable the level of disconnection that we have, which culture and religion instigate. As a woman, my body was always a source of shame, guilt and fear. Fear of the physical pain that it will inflict upon me and of its potential to become an object of psychological and physical abuse and violence. A woman's body is a scary place to live in, and it will continue to be if society does not address the root cause of these issues.

Even though this condition does not define me as a person or as an artist, it propelled me to where I am now. It is an unavoidable part of my life story and my work. Over the years, I also realized that what I thought was an individual and lonely process was actually collective. Often, without telling the stories behind my artworks, people, particularly women, would relate to them, be moved and questioned by them. That's the beauty of art! Even though exhibiting always comes with emotional challenges, knowing that sharing my personal journey has the potential to impact the world motivates me to continue doing it, despite all the real-world obstacles I face every day.

Lisboa: *Have you felt that having an undiagnosed medical condition has determined your experiences of certain groups (for example, doctors as purveyors of power over the bodies of their patients?).*

Palma: I still feel nervous every time I have a doctor's appointment. It appalls me how little research has been done so far on the female reproductive system. Despite so many medical advances, the female body remains a mystery to Western medicine; for instance, women are still underrepresented in drug trials resulting in overmedication, hence unnecessary side effects. This is just one example. There might be a few protocols to follow but none of them is made to identify and address the underlying causes. Because I could not accept this reality I had to try to look for answers. I read several books and scientific papers in order to gain a better understanding of my condition, to begin to help myself, to have the language to discuss it with the health professionals and be taken seriously. Nevertheless, many times I felt that I was being gaslighted and my symptoms were dismissed or overlooked. Gender bias in health is a cruel reality that I have experienced myself.

As a woman, I grew up believing that I could not trust my body. We normalize pain, hunger, body dysmorphia and so forth. Some of us are lucky enough to be taught the basics of sexuality and the female reproductive system, yet the basics are not enough to help us develop self-knowledge and make informed decisions. How disempowering is this? Taking ownership of our bodies, as in learning more about them, listening, and trusting, but also taking responsibility, is a way to liberate us from deep-rooted transgenerational objectification.

Lisboa: *The imperiled body (scarred, bleeding, in pain) seems to be a strong trope in your work. Do you connect that in any way to the work of Paula Rego?*

Palma: With regard to the visual language, I don't see a connection between our work apart from having a strong drawing component. However, I was always drawn to the psychological and social-political aspects of Paula's work. We might express ourselves differently, but perhaps we might be haunted by the same 'demons'.

The imperiled body in my work shows my attempt to dissect myself, searching for the physical, psychological and spiritual causes of my condition. Because my practice is so personal, it puts me in a very vulnerable position, not only because it exposes me but also because seeking the truth implies being willing to face our darkest side. In that way, I do see a connection between our work.

Lisboa: *There is also in some of your works a component of race (the models you choose). Can you say a bit more about that?*

Palma: To be completely honest, I don't know… I don't think I have ever reflected on it.

However, one of the things that I love the most about London is its diversity—all nationalities, religions, ethnicities, etc. I always found it so enriching! This is likely to influence my creative choices. I believe that the work of any artist reflects, conscious or unconsciously, not only who they are but also their context.

Lisboa: *Tell me something about the physical reality of making your works? How do you choose certain media? Tell me something about the processes involved.*

Palma: Although I have always considered myself a pragmatic person, I'm the opposite when it comes to my practice. For me, creating means improvising and acting according to how I feel, with all the challenges and discomfort that come with it. So even though the aesthetic choices are mostly intuitive, the practical aspect of my creative process reflects real-world constraints such as the space and resources available.

Drawing is the foundation of my practice and everything I do starts with a drawing, even if it ends up covered in paint. It allows me to express myself in the most authentic way and to 'put it all out', then painting brings everything into balance. Writing comes last to complete the work if the lines and brush strokes were not enough.

The starting point of my art works can be a line, a text, an image, my own body or objects from my collection. I like to be surprised by what comes out of my hands, mind and soul. I like that nothing ever goes according to plan, I like seeing the composition unveil itself as it reveals new parts of myself. Every new visual composition brings aesthetic puzzles that I enjoy solving. Saying this, I must highlight that my creative process gives me as much satisfaction as it does frustration. It can be very painful when I can't find solutions or I am sucked into a traumatic memory or a difficult truth. Sometimes, completing a piece feels like a relief.

Lisboa: *Have I not asked you anything that you would have liked to have been asked?*

Palma: I don't think so. You have asked me some of the most interesting and pertinent questions I have ever been asked in an interview. Thank you very much for your genuine interest in my work and for trying to find out what's beyond the pictures.

Websites

Ana Palma, https://ana-palma.com/

'Exhibitions', *Ana Palma,* https://ana-palma.com/exhibitions/

'Femina', *Art Rabbit,* https://www.artrabbit.com/events/ana-palma-femina

Instagram, https://www.instagram.com/p/CHtUc-7goP2/

In memoriam: Paula Rego and the Stories Left Untold

Helder Macedo

(Translated by Maria Manuel Lisboa)

It is Suzette—Suzette Macedo—not I, who should be writing this now, in this our life forever shared. She was, like Paula, a story-teller. Stories made from words, skilfully moulded to suit the listeners, making them part of those who heard them. But now it is as if the suspended hand had continued to draw outside the boundaries of the page. The last time they met, on the occasion of Paula's last show before she died, both in wheelchairs, they laughed at each other, holding outstretched hands. On the day of Paula's funeral I managed to take Suzette to the church where, on Paula's instructions, a farewell mass was to be said for her. The Church of the Immaculate Conception, in one of those steep alleys in Hampstead. A choice only on the surface dissonant from her pictures about women's freedom to chose either to bear children or not. Suzette saw Paula's children at a distance in the church, recognized them and said: 'Look, Paula's children! I'll ring her and tell her I saw them'.

Quite so. For decades they rang one another every Sunday, long conversations interspersed by laughter. And when they met they told each other stories, each in her own way. On Suzette's nineteenth birthday, Nick Willing, Paula's son, brought her a print depicting a reclining woman with two upright female figures drifting above her. Guardian angels? Watchers at a wake? It is impossible to say whether the woman is dead or whether the custodial shadows are alive. Nick, very kindly, said it was a present from his mother. And yes, it might have been, if

Paula had still been capable of it.

It's not as though I too, wasn't Paula's friend. When she rang, if I happened to pick up the phone, we would chat for a while—literature, politics, news, facts, transitive verbs, grown-up talk. But with Suzette it was different, it was as though they were childhood friends, or rather, as though they were children again because they were friends. And then things would happen. On one occasion we met in Portugal, joined by other friends—poets, painters—in Paula's beautiful house in Ericeira (see Chapter 4), a stretch of coastline where the sea is always wild. Vic Willing—Paula's husband—who always grasped everything about Paula with razor-sharp intelligence, was still alive. Menez, the Portuguese painter of our generation who, next to Paula, I most admire, was also still alive. It was a time when we were happy and didn't know it.

The house (Quinta da Ribeira da Baleia) was a mansion with frescos on the walls, engraved ceilings and a garden with thick shrubbery long left untrimmed. Colourful rugs under the lumpy trunk of an oak tree. Wine and soft drinks before lunch. The exuberant setting of an impressionist painting transferred further south. Until suddenly the air grew thick, the grass appeared to have grown, and Suzette asked uneasily: 'Are there snakes here?' and Paula, with that amiable smile that revealed the unexpected predatory teeth: 'Yes'. Nothing more. A little girl's voice. We relaxed. It was a way of saying yes to say no. But later she got up, walked behind the tree and came back with little dancing steps, holding something in her upturned skirt and singing 'Lalarilalala' like in a children's circle game. And suddenly, no longer smiling, she threw a snake at us. 'I killed it this morning'. Her voice that of a fearless woman. I maintain that the snake was conjured up by Paula because Suzette asked about it. These two friends imagined things that became real.

Paula Rego became the artist unanimously acclaimed who justified the highest honours the UK could bestow on her. They even made her a Dame of the British Empire, as if such a thing still existed. Her death made front-page news in the British press. All of it, no more than she deserved. In times past, however, she had received some paternalistically condescending reviews by some of the mandarins of the arts in Britain. One particularly obtuse commentator, who probably has since joined the chorus of homage, even said she couldn't draw. That was before several British fellow-artists recognized her extraordinary quality and some even tried to imitate her drawings and paintings. And her critics then discovered that she was 'one of us'.

Be that as it may, let us not forget that the importance of her work was first recognized back in her homeland. That other country with which she maintained a constant dialogue. Exchanging ideas—sometimes images—with artists unknown in Britain. For example—or above all—with Menez, whose work would be music had it not been poetry, and poetry had it not been painting. Each as different from the other as they were akin to one another. Which of course does not diminish in the slightest—rather emphasizes—Paula Rego's unparalleled creativity, which Anglo-Saxon culture in good time adopted as its own. But it also suggests that there are still paths to be explored in a body of work that is both so all-encompassing and so specific, as much a part of other cultures as it is of that from whence she came and which was to remain hers till the end. Which is just as well. Because it means that there are still many stories to be told.

Helder Macedo, London, January 2023.

Helder Macedo is Emeritus Professor of Portuguese and Fellow of King's College London. An active opponent of the Portuguese dictatorship, he returned briefly to Portugal after the 'Carnation Revolution' of 25 April 1974 and was in government as Secretary of State for Culture. He is also a poet and a novelist.

A long-time friend of Paula Rego and her family, he was married to Suzette Macedo, who was one of her closest friends. It is one of life's cruelties that just as Paula went only partly gently into that good night with some of her memory erased, Suzette followed not long afterwards suffering from the same problem. But if/when they met again, no doubt it was with a giggle. *Sempre traquinas* and with their souls intact.

Index

abjection 16, 62, 154
abortion 5, 120, 141–142, 150, 153, 158–159, 165, 170, 185, 190
absence 5, 13, 57, 73, 89–90, 113, 153, 155
Adam and Eve 148, 151, 154, 161–162, 167, 174
agency 10, 46, 73, 157
Aleijadinho. *See* Lisboa, Antônio Francisco ('Aleijadinho')
Alves de Paula Martins, Adriana 36
amenorrhea 5, 159–160, 162–163, 170, 174, 190
Ancell, Matthew 17
Andersen, Hans Christian 135
Applegate, Christina 94
Aristophanes 158
Aristotle 18
Atwood, Margaret 120, 148, 161

Bacon, Francis 92, 111, 126
Ballweg, Mary Lou 153
Bamberger, B. J. 152
Bandeira, Manuel 110
Barbosa, Joaquim 28
Baroque, the 5, 8, 11, 22–24
Barthes, Roland 34, 50
Bataille, Georges 168, 170
beauty 18, 66, 90, 121–122, 174, 191
Beckett, Samuel 87–88, 111, 113
Beloso, Lani 149
Bersani, Leo 97–99
body, the 2, 4, 9–11, 15–18, 27, 36, 48, 60–62, 72, 77, 89–90, 101, 105, 107–108, 111, 119, 130, 137, 139, 142, 148–151, 153, 155, 158, 160–163, 168, 170–171, 176, 184, 189–193, 197
Bourdieu, Pierre 9–10
Bowie, David 96
Braidotti, Rosi 61, 78–79

Brine, Kevin R 121
Brontë, Charlotte 33, 139, 188
Brothers Grimm 135, 139

Caeiro, Alberto 4, 99–101
Campos, Álvaro de 53, 88
Carroll, Lewis 31, 65, 119
Carter, Angela 138, 140, 143
Carter, Kevin 2–3
Castelo Branco, Camilo 4–5, 31–32, 36–37, 41–45, 47–53
castration 78, 133, 139, 152
Catenaccio, Claire 17–18
Chaucer, Geoffrey 94
Chicago, Judy 149
childhood 107, 110, 135, 138, 140, 196
children 2–3, 5, 12, 22, 35, 43–44, 46, 48, 51, 59, 62, 73, 80, 92, 107, 110, 135, 137–138, 142, 151, 158, 165, 167, 171, 174–175, 187, 195–196
Christianity 14, 23–24, 31, 53, 59, 120–121, 125, 134, 153, 166
Ciletti, Elena 121–122
conflict 2–3, 17, 22, 42, 44, 47, 158
Congreve, William 135
Cooke, Lynne 102–103
Correia, Natália 113
Couzens, Wayne 137
Covington, Sarah 18
Craveirinha, José 110
culture 19–20, 22, 32, 35, 66, 149–150, 154, 161, 188–189, 191, 197

Dalcastagné, Regina 70
Dead Poets' Society (film) 34
death 2, 11–13, 24, 27, 37, 40–41, 44, 47–50, 58, 63, 71–73, 75–76, 78, 80, 89–90, 95, 97–100, 103, 105, 110, 113, 125, 135, 142, 158, 160, 163–168, 175–176, 190, 196
Deleuze, Gilles 61, 78, 103

Delilah (biblical figure) 124–125
democracy 18, 21, 41, 60, 189
Derrida, Jacques 33, 58, 61, 64–65, 73, 78, 96, 113, 150, 170
desire 37, 42, 85, 98, 109, 154
Dickinson, Emily 119
disability 1–2, 5, 8, 10, 27, 105, 133
Disability Studies 1–2
dogs 9, 17, 19, 70, 126–131
Douglas, Mary 10
Douglass, Ellen 67–68
Duffy, Carol Ann 140
Dury, Ian 1

Eakin, Marshall C. 19–21
Eden/Garden of Eden 148, 162
Eliot, T. S. 101
Éluard, Paul 92
emotion 87, 90, 104, 130, 142
Engels, Frederick 33
Enslen, Joshua Alma 67
ethics 61, 102, 112
Euripides 165
exile 37, 39–40, 43, 46–47, 104

Farrell, Kaitlyn 131
fascism 185
feminism 33, 35, 61, 112, 149, 188
fertility 153, 161, 172, 190
Fitz, Earl E. 67
Foucault, Michel 10, 61–62
Fragonard, Jean-Honoré 126, 128–130
Freyre, Gilberto 21–22
Friedlander, Saul 35

Gallagher, Catherine 35
gender 5, 9, 35, 62, 65–66, 70, 130, 151, 155–156, 158, 160, 187–189, 191
Gentileschi, Artemisia 122–123, 125
Gobineau, Arthur 19
Goya, Francisco 94
Grabato Dias, João Pedro 57–58
Gramsci, Antonio 34
Greenblatt, Stephen 35
grief 48, 165, 172, 174

Griffin, Randall 18

Hawthorn, Jeremy 36
Hemingway, Ernest 1
Hendrickson, Julia V. 154
Herculano, Alexandre 41–42, 48
Hippocrates 85
Hirst, Damien 96–97
Hockney, David 94, 126
Hogarth, William 126, 130–133
Holiday, Billie 94

identity 15, 45, 65, 160, 187, 191
immortality 72, 108, 126, 168, 186
inequality 21–22, 60, 188

Jameson, Frederic 32
Jesus 15, 24–26, 53, 67, 91, 134, 152, 176
Judith and Holofernes 120–124

Kahlo, Frida 94, 158
Kipling, Rudyard 141, 157
Klee, Paul 94
Klobucka, Anna 60–61
Koivunen, Anu 103–104
Koo, Kathryn S. 10
Kosoi, Natalie 96

LaBute, Neil 147
Lacan, Jacques 78
Lady Gaga 94
Lange, Dorothea 94
language 23, 33, 59, 63–65, 72–73, 77, 160, 190, 192
Lazzarini, Elena 18
Lee, Janet 155
Lefebvre, Henri 90
Leviticus 150, 152, 166–167
Lipstadt, Deborah 35
Lisboa, Antônio Francisco ('Aleijadinho') 4–5, 7–9, 11–16, 18–20, 22–27
Lispector, Clarice 4–5, 57–68, 71–73, 76–80
Little Red Riding Hood 136, 139
longing 46–47, 85

Lycett, Andrew 157
Lyotard, Jean-François 33

Macedo, Suzette 195
MacNeice, Louis 162
Mandziuk, Roseann 155
Manet, Édouard 94
Manic Street Preachers 2–3
Marx, Karl 33–34
masculinity 66, 71, 77, 128, 155, 171
Matisse, Henri 94
McCracken, Peggy 155–157
McCracken, Scott 95, 108
McEwen, John 86, 89, 95, 102, 107–108, 110–112
Meireles, Cecília 7
memory 24, 46, 50, 107, 110, 193, 197
Menez 196–197
menstruation 5, 148–157, 161–163, 167, 170, 190
Merleau-Ponty, Maurice 10
Michelangelo 8, 94
Milam, Jennifer 130
Millay, Edna 152
Milton, John 126
miscarriage 94, 148, 174, 190
Monet, Claude 94
monstrosity 16, 67, 126
motherhood 136–137, 148, 151, 154, 159, 161, 171
multiple sclerosis (MS) 5, 85, 90, 93–95, 101, 103, 107, 109, 111, 126, 128, 133, 183
mysticism 23, 166
mythology 16, 46, 49, 126, 172, 174

New Historicism 32–35
Nietzsche, Friedrich 102, 111
Nina Rodrigues, Raimundo 19, 21–22
Nunes, Lila 5, 183–186

Oliver, Mary 57

pain 2–3, 15, 18, 28, 58, 87, 89, 93–94, 111, 135, 142, 148–151, 154, 161–164, 167, 170, 191–192
painting 5, 18, 22–23, 86, 91–93, 95, 100, 102–108, 112, 130, 149, 184–185, 193, 196–197
Palma, Ana 4–5, 147, 150, 159–160, 162–174, 187–190, 192–194
Paquette, Gabriel 41
performance art 99, 158, 175
Perry, Walter 90
Pessoa, Fernando 31, 37, 46, 48, 87–88, 100
photography 2
Plath, Sylvia 92
Plato 9–10, 16, 65, 126
politics 5, 10, 14, 17, 20, 22, 27, 32–33, 36, 38, 40–44, 47–50, 52, 60–61, 65–66, 70, 74, 78, 111–112, 119, 147, 155, 188–189, 192, 196
presence 24, 70, 75, 87, 89, 91, 102–104, 108, 112, 188–189
psychology 52, 170, 191
puberty 149, 154

Queirós, Eça de 37, 41, 48, 51, 53

race 1, 4, 8, 13–14, 18–22, 27, 52, 65, 193
Racine, Jean 97–99
racism 19–21, 143
rage 49, 122, 174
Rank, Otto 121
Realism 32–33, 37–38, 41, 48–49, 51–52
rebellion 39, 175
Rego, Paula 4–5, 87, 92–93, 95, 100, 104–106, 113, 119–120, 122, 124–128, 130–134, 136, 139–145, 147, 150–151, 159, 162, 183, 186–188, 192, 195–197
Reischer, Erica 10
religion 12, 120, 152, 188–189, 191, 193
Rhys, Jean 137
Ricasoli, Corinna 24
Rocha-Trindade, Beatriz 44–45
Romanticism 37–38, 41, 44, 47–49
Romero, Sílvio 19–22
Ronsard, Pierre de 98–99, 147

Rossetti, Dante Gabriel 161
Rothko, Mark 96, 99–100

Sandler, Irving 96
Santesso, Aaron 133
Sá, Olga de 41, 56, 59–60
Sappho 160
Sartre, Jean-Paul 67, 96, 101, 103
Schneemann, Carolee 149
self-portrait 90–91, 102–104, 148, 150, 163
Sellberg, Karin 61
Selvidge, Marla 152
Senna, Marta da 67
Serota, Nicholas 86
sexuality 21, 65, 130, 142, 160, 168, 187, 190–192
Shakespeare, William 16–17, 33, 89, 127, 143, 157
Shelley, Mary 16
silence 28, 71, 73–74, 76, 89–91
Silence of the Lambs (film) 80
Silva, João Baptista da 41
Sjöö, Monica 151
slavery 8, 12, 15, 18–19, 21–23, 28, 35
Snow, Peter 87
Steinem, Gloria 149
Striff, Erin 158
suffering 24, 85, 111, 149, 183, 197
symbol 10, 85, 90, 104, 126, 131

Tamber-Rosenau, Caryn 122
Tate, Andrew 128, 137, 153
Tiegs, Vanessa 148
Titus-Carmel, Gérard 96
Tolstoy, Leo 2
Toulouse-Lautrec, Henri de 94
trauma 5, 15, 18, 59, 139, 171
truth 18, 31, 33, 35–36, 50, 53, 63, 79, 119, 143, 168, 174, 193

Van Gogh, Vincent 94
Vicuña, Cecilia 149
violence 5, 127, 137, 141–143, 158, 189, 191

vulnerability 73, 149–150, 193

Waiting for Godot (film) 87
Walsh, Timothy 89–90
war 21, 31–32, 40, 47, 59, 77, 97, 112, 121, 148, 156, 158
Warfield, William 7
Watteau, Antoine 128–129
wealth 21, 46, 48, 65–66, 71, 112
Willing, Nick 91, 95, 112, 127, 190, 195
Willing, Victor 4–5, 85–96, 99–113, 126–127, 133–134, 183, 196
womanhood 121, 149, 154
Woolf, Virginia 62, 136
writing 34, 59, 61–66, 70, 72, 77
Wyeth, Andrew 18

Yates, Bart 85
Yeats, W. B. 32, 98, 109
Young, Silvia 156

About the Team

Alessandra Tosi was the managing editor for this book.

Adèle Kreager proof-read this manuscript and compiled the index.

Jeevanjot Kaur Nagpal designed the cover. The cover was produced in InDesign using the Fontin font.

Annie Hine typeset the book in InDesign. The main text font is Tex Gyre Pagella and the heading font is Californian FB.

Jeremy Bowman produced the PDF, paperback, and hardback editions and created the EPUB.

The conversion to the HTML edition was performed with epublius, an open-source software which is freely available on our GitHub page at https://github.com/OpenBookPublishers

Laura Rodríguez was in charge of marketing.

This book was peer-reviewed by Leonor Oliveira, Institute of Art History, Universidade NOVA de Lisboa, and an anonymous referee. Experts in their field, these readers give their time freely to help ensure the academic rigour of our books. We are grateful for their generous and invaluable contributions.

This book need not end here...

Share

All our books — including the one you have just read — are free to access online so that students, researchers and members of the public who can't afford a printed edition will have access to the same ideas. This title will be accessed online by hundreds of readers each month across the globe: why not share the link so that someone you know is one of them?

This book and additional content is available at
https://doi.org/10.11647/OBP.0500

Donate

Open Book Publishers is an award-winning, scholar-led, not-for-profit press making knowledge freely available one book at a time. We don't charge authors to publish with us: instead, our work is supported by our library members and by donations from people who believe that research shouldn't be locked behind paywalls.

Join the effort to free knowledge by supporting us at
https://www.openbookpublishers.com/support-us

We invite you to connect with us on our socials!

BLUESKY	MASTODON	LINKEDIN	INSTAGRAM
@openbookpublish .bsky.social	@OpenBookPublish @hcommons.social	open-book-publishers	openbookpublishers_

Read more at the Open Book Publishers Blog
https://blogs.openbookpublishers.com

You may also be interested in:

Essays on Paula Rego
Smile When You Think about Hell

Maria Manuel Lisboa

https://doi.org/10.11647/OBP.0178

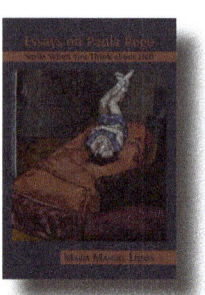

Gender-Based Violence in Arts and Culture
Perspectives on Education and Work

Marie Buscatto, Sari Karttunen and Mathilde Provansal (eds)

https://doi.org/10.11647/OBP.0436

Troubled People, Troubled World
Psychotherapy, Ethics and Society

Michael Briant

https://doi.org/10.11647/OBP.0416

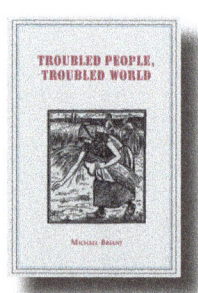

The Struggle You Can't See
Experiences of Neurodivergent and Invisibly Disabled Students in Higher Education

Ash Lierman

https://doi.org/10.11647/OBP.0420

www.ingramcontent.com/pod-product-compliance
Lightning Source LLC
Chambersburg PA
CBHW061250230426
43663CB00022B/2963